NEXT-GENERATION ENTERPRISE SECURITY AND GOVERNANCE

Security, Audit and Leadership Series
Series Editor: Dan Swanson
Dan Swanson and Associates, Ltd., Winnipeg, Manitoba, Canada

Security, Audit and Leadership Series series publishes leading-edge books on critical subjects facing audit executives as well as internal and IT audit practitioners. Key topics include Audit Leadership, Cybersecurity, Strategic Risk Management, Auditing Various IT Activities and Processes, Audit Management, and Operational Auditing.

Corporate Defense and the Value Preservation Imperative
Bulletproof Your Corporate Defense Program
Sean Lyons

Mastering the Five Tiers of Audit Competency
The Essence of Effective Auditing
Ann Butera

Software Quality Assurance
Integrating Testing, Security, and Audit
Abu Sayed Mahfuz

The Complete Guide to Cybersecurity Risks and Controls
Anne Kohnke, Dan Shoemaker, Ken E. Sigler

Operational Assessment of IT
Steve Katzman

A Guide to the National Initiative for Cybersecurity Education (NICE) Cybersecurity Workforce Framework (2.0)
Dan Shoemaker, Anne Kohnke, Ken Sigler

Securing an IT Organization through Governance, Risk Management, and Audit
Ken E. Sigler, James L. Rainey, III

Leading the Internal Audit Function
Lynn Fountain

NEXT-GENERATION ENTERPRISE SECURITY AND GOVERNANCE

Edited by
Mohiuddin Ahmed, Nour Moustafa, Abu Barkat,
and Paul Haskell-Dowland

CRC Press
Taylor & Francis Group
Boca Raton London New York

CRC Press is an imprint of the
Taylor & Francis Group, an **informa** business

First edition published 2022
by CRC Press
6000 Broken Sound Parkway NW, Suite 300, Boca Raton, FL 33487-2742

and by CRC Press
4 Park Square, Milton Park, Abingdon, Oxon, OX14 4RN

CRC Press is an imprint of Taylor & Francis Group, LLC

© 2022 Taylor & Francis Group, LLC

ISBN: 978-0-367-63962-4 (hbk)
ISBN: 978-1-032-24775-5 (pbk)
ISBN: 978-1-003-12154-1 (ebk)

DOI: 10.1201/9781003121541

Typeset in Sabon
by MPS Limited, Dehradun

Dedicated to

"My Loving Son: Zaif"

Mohiuddin Ahmed

Contents

Preface

INTRODUCTION

The Internet is making our daily life as digital as possible and this new era is called the Internet of Everything (IoE). The key force behind the rapid growth of the Internet is the technological advancement of enterprises. The digital world we live in is facilitated by these enterprises' advances and business intelligence. Consequently, those enterprises need to deal with gazillions of bytes of data, and in today's age of General Data Protection Regulation, enterprises are required to ensure privacy and security of large-scale data collections. However, the increased connectivity and number of devices used to facilitate IoE are continually creating more room for cybercriminals to find vulnerabilities in enterprise systems and flaws in their corporate governance.

Ensuring cybersecurity and corporate governance for enterprises should not be an afterthought or a huge challenge. In recent times, the complex diversity of cyber-attacks has been skyrocketing, and zero-day attacks, such as ransomware, botnet, and telecommunication attacks, are happening more frequently than before. New hacking strategies bypass existing enterprise security and governance platforms with increasing ease by using advanced persistent threats. For example, in 2020, the Toll Group firm was exploited by a new crypto-attack family for violating its data privacy, where an advanced ransomware technique was launched to exploit the big corporation and a request a huge figure of monetary ransom. Even after applying rational governance hygiene, the cybersecurity configuration and necessary software updates are often overlooked when they are most needed to fight cyber-crime and ensure data privacy. Therefore, the threat landscape in the context of enterprises becomes wider and far more challenging. There is a clear need for collaborative work throughout the entire value chain of the network.

In this context, this book will address the cybersecurity and cooperate governance challenges associated with enterprises, which will provide a bigger picture of the concepts, intelligent techniques, practices, as well as open research directions in this area. In addition, the proposed book will serve as a single source of reference for acquiring knowledge on the technology, process, and people involved in the next-generation's privacy and security.

CHAPTERS

The book covers some key aspects of enterprise security and governance. Chapter 1 covers the interesting threat intelligence paradigm for enterprises. Chapter 2 covers effective IT governance from the project management perspective. Chapter 3 highlights the risks associated in enterprise setup. Chapter 4 showcases some insights on incident response techniques for next generation enterprises. Chapter 5 covers cyber-enabled crime for industrial enterprises. Chapters 6 and 7 cover the enterprise data and cloud facilities for enterprises. Chapter 8 focuses on an application of enterprise security in intelligent transportation. The last chapter of the book includes policies associated with futuristic communication, e.g., the sixth generation mobile network.

Editors
Mohiuddin Ahmed, Nour Moustafa, Abu Barkat, and Paul Haskell-Dowland

It is another incredible book editing experience and we extend our sincere gratitude to the publisher for facilitating this process. This book editing journey enhanced our patience, communication, and tenacity. We are thankful to all the contributors, reviewers, and publishing team. Last but not least, our thanks to our family members, whose support and encouragement contributed significantly to completing this book.

Mohiuddin Ahmed
Nour Moustafa
Abu Barkat
Paul Haskell-Dowland

Contributors

Mohiuddin Ahmed has made practical and theoretical contributions in cybersecurity and big data analytics for several application domains. His research has a high impact on data and security analytics, false data injection attacks, and digital health. Mohiuddin has led edited multiple books and contributed articles in The Conversation. He has over 50 publications in reputed venues and a Senior Member of IEEE. Mohiuddin secured the prestigious ECU Early Career Researcher Grant for investigating the effectiveness of blockchain for dependable and secure e-health. He also secured several external and internal grants within a very short timeframe.

Keyvan Ansari received the PhD degree in computer science from the Queensland University of Technology (QUT), Brisbane, QLD, Australia, in 2014. From 2014 to 2016, he was an associate lecturer with the School of Electrical Engineering and Computer Science, QUT. In 2016, he joined the University of the Sunshine Coast, where he currently undertakes research and lectures in Computer Science and ICT with the School of Science, Technology and Engineering. His research interests include pervasive communications and computing, covering topics ranging from connected vehicles and Internet-of-Things to cyber security. He has co-chaired and has been a member of technical program committees of several international conferences and workshops and has been an Editorial Board Member and a Reviewer of several international journals and magazines.

Hadrian Geri Djajadikerta is an associate professor of Accounting at Edith Cowan University, Australia. Hadrian has over two decades of research, teaching and academic leadership experiences, including Associate Dean Research, Head of Commerce Discipline, MBA and Postgraduate Director, and Chair of Accounting. He has numerous quality publications, competitive research grants and supervised more than a dozen PhD students to completion. He has also been awarded both Vice-Chancellor's Award for Excellence in Research Supervision and Vice-Chancellor's Award for Excellence in Teaching. His main research focuses on sustainability and sustainability reporting, corporate governance, strategic management accounting, behavioural accounting, and corporate social responsibility.

Frank den Hartog received the MSc degree in applied physics from Eindhoven University of Technology, and the PhD degree in physics from Leiden University, both in The Netherlands. From 1998 to 2003, he worked for the telecom operator KPN. He then was a Senior Scientist with the research organization TNO, where he acquired and led various large collaborative research projects in the field of Internet of Things. From 2012 to 2016, he was the Chair of the Technical Working Group of the worldwide Home Gateway Initiative industry consortium. In 2018, he became an associate professor and director of Postgraduate Studies at UNSW, Canberra, Australia, specializing in complex systems security. He has co-authored 73 peer-reviewed articles, 67 contributions to standardization, and seven international standards. He holds 16 patents in Europe and the US. Prof. Den Hartog is a Senior Member of IEEE and a member of ACM, TelSoc, and AISA.

Khondokar Fida Hasan has a PhD in Computer Science from Queensland University of Technology (QUT). He awarded the High Achiever Research Award in 2018 from QUT. In his academic career, he taught several courses in the area of Cybersecurity and Computer Networking and supervised 50+ MIT students. He held different academic and administrative positions thoughout his career including Head (Acting) of the school. In recognition, Fida Hasan awarded the Fellow of HEA, UK, for the excellence of his teaching and research practice in higher academia. His current research interests includes solving security, privacy and trust issues in cyber physical system including Internet of Things and Intelligent Transportation System.

Craig Jarvis is an independent cyber security strategist completing a PhD in Cyber Security & History at Royal Holloway, University of London. Craig holds master's degrees in Cyber Security, International Security, and Classical Music, and studied history at Oxford University. Craig is the former chief technology officer at DXC Security, one of the world's largest providers of managed and consultancy cyber security services. As well as leading technology strategy, Craig founded DXC's Security Labs and oversaw strategic intelligence. During this role, Craig worked with global CISOs to develop robust enterprise security architectures. Craig's first book, Crypto Wars – The Fight for Privacy in the Digital Age: A Political History of Digital Encryption, was published by CRC Press in 2020.

Raja Jurdak is a professor of Distributed Systems and Chair in Applied Data Sciences at Queensland University of Technology, and Director of the Trusted Networks Lab. He received the PhD in information and computer science from the University of California, Irvine. He previously established and led the Distributed Sensing Systems Group from

2011–2019 at CSIRO's Data61, where he maintains a visiting appointment. He also spent time as visiting academic at MIT and Oxford University in 2011 and 2017. His research interests include trust, mobility and energy efficiency in networks. Prof. Jurdak published over 190 peer-reviewed publications, including two authored books most recently on blockchain in cyberphysical systems in 2020. He serves on the editorial board of Ad Hoc Networks, and on the organising and technical program committees of top international conferences, including Percom, ICBC, IPSN, WoWMoM, and ICDCS. He was TPC co-chair of ICBC in 2021. He is a conjoint professor with the University of New South Wales, and a senior member of the IEEE.

Nickson M. Karie received his PhD degree in computer science from the University of Pretoria, South Africa, in 2016. Currently, Nickson is a Cybersecurity CRC Research Fellow at Edith Cowan University, Security Research Institute, Perth, Western Australia. He has more than 10 years of experience in academic research, teaching, and consultancy in different countries including India, Kenya, South Africa, Swaziland, and Australia. His research interests include intrusion detection and prevention, information and computer security architecture, network security and forensics, mobile forensics, and IoT security. He is also actively engaged as a high impact international conference and journal author and reviewer.

Roberto Musotto is Research Fellow in Cybersecurity and Law at the School of Business and Law and at the Cyber Security Cooperative Research Center (CSCRC). He is an Italian-qualified lawyer (*Avvocato*) with expertise in serious crimes and their economic implications, focusing on commercial, corporate, and cyber aspects. He has advised international institutions across the world on cybercrime organizations, cyber policies, and strategy.

Mohsen Aghabozorgi Nafchi obtained a Master of Information Technology from Shiraz University (Iran) in 2013. Since then, he has been teaching at the Department of Information Technology (IT) of PayameNoor University at Shahrekord, Iran. He is doing researching in different subjects especially Human Computer Interaction (HCI), Psychology, User Experience, Educational Technologies, Security and Privacy. Also, Social Media, Quantum Intelligence, Smart Healthcare, Blockchain, Internet of Things, Data Mining, Big Data, Learning Analytics, Opinion Mining, machine learning and Deep Learning are other most his interested areas for continuing to carry out fundamental research. At last, His main aim is to use new technologies for improving the quality of life of humanity not to destroy environment and mankind.

Brian Nussbaum is an Assistant Professor in the College of Emergency Preparedness, Homeland Security and Cybersecurity (CEHC) at the

University at Albany. He also serves as an affiliate scholar at the Center for Internet and Society (CIS) at Stanford Law School. His research has been published in the *Journal of Cyber Policy, Computer Law & Security Review, the Journal of Financial Crime, Public Integrity, Business Horizons,* and *Global Crime.* He formerly served as an intelligence analyst with the state of New York's homeland security agencies.

Antony Overall received a Master's Degree in Information Technology (Cyber Security and Networks) from the School of Engineering and Science, Queensland University of Technology (QUT), Australia. He is currently an associate at PwC Australia working in Cyber Security and Digital Trust working the assurance division. His research interest includes Intelligent Transportation Systems and Security Governance.

Gowri Ramachandran is a research fellow at the Queensland University of Technology. He received his PhD from imec-DistriNet, KU Leuven, Belgium, and worked as a postdoctoral researcher at the University of Southern California for three years. Gowri's research interests revolve around the Internet of Things, smart cities, and supply chains. He is broadly interested in solving trust, performance, and scalability issues involving decentralized architectures and blockchain technologies.

A. N. M. Bazlur Rashid received the BSc degree in Computer Science and Engineering from Rajshahi University of Engineering and Technology, Bangladesh, in 2004, and the MSc degree in Information and Communication Technology from the Bangladesh University of Engineering and Technology, in 2010. He is currently pursuing the PhD degree with the School of Science, Edith Cowan University, Australia. From 2005 to 2010, he has served in different organizations in different roles, such as database administrator and programmer. In 2010, he joined Comilla University, Bangladesh, as a lecturer at the Department of Computer Science and Engineering. Since 2012, he has been an assistant professor (Computer) with the Bangladesh University of Textiles. He is the author of a number of conference and journal articles in reputed venues. His research interests include cybersecurity, Big Data analytics, evolutionary computation, machine learning, data science, feature selection, knowledge discovery, and decision support systems.

Tahmina Rashid is an associate professor in International Studies, at the University of Canberra, Australia. Her previous work includes "Contested Representations: Punjabi Women in Feminist Debates in Pakistan" and "International Development: Linking Academia with Development Aid & Effectiveness".

Saiyidi Mat Roni is an academic in the School of Business and Law at Edith Cowan University, Australia. He has over two decades of experience in academia, teaching as a lecturer in accounting and finance. He has been actively consulted by researchers across multiple disciplines on data analysis. Saiyidi has also been invited to deliver trainings in statistical analysis for research students and academics in Australia as well as abroad. He is also the lead author of two statistical books published by Springer. Saiyidi's primary research interests are the behaviour side of accounting, information systems, and the emerging technologies that are changing the accounting, auditing, and finance landscape.

Matthew Ryan is a cyber resilience expert for the Australian Prudential Regulatory Authority (APRA). He has previously performed senior cybersecurity roles for organisations such as the Commonwealth Bank of Australia, Deloitte, and the Australian Defence Force. He completed multiple master's degrees before receiving his doctorate from the University of New South Wales in 2020 for his research into the rise of ransomware. In his current role, he is responsible for the ongoing development of prudential cyber security standards, and for evaluating the cybersecurity and technology resilience for many of Australia's largest financial institutions. Concurrently he is a cyber security researcher at the UNSW specializing in enterprise cybersecurity, strategy, and risk management practices.

Munir Ahmad Saeed is currently enrolled in Doctor of Project Management and his research is focused on investigating Benefits Management Practices in the Australian Public Sector organizations. He is working as a lecturer at the College of Business and Management, Canberra Institute of Technology. He won Walt Lipke award for best research article from Project Governance Control Symposium (PGCS) 2020. He has published various book chapters and conference papers. Saeed has worked as a journalist for 10 years and has an abiding interest in politics and social issues. He holds bachelor of Arts, bachelor of Business, Master of English Literature and Master of Project Management.

Zahra Alidousti Shahraki received her master degree in computer architecture at university of Isfahan, Iran (2011–2014). Since then, she is teaching at Technical and Vocational university of Shahrekord, Iran (Oct 2014–Now) and also she is research director of Researcher's Women community in Shahrekord, Iran (Oct 2019–now). Her interest is the study of the topics of Quantum intelligence, Human Computer Interaction (HCI), Psychology, User Experience, Educational Technologies, Cognitive Science, Security, Privacy, Computer Architecture, Image Processing, Machine Learning and Deep Learning. She is doing research about new artificial intelligence technologies and effects of them in societies. In her research, she always wants know more about how we can develop new technologies and what effects are to be expected on humanity.

Leslie F. Sikos is a computer scientist specializing in artificial intelligence and data science, with a focus on cybersecurity applications. He holds two PhD degrees and 20+ industry certificates. He has worked in both academia and the industry, and acquired hands-on skills in datacenter and cloud infrastructures, cyberthreat management, and firewall configuration. He made contributions to major cybersecurity projects in collaboration with the Australian Government's Defence Science and Technology Group, CSIRO's Data61, and the Cyber Security Cooperative Research Centre. He is an active member of the research community as an author, editor, reviewer, conference organizer, and speaker, and a member of industry-leading organizations, such as the ACM and the IEEE. He contributed to international standards and developed state-of-the-art AI systems. Dr. Sikos published more than 20 books, including textbooks, monographs, and edited volumes.

Terri Trireksani is the honors coordinator and a lecturer in Accounting at Murdoch University, Australia. An experienced academic, Terri is committed to her research, teaching, and supervision of PhD students. She has been awarded a national Australian Learning and Teaching Citation Award for an Outstanding Contribution to Student Learning and Vice-Chancellor's Citations for Excellence in Enhancing Learning. She is also a recipient of several research and teaching grants. Before joining academia, she was an accounting practitioner and consultant. Her research interests are in the areas of sustainability reporting, accounting education, and management and accounting issues in Indonesia and Australasia.

Abu Barkat Ullah attained his PhD in Computer Science from UNSW Australia in 2009. His research expertise encompasses cybersecurity and safety, data analytics, decision analytics, evolutionary optimization and covers a wide range of applications. He has the experience and expertise in delivering Higher Education, research in IT and Cyber Security for domestic and international institutes and universities. Before joining the University of Canberra, Dr. Abu Barkat Ullah was the Head of the Department of Cyber Security and Games at Canberra Institute of Technology, Canberra, Australia. He has set up a Security operations centre for cyber training (TSOC) at CIT, jointly with Aust Cyber, Fifth domain. This project for National Cyber Security Education and Training, CIT (in partnership with Fifth Domain and AustCyber), was awarded winners of the '2019 ACT Industry Collaboration Award'. He was a member of CIT's Academic Council and Corporate Resources Committee. Dr Barkat Ullah is a member of a number of professional bodies. He has received several awards and recognition for his career achievement, including 'CIT Board Award' for Leadership, Industry engagement and Business growth.

Chapter 1

Enterprise Threat Intelligence

Craig Jarvis
Independent Cyber Security Strategist

CONTENTS

DOI: 10.1201/9781003121541-1

1

1.1 INTRODUCTION: SECURITY RISK & INTELLIGENCE

Security is dependent upon threat insights, otherwise known as intelligence. Without intelligence enterprises are unable to calibrate controls – they are blind, or at best, myopic. Cyber defense requires fighting battles on multiple fronts. Unlike in conventional warfare, enterprises cannot return fire – they must absorb the punishment of distant enemies. Occasionally, adversaries loiter closer to home, perhaps even within their own citadels. Enterprises must also be fortified against the carelessness of their own forces, whose mistakes may cost battles that at worst lead to corporate demise. To avoid such eventualities enterprises must be hardened against compromise, and incident response must be rehearsed – for history suggests breaches are all but inevitable. Post-compromise, enterprises are judged not only in the court of public opinion, but in regulator's offices, the rulings from whence could render billions of dollars in fines. Two principal factors determine the scale of such penalties: were proportionate defensive controls implemented? and, was breach response effective? Meeting the first of these requirements necessitates an enterprise risk assessment. Breach risks include confidentiality losses via stolen intellectual property or personally identifiable information (PII), integrity damage, such as the altering of bank balances, and availability impacts, such as extortionists encrypting enterprise assets. An evolving additional risk is that attackers endanger human safety, such as via the manipulation of traffic lights, or of manufacturing processes – such risks are rapidly transitioning from science fiction to science fact. The impact of these risks manifesting includes brand damage, competitive advantage forfeit, financial loss, and even enterprise extinction. Breaches are also often resume-generating events for executives, in particular the CEO, CIO, and CISO. A 2020 Ponemon study estimates breaches with less than 99,730 client records stolen cost enterprises an average of $3.86m. The same study found compromises of 1 to 10 million records resulted in an average $50m loss, whilst breaches exceeding 50 million records cost businesses an average $392m [1]. As regulations are made stringent, more of these costs are associated with fines. For example, Capital One was fined $80m for a 2019 breach that compromised the credit applications of 100 million users [2]. An even more severe £183m (~$250m) fine was issued to British Airways after a 2018 breach exposed 500,000 customer records, this was later reduced to £20m (~$26m) in recognition of the crippling impact the pandemic was having on the airline sector [3]. Cyber Defense Consultancy Director Dan Baker, who has worked with scores of technology executives, comments, "it isn't fear of criminals, it's fear of regulations that drives enterprise security investment" [4]. We can expect further large fines in the coming years.

Intelligence enables defense calibration minimizing breach risk. It is said that intelligence is the world's second oldest profession.[1] One of the first warfare philosophers, Sun Tzu, commented around 2500 years ago that, "the reason the enlightened prince and the wise general conquer the enemy whenever they move and their achievements surpass those of ordinary men is foreknowledge [intelligence]" [5, p. 144]. At its best, intelligence locates adversaries, reveals their intent and capabilities, and allows the devising of defensive countermeasures to diminish, or even remove, associated risks. Cyber security is critically dependent on intelligence. Traditional bricks and mortar enterprises had few exposure points. Security resided in physical security measures such as guards, and industry-specific controls such as merchandise alarm tags. Digital transformations, accelerated by the pandemic, have resulted in what scholar Frances Cairncross terms the "death of distance" – physical distance no longer hinders adversaries [6]. Therefore, enterprises now face a greater number of more diverse threats. The threat actors are often well-funded, highly skilled, and extremely persistent. Intelligence allows assessment of these disparate threats and controls calibration. Intelligence is also crucial in reducing an overwhelming number of security alerts to reveal critical events, and in improving the performance of the second factor regulators use in determining breach fines: incident response. Ultimately, intelligence enables better business decisions.

1.1.1 Chapter Roadmap

This chapter explores each threat group and offers selective countermeasure recommendations. In Section 2 organized crime is explored, with examination of identity theft, financial and asset systems targeting, extortion, and infrastructure squatting. Nation states are the focus of Section 3, with espionage, financial-gain operations, sabotage, and influence activities all explored. Section 4 provides an overview of hacktivism, which, whilst currently at a historical nadir, remains a problem to enterprises with particularly immature defenses. Section 5 considers the emerging challenge of cyber terrorism, whilst Section 6 assesses the risks of insider threats. Finally, Section 7 examines future threats including artificial intelligence, adversarial machine learning, quantum-insecure cryptography, and the vulnerability of cyber-physical systems on which our societies are dependent.

1.2 ORGANIZED CRIME

Cybercrime represents the majority of enterprise attacks [7, p. 9]. Criminals manage their operations as multi-national high-revenue businesses and focus heavily on innovation. A rich and collaborative criminal eco-system underwrites the industry's prodigious success. Adversarial capabilities range from misguided self-taught teens, to organized criminal enterprises the sophistication of which rivals some nation states. Cybercriminals typically operate from jurisdictions beyond the reach of their victim's governments. For instance, criminal marketplaces often forbid their products use in the Commonwealth of Independent States (CIS), the home of a high concentration of cybercriminals [8], 22:00].[2] Malware may enforce geographic filters to ensure such diktats are not violated. Cybercriminals may also bribe local law enforcement to turn a blind eye to their operations, with the caveat that the criminal's activities must not target countries with which their government has good relations (for Russia, the CIS). In short, cybercrime offers perpetrators a drastic risk reduction in comparison to physical crime, a reality which has driven cybercrime's vertigo-inducing growth. There are several methods cybercriminals use to part enterprises from their profits.

1.2.1 Identity Theft

Identity theft involves criminals using stolen PII to impersonate victims for financial fraud. For instance, the threat actor may acquire credit in the victim's name before using that credit to make large purchases, which can then be cashed-out via black market resales. Such operations require a network of criminals involved at different stages of the attack chain, from malware authors, to money mules. Attackers can also sell the pilfered details online; such datasets are increasingly rich as attackers harvest victim's browser settings enabling an emulation of their digital identity, thus reducing the chance of anti-fraud detection. In 2020, the average dark web price for the details of a stolen credit card with an account balance of up to $5000 was just $20, physical cloned credit cards started at $15 [9]. However, identity theft is trending downwards [10]. This is because improving cyber security is removing the lowest hanging fruit upon which criminals feast, and as extortion attacks offer easier and swifter monetization. Initial access for identity theft is often achieved with spear-phishing, technical vulnerability exploitation, or via access brokers (actors who breach a network before selling their access, Mandiant assessed 2% of intrusions they investigated during 2020 were for this purpose) [11, p. 19]. Lateral movement typically occurs quickly, with the database servers almost always the destination from where PII is stolen.

1.2.1.1 Countermeasures

Database security is imperative to countering the bulk loss of PII. Sensitive data requires a well-documented lifecycle with encryption applied wherever possible. **Identity and access management** is also crucial. A **least privilege** model should limit the ability of entities to read from PII databases. Where possible **two-factor authentication**, ideally hardware (U2F) security tokens, should be used, especially for those with sensitive accesses. **Cloud security** is another common ingress method, with security firm checkpoint noting misconfiguration as the main associated problem [12, p. 23]. Such misconfiguration often leads to exposed credentials which can enable breach – enterprises should make use of tools such as GitHub's secret scanning to continually monitor for exposed credentials. Security firm Trustwave's SVP of Strategy Marco Pereira comments, "most people don't truly understand the profound security implications of [the] cloud, it's like our understanding of the Internet 25 years ago" [13]. Cloud security should be a focus to manage all threat actors, as should **patching. Dark web monitoring** should be considered for stolen data identification. Enterprises should also consider defensively searching client email addresses against breach lists, such as www.haveibeenpwned.com. Any available credentials on the dark web will often become part of a credential stuffing attack, whereby the username and password are tried against multiple websites as an attacker hopes to find an instance of password reuse. Where breached account owners are identified they can be notified, and provided security recommendations.

1.2.2 Financial & Asset System Targeting

1.2.2.1 Payment Card Attacks

Targeting of enterprise points of sale (PoS) infrastructure is becoming more challenging due to security advances. Chip and pin technologies are also minimizing the locations at which stolen credit cards numbers alone can be used. Additionally, the rise of extortion-oriented attacks have caused criminal groups, such as Russia-based Carbon Spider, to transition from PoS attacks to ransomware [11, p. 6]. There are two main PoS targets – PoS physical infrastructure, such as retailer payment terminals, and online payment systems. Verizon found that only 0.8% of breaches were directed at PoS terminals in 2019, marking a "notable decrease in the last few years" [7, p. 37]. To access PoS terminals attackers typically first compromise the enterprise network before pivoting into PoS infrastructure. RAM scrapers are then used to extract card details from the PoS' memory. Exploiting e-commerce payment methods typically requires breaching the host website before injecting code, often JavaScript, into the payment system to harvest card details. These attacks are known as cyber skimming or formjacking, and are rising as attacks against physical PoS diminish. Attackers also abuse online payment systems to test the validity of credit cards acquired elsewhere, and to attempt to guess card verification numbers (transactions are aborted before completing to avoid detection). One CISO of a national retailer comments, "this problem is vast and everywhere [...] the danger is it prevents legitimate transactions acting as an unintended denial of service attack" [14].

1.2.2.1.1 Countermeasures

Network segregation is vital for defending payment systems, as is making the enterprise itself harder to compromise, thus reducing the possibility of lateral movements into PoS infrastructure. **File integrity monitoring** is helpful for e-commerce payment infrastructure modification detection. Third-party services, such as analytics, used at the digital point of sale should be minimized to reduce the chance of an attack occurring via a third party. Users with code modification privileges should use **2FA**, ideally with U2F tokens. **Basic hygiene** such as the use of web application firewalls, vulnerability scans, and penetration testing will also help protect the environment. PCI Security Standards Council guidance should also be applied to PoS infrastructure.

1.2.2.2 Business Email Compromise (BEC)

BEC occurs when an enterprise employee is socially engineered (i.e., tricked) into making a fraudulent asset transfer to an attacker.[3] Social-engineering exploits human emotions and behavior, in particular greed, curiosity, fear, and the desire to be helpful [11, p. 15]. In BEC attacks, social engineering usually occurs via an email exchange, but may include telephony. Typically, financial assets are transferred, though attackers may seek other assets suitable for resale, or even sensitive data. To socially engineer the target the attacker makes the request whilst masquerading as a colleague of the target, or as another trusted third party. Threat actors often collect open-source intelligence (OSINT) to enable BEC attacks. They may also breach the enterprise to study its financial transfer procedures, and to identify suitable entities as whom they can masquerade. Mo Philip, a CISO and former financial regulator comments:

> I've seen many successful BEC attacks, attackers do lots of reconnaissance, they know the language, frequency, and cadence of financial transactions - that makes requests more plausible and therefore more likely to be successful [...] criminals have made off with billions of pounds as a result [15].

Typically, the transfer request is instilled with a sense of urgency to prevent request vetting time. For example, the likely Russia-based Cosmic Lynx attackers impersonate an enterprise's CEO and asks the target employee to work with "external legal counsel" to arrange a "time-sensitive" acquisition payment – the employee's discretion is sought during this "highly sensitive" transaction [16, pp. 4–5]. Another attacker approach is to hijack an existing email thread with a trusted supplier. In this scenario an adversary hijacks a thread and replies to, or forwards, the message, either masquerading as an existing correspondent, or imitating another individual, commenting that an invoice urgently requires payment. The established thread which includes legitimate messages from colleagues causes the target to think they are amongst trusted parties, making them less likely to challenge the transfer request. International BEC damages amounted to $26b in total costs during 166,000 incidents between June 2016 and July 2019, according to the FBI. The money mostly went to China and Hong Kong [17]. The funds are then typically laundered through a series of accounts. Alternatively, currency is withdrawn and laundered through cash-heavy businesses, such as casinos, where cash is exchanged for chips, before being converted back to a cheque suitable for a bank deposit.

According to the Anti-Phishing Working Group (APWG), a collection of 2000+ organizations, the average Q4 2020 BEC demand was $75,000. Whilst some attackers request six and seven figure sums, criminals perhaps see lower values as the sweet spot. Smaller amounts are less likely to trigger financial and audit controls, and may be deemed of insufficient value to subsequently justify a corporate investigation or legal action. The APWG found gift cards, of an average value of $1260, were requested in 60% of Q4 2020 attacks, 13% of attacks instructed payroll diversions, whilst 22% solicited bank transfers, the remaining 5% requested other payment methods [18, pp. 6–7]. Gift cards are appealing as more employees of lower seniority are empowered to transfer them, and the smaller values may not trigger alerts. Black market services are available to exchange gift cards for Bitcoin [19, p. 49]. The APWG also found around 75% of BEC attack emails originated from free webmail accounts. In the other cases domains were registered by the attackers, these were likely domains which emulated their masquerade entities' domain, a practice known as typo squatting – bulletproof hosting services, which, with the exception of child abuse content, will not remove hosted content or co-operate with law enforcement, are often used [18, p. 5]. BEC will likely continue to uptrend as the pandemic has made BEC more appealing, Philip comments, "Given the trend towards more remote working there are increased chances for BEC successes as transfer authorities are less likely to be physically co-located [reducing the chance of attack detection]" [15].

1.2.2.2.1 Countermeasures

BEC defense requires a well-trained staff and **hardened business processes**. Philip comments, "Technical controls are getting better, but individuals remain the weakest link" [15]. Those employees empowered to make asset transfers should receive additional **counter-BEC training**, including ongoing simulation tests to inculcate constant awareness. Asset transfer business processes should be clear; transfer authorities must be empowered to deny transfers when the requestor does not adhere to such processes. Where possible, transfer requests should be made in person to mitigate forgery potential, though in global enterprises this may be challenging. **Multi-person authorization** should be used, with asset transfers countersigned by further transfer authorities (who should ideally be contacted in person or via telephone by the requestor, as well as by email to reduce the chance of a BEC-induced authorization). At least **two-factor authentication, ideally hardware (U2F) security tokens,** should be used to authorize asset transfers. **Domain-based Message Authentication, Reporting & Conformance** (DMARC) can help prevent adversaries masquerading as enterprise employees, and potential typo squatting domains should be defensively registered. These measures should be underpinned by **robust security hygiene.**

1.2.2.3 Direct Financial System Attacks

Whilst BEC is mostly an indirect, human-dependent attack, being reliant on unwitting employee facilitation, financial attacks not relying on inadvertent insider aid are also a substantial enterprise threat. In direct financial system attacks an enterprise is breached before the threat actor conducts asset transfer process reconnaissance to gain the necessary insights and credentials to execute a transfer. These attacks often take months to complete. Carbanak are one of the most notorious criminal groups in this category. Investigative bodies assess Carbanak has stolen more than $1b from 100 financial institutions. Each attack took two to four months. Spear phishing enabled enterprise breaches, before attackers identified the financial transfer authorities and recorded their computer screens to study the transfer processes. As well as direct transfers, threat actors at times programmed their target's ATM fleets to disperse thousands of dollars, an attack known as Jackpotting, to their awaiting operatives [20]. Financial enterprises are not alone in being targeted. As financial organizations have fortified their defenses against this type of attack, adversaries have targeted other verticals, as all companies have financial transfer systems. Corporate reward or gift card systems, the latter particularly prevalent in the retail sector, are also targeted. In one case, an attacker submitted employee reward nominations from one compromised account before approving them with another compromised account [19, p. 49]. Crypto currency financial exchanges have also been breached with severe losses resulting from direct transfers. For instance, $460m was stolen from Mt. Gox in 2014, and $500m from Coincheck in 2018 [21].

1.2.2.3.1 Countermeasures

Direct financial attacks are executed by some of the most advanced adversaries enterprises confront. As well as the **BEC risk reduction** measurespreviously outlined, defense-in-depth is vital for early detection. The long surveillance period often required for asset transfers attacks offers defenders ample detection time; monitoring solutions should incorporate **user and entity behavior analytics** (UEBA). Given financial institutions invest heavily in cyber security, one problem often identified in the wake of direct financial attacks is that their security software was not performing as expected. Security firm Crowdstrike observes, "Time and again, CrowdStrike observed successful intrusions in environments where security controls were in place that could have successfully blocked attacks, but were not configured by the organization to do so or were not fully deployed across the environment" [22, p. 65]. **Continuous security validation** (CSV) tooling should be considered to address this issue. CSV allows an organization to verify if security controls are functioning as expected, and to map controls against attack frameworks such as Miter's ATT&CK matrix. Such practices are niche now, but will become standard in the coming years, and are vital for managing complex control estates.

1.2.2.4 Crypto Currency Attacks

Crypto currencies theft continues to be a criminal priority. The decentralized nature of currencies such as Bitcoin and Monero limits law enforcement's ability to identify ownership. Digital laundering facilities offer a further investigative obfuscation layer. Cambridge University estimates that Bitcoin mining alone accounted for 0.31% of global energy consumption in 2020 – more than the estimated national usage of Austria or Columbia [23]. Whilst legitimate miners hire or build compute power to digitally excavate crypto currencies, criminals breach enterprises to steal compute and mine, a practice known as crypto-jacking. Checkpoint estimated 21% of 2020 cyber-attacks were crypto-jackers [24, p. 35]. Cryptojacking is pernicious for several reasons. First, there is the stolen compute cost. However, theft of large compute volumes risks rapid detection, particularly on cloud infrastructure, therefore attackers may steal low compute volumes to remain unnoticed. Second, resource theft can impact the performance of other enterprise assets, though this may also risk rapid detection, therefore some miners only operate at times of low compute demand. For instance, the Monero Madness miner only runs after a machine's user is idle for 60 seconds [25]. Whilst crypto miners degrade performance and increase compute costs, the more acute risk is the attacker's enterprise access facilitating more impactful breaches.

1.2.2.4.1 Countermeasures

As well as defense-in-depth, particular focus should be on **monitoring compute resource for unusual spikes.** Other steps such as using **anti-cryptomining browser extensions** and **ad-blockers** to prevent breach vector is helpful. Enterprises should disable JavaScript, often used by cryptominers, where possible – though there is a substantial security-usability trade-off with this control. Anti-virus (AV) is competent at detecting all but the newest crypto miner variants.

1.2.3 Extortion

1.2.3.1 Denial of Service (DoS)

DoS attacks aim to exhaust resources so a service, or services, cannot function. Most commonly, threat actors use stolen resources, such as a Botnets, to mount distributed DoS (DDoS) attacks. The large number of unprotected IoT devices is contributing towards the potency of DDoS Botnets. For instance, Mirai, a Botnet comprising mostly IoT devices, disrupted Amazon, Netflix, and Twitter in 2016 [26]. The size of attacks continues to grow, with the largest exceeding 2.5 TB per second by early 2021 [7, p. 36], [27]. DDoS offensives come in a variety of forms, the simplest being volumetric attacks whereby a high volume of requests are made of a resource, such as a website, in an attempt to overwhelm the server and prevent the returning of legitimate requests. Variants of this attack can include state exhaustion attacks, whereby the system's concurrent connection capacity is exceeded by the attackers conducting a SYN flood, an attack where the first part of a TCP connection is initiated but the connection is never completed. This leaves the system keeping a partial TCP connection open in anticipation of a response that will never arrive – when enough connections are partially instigated the server will no longer have capacity to instigate new connections. Another DoS method targets application logic. For instance, large request volumes can be sent to resource intensive operations, such as database writes likely to include SQL joins. Attacks can also be reflective – an adversary may spoof the IP of their target and request a service, such as a DNS resolution which is then reflected to the target. DoS attacks are increasingly multi-vector, using a combination of these methods to mount their offensive. DDoS attacker monetization is typically via extortion, known as Ransom DoS (RDoS). Typically, RDoS attacks occur in three stages: a brief attack demonstrates capability; a ransom is delivered; a full DoS attack occurs unless the ransom is paid. This pattern evolved after a spate of attacks where new adversaries masqueraded as known threat actors in an attempt to scare targets into capitulation, these charlatans lacked DoS capabilities [28]. It is also possible that an enterprise competitor may hire attackers to execute a DoS attack during a commercially expedient moment. Competitor instigated DoS attacks occurred during the 1990s, such as between online gambling rivals on occasion of key sporting events. However, evidence for such attacks more recently is limited. One example is when an employee of Cellcom, a Liberian mobile phone provider, hired a British national to conduct a DDoS against its business rival, Lonestar, in 2016 [29]. The attack intermittently blocked Liberia's entire Internet connection over a two-day period. Despite the dearth of case studies, a Kaspersky poll found a large proportion of victims believed their DDoS attacks were competitor-instigated [30]. This could reflect Kaspersky's primarily Russian client base, a jurisdiction where the rule of law is not always robust, and therefore such sentiments may not be globally representative. Where corporations chose to attack their competitors, they will find DoS services can be hired via DarkWeb forums for as little as $10 [9].

1.2.3.1.1 Countermeasures

DoS attacks should ideally be blocked at the network level to prevent application layer impact. **DoS protection services** can be procured from numerous suppliers, including the major cloud providers. Such providers use analytics to identify and block likely malicious requests. However, DoS protection mechanisms will likely impact at least some legitimate traffic. Therefore, it is important to **use log analysis to profile your traffic before an attack**. For instance, if your resource has never received Cambodian requests, then during an attack such requests can likely be blocked with minimum impact on legitimate requests. Enterprises can also use **Anycast**, rather than Unicast, addresses for incoming web requests. This enables the workload to be spread over several assets, rather than allowing attackers to focus on a single resource-constrained server. **Microservice architectures** are more resilient than monolithic architectures to DoS attacks as they can autoscale, rapidly replicating system components, such as APIs, as well as middleware, such as load balancers to endure traffic floods. Techniques such as **SYN cookies** can help identify requestors complicit in SYN floods, and **CAPTCHAs** can aid in distinguishing human over bot requests. Enterprise architects should design their systems for **graceful degradation**, rather than outright failure, in anticipation of DoS attacks. Techniques such as HTTP throttling, constraining bandwidth-egress requirements, and offering scaled back service versions, such as Gmail's SimpleHTML, can all aid in mitigating and minimizing DoS attack impacts. Managing ransom demands will be explored during ransomware countermeasures.

1.2.3.2 Ransomware

Whilst ransomware first victimized consumers, enterprise targeting, known as big game hunting (BGH), became the vogue post-2017 [12, p. 30], [31]. John Maynard, previously Security VP at Cisco and now CEO of security firm Adarma, stated that 66% of all Cisco's incident response work concerned ransomware in 2020, and it was not only poorly funded public institutions being victimized, Maynard comments, "Very large enterprises with mature security are also suffering attacks" [32]. BGH Ransomware is harder to detect than commodity ransomware; code is often custom written and uniquely packed for each victim – known bad detection methods such as signatures are often ineffective. Ransomware enterprise infiltration is achieved via multiple methods. FBI's Agent DeCapua states that Remote Desktop Protocol (RDP) brute force attacks, where username and passwords are guessed, account for 70–80% of breaches – Sophos concurs recognizing RDP as the top ransomware vector [8], [11:17], [33]. Spear phishing and unsecured network services provide additional ransomware ingress points [12, p. 30]. Supply chain attacks, such as those against managed service providers, are also effective. Successful compromise of such entities enables ransomware deployment to vast numbers of clients via remote management software [22, p. 65]. Access brokers provide another attack vector. For instance, XDedic Marketplace was, according to DeCapua the, "biggest RDP marketplace in the world [before being taken down], it's where lots and lots of ransomware actors would go and purchase access to their victim's networks," Decapua adds, "a lot of ransomware hackers aren't sophisticated hackers, they're buying network access and deploying ransomware, we find this all the time" [[8], 7:17]. Ransomware is also a contingent plan when attackers breach enterprises yet cannot achieve their primary objective. For instance, one attacker, known as UNC1733, turned to ransomware within a day of failing to acquire payment card information [19, p. 35]. Attackers may also use multi-faceted extortion attacks, perhaps extracting confidential data before deploying ransomware. Malware-as-a-service providers, such as Venom Spider, have introduced ransomware modules making it easy for cybercriminals to augment their traditional data-theft operations with encryption-based attacks [22, p. 4]. Criminals are also embracing penetration testing tools, most notably Cobalt Strike, which was leveraged in 66% of the ransomware attacks Cisco investigated as of late 2020 [34]. Tools of such sophistication are no longer a pre-requisite for ransomware deployment – the attacker's technical entry threshold is continually lowering. FBI's DeCapua comments:

> If you want to create your own Ransomware the code is there, very advanced versions of ransomware are available on GitHub you just take it, the disclaimers are its for educational purposes only, you change the virtual wallet to your wallet, your write any note that you want, and you can deploy it on a victim system [[8], 9:10].

Even if ransomware is the primary intent, attackers increasingly steal enterprise data for additional leverage should a victim refuse to pay the decryption ransom. This trend is the result of more robust enterprise back-up procedures. Even when ransomware successfully targets backups many enterprises refuse to pay the ransom [35, p. 23]. Threatening to leak sensitive corporate data further induces payment, and can facilitate additional extortion after a decryption ransom is paid. Attackers have settled on a common toolset for data extraction using living off the land (LoTL) techniques, whereby pre-existing system utilities that often go undetected by AV are used. These tools include Total Commander – a file manager with built-in FTP client, 7Zip, WinRAR, pSFTP (Putty SFTP client), and Windows cURL [33, pp. 5–6]. Purloined data is often sent to locations that will not draw attention, such as Google Drive or Amazon S3 buckets [33, p. 7]. When client data is stolen, attackers are becoming media savvy during ransom extraction. As early as 2016, "the Dark Overlord" (TDO) pioneered the leaking of small amounts of stolen data on Tor-based dedicated leak sites (DLS) when enterprises refused to pay the encryption ransom.[4] TDO then alerted the media that the enterprise had failed to protect their client's data, and were unwilling to pay the ransom to prevent further data leakage [36]. Consequently, the enterprise endures negative media coverage, as well being implored by their clients and partners to pay the ransom and prevent further privacy violations. Some attackers even release the data small percentages at a time, prolonging the victim's agony and further giving them the opportunity to pay the ransom when they start to experience the damage being caused. An example of ransomware and data theft occurred when Utah University was attacked in 2020. Whilst defenses stopped the encryption when only 0.02% of server data was encrypted, the University subsequently paid $457,000 to prevent student's confidential data being leaked. The insurer and university each contributed towards the payment [37]. News reports indicate the attacker was likely NetWalker, a group that in a four-month period in 2020 made at least £25 m from similar operations [38]. For some malware families such as REvil, stolen files are available for anyone to purchase directly from their website, offering criminal revenue streams when enterprises do not pay to prevent their data from being leaked [33, p. 5]. Crowdstrike comments that by 2021, "Data theft and the use of DLS' have arguably become as engrained in the BGH ransomware operation as the encryption process itself" [11, p. 23]. Even if ransomware does not seek to first steal data, encryption is not necessarily its priority on execution. The encryption process is computationally expensive and time-consuming. Therefore, disabling security controls is often the first priority to ensure detection does not occur during encryption operations [31, p. 4]. Additionally, attackers may need to move laterally, circumvent defenses, locate privileged domain accounts, and identify backups before encrypting files. Mandiant found that ransomware was within a network for an overall median dwell time of 5 days during 2020 before discovery, suggesting that the encryptors were yet to execute [11, p. 13].[5] This gives defenders with strong detection capabilities the chance to stop the attacker before encryption commences.

Enterprises sometimes covertly pay ransoms, especially as such an act may be illegal in their jurisdiction. Sophos found 26% of enterprises pay the ransom, with criminals decrypting environments in 95% of those breaches

[31, p. 3]. The FBI estimates that between 2013 and 2019, $144m was paid to extortionists in Bitcoin alone, with Ryuk ransomware generating $61m [8], 8:34]. Ransom demands range from tens of thousands, to millions of dollars – one of the highest being a $50m ransom demand of Acer in 2021 [39]. This is separate from the ransomware-related enterprise costs resultant from associated downtime, incident response, equipment replacement, brand damage, and potential regulatory fines. The average 2020 ransomware incident cost according to Sophos was $730k for enterprises that refuse to pay ransoms, and $1.44m for those that capitulate [31, p. 2]. However, this cost is often far exceeded by large enterprises. For instance, the 2017 Not-Petya attacks cost pharmaceutical company Merck around $1.3b [40]. Cyber insurance can offset some ransomware risk; however, policies have high excesses and are increasingly expensive. Cyber insurance is also believed to be contributing to the ransomware epidemic. Emsisoft's Fabian Wosar comments, "Cyber insurance is what's keeping ransomware alive today. It's a perverted relationship. They [insurers] will pay anything, as long as it is cheaper than the loss of revenue they have to cover otherwise" [41]. The ransom payments further cause the industry to grow, and more companies to take out expensive cyber insurance policies.

1.2.3.2.1 Countermeasures

As well as general security hygiene, **backups** must be regularly created, routinely tested, and at least one copy should be kept offline. **Endpoint controls** are particularly important, as is **rapid OS patching** – 60% of breaches could have been prevented by patching according to a 2019 study, which also found it took an average 16 days to patch a critical vulnerability [42, p. 5]. More than 18,300 vulnerabilities were reported in 2020, a 183% increase from 2015 [43]. Therefore, patching should be prioritized using the Common Vulnerability Scoring System (CVVS) and other variables such as the availability of exploits. Whilst much attention is placed on zero-days, of which there were only 29 in 2020, vulnerability scanning experts Tenable argue:

> Unpatched vulnerabilities are a bigger problem than zero-days [...] This low-hanging fruit is favored by nation state actors and run-of-the-mill cybercriminals alike. While zero-day vulnerabilities are often leveraged as part of targeted attacks, unpatched vulnerabilities are targeted en masse, posing a much greater threat [42].

Security tooling is improving at identifying ransomware; it is helpful as some ransomware traits are hard to obfuscate. For instance, successive document encryption is often detectable via associated calls to system APIs. Other measures include **account lockout policies** and **2FA** to prevent account hijacking, **disabling RDP and SMB** where possible, and ensuring robust lateral movement controls (e.g., microsegmentation). Services such as RDP should be placed behind firewalls that first require users to connect via a VPN or a zero-trust mechanism.

Moral complexity engulfs whether enterprises should pay ransoms. The ideal, and most virtuous, policy is never to yield. However, for some enterprises there are compelling arguments for capitulation. For instance, consider a hospital where inaccessible patient records or critical infrastructure could cause fatalities. In another scenario, consider a manufacturer that is the foundation of a local communities' economy, perhaps the cyber-physical systems (CPS) that control its factory operations become encrypted by an attacker, and is too esoteric and expensive to be replaced [43].[6] The demise of this business could cause hundreds of job losses and ruin a once prosperous community. There are many further scenarios where ransom payment may be considered the lesser evil. This was the case when the University of California San Francisco School of Medicine had some of their servers encrypted during the pandemic. The attackers, believed to be the Netwalker gang, demanded what is reported to be a £3m ransom. The BBC was able to observe the bartering process, which may have been conducted by a professional negotiator such as Coveware, rather than the victim itself. During the negotiation the attacker spurned offers below their demand, stating the victim should keep the money, "to buy McDonalds for your employees." Subsequently, the adversary did accept $1.14 [44]. Regarding their surrender, the University stated, "The data that was encrypted is important to some of the academic work we pursue as a university serving the public good" [45]. On the other side of the equation, one must consider the ransom's destination. Whilst some payments may enable extortionists to spend the next year on a warm beach with a cold beer, other ransoms will further fund cybercrime, thus perpetuating the problem, and may even enable more unsavory pursuits such as child exploitation or terrorism. There are no easy answers. Even when the ransom is paid there are no guarantees the enterprise's data will be decrypted, and such a capitulation may set a precedent for future attacks. There is no clear sight as to how the ransomware problem could end, security firm CrowdStrike's CEO George Kurtz comments, "This merciless ransomware epidemic will continue, and worsen, as long as the practice remains lucrative, and relatively easy and risk-free" [22, p. 2].

1.2.4 Infrastructure Squatting

Enterprise breaches are also used to facilitate attacks against third parties. According to Verizon, infrastructure squatting is the second most frequent breach purpose [7, p. 10]. However, Mandiant found only around 3% of their 2020 incident responses were likely for attacker infrastructure squatting [11, p. 19]. As well as offering criminals deniability, using an enterprise's infrastructure may enable the attacker to create a trust relationship with their targets they could otherwise not build. For instance, a malicious communication from a genuine bank email address is more likely to be successful than a spoofed email. In another example, infrastructure squatting often facilitates Botnet augmentation.

1.2.4.1 Countermeasures

General defense-in-depth practices, as well as a focus on web security, can help diminish the risk of infrastructure squatting.

1.3 NATION STATES

Terminology is important when discussing nation state threats. The industry language of an enterprise having suffered a cyber-attack is not the equivalent of a traditional physical nation state attack. A cyber-attack for instance, in accepted industry parlance, could be an attempt to exploit a server vulnerability to gain enterprise access, whereas a physical nation state attack may be the armed incursion into a country by a foreign actor. Espionage is a more apt descriptor for the majority of state activity, it being most simply described as the covert collection of information. Espionage and cyber-espionage broadly equate. Espionage is an established part of international relations, and is not always negative: consider a nation that believes its neighbor intends war despite its leader's contrary narrative, intelligence collection may provide assurance that peace is in fact their neighbor's intent. Cyber sabotage is closer in analogy to a traditional nation state attack, though such equivalence is still flawed, as cyber sabotage could range from a DDoS attack that temporarily disables a government website, an action with no obvious physical equivalent, to the disabling of air defenses, or the incapacitation of power plants. States also conduct influence operations, in the same way they have for generations, using the Internet, though often, such as in the Russian attempted manipulation of the US election, these operations often do not require the breaching of organizations.

1.3.1 Espionage

The earliest indirect nation state cyber-espionage incident occurred in the mid-1980s when the KGB paid German hackers to breach US government systems [46]. In the mid-1990s, another operation of likely Russian origin, Moonlight Maze, represented the first direct nation state operation [44]. Given the secretive nature of espionage, it is possible these were not the first such acts. Mandiant reports that 29% of attacks they investigated during 2020 were likely for intelligence gain [11, p. 19]. The growth of cyber-espionage is unsurprising as it offers many advantages over traditional espionage. First, cyber-espionage can be conducted from a nation's home territory; reducing the risk to the threat actor of being imprisoned in a foreign jail should the operation go awry. Second, cyber scales in a way human intelligence (HUMINT) cannot. Third, cyber is more responsive; HUMINT source cultivation takes months or years, in contrast, once a cyber-espionage capability is established, targeting and exfiltration can occur in days or even hours. However, one should acknowledge that cyber lacks the ability to pose emotionally oriented questions, such as asking a target's confidant "do you feel X will do Y given Z?" Finally, cyber attribution is harder than traditional attribution. Nation states are increasingly designing false flags into their operations, often frustrating attribution to all but the most technologically advanced states. Even when seemingly irrefutable attribution evidence is presented, including named individual perpetrators within the threat actor's state, the accused may practice what has come to be branded as implausible deniability. Implausible deniability is possible as there are no internationally agreed cyber-espionage (or cyber-sabotage) norms. Many developed nations are exploiting this absence of norms, and there is little chance of prosecuting associated government agents, as such measures may bring forth unwanted reciprocity and other unintended consequences. Cyber-espionage meets numerous national security requirements, including intelligence collection against foreign nations, enemies of the state, and dissidents. For instance, when the US Office of Personnel Management (OPM) was breached, likely from at least 2012, the attacker, attributed as China by the FBI, stole 19.7 million investigation records of government employees and contractors holding sensitive security clearances [47,48]. This rich data set could not only aid in the identification of American intelligence officers deployed to Beijing, but could also enable the crafting of bespoke tactics when attempting to recruit Americans to spy for China. Such bulk data sets are of high value to nation states. Bulk communication records are particularly crucial during target profiling. In 2018, security firm Cybereason assessed it was highly likely that China breached a telecoms company serving 200m users – call records were the target [49]. Many similar breaches have occurred. Some nations also target enterprise's intellectual property. NSA director General Keith Alexander stated in 2012 that intellectual property theft from US companies represented the, "greatest transfer of wealth in history," the problem has only got worse since Alexander's assessment [50]. The US has attempted to discourage the theft of intellectual property with only fleeting success. For now at least, in contradiction to the physical world, enterprises will have to protect themselves from nation state aggressors in cyberspace, knowing failure presents an existential threat.

Nation states employ the full spectrum of technical methods to achieve breaches. Their resources can include zero-day attacks. However, most frequently, nation states are economical with the deployment of their cyber arsenal, tending to rely on the minimum sophistication tooling required to achieve their objectives in order to keep their key assets for future use – quite often nation states use commodity malware, which can complicate attribution by causing their operations to become shrouded in the veil of criminality [43]. LoTL techniques are also increasingly popular, with tools such as PowerShell and Windows Management Instrumentation (WMI) used for post-breach actions. Supply chain vectors are also used by nation states to breach targets due to their established trust relationship with numerous entities. One example is the breach of multiple managed security services providers, likely by China [51]. Such operations enable the attackers to leverage the target's trusted access to hundreds of enterprises.

1.3.1.1 Countermeasures

Despite the challenge provided by nation states, the risks can be managed. Enterprises must practice **defense-in-depth**, apply **zero trust principles**, and always adhere to the **assume compromise doctrine**, which dictates a continual monitoring and hunting for adversaries within the enterprise network. **UEBA** should be used to detect anomalies suggestive of breaches. CrowdStrike track a metric called "breakout time," the duration for a threat actor to transition from an initial system foothold to lateral movement. Within all CrowdStrike's 2019 investigations the average attacker breakout time was 4 hours 37 minutes [22, p. 10]. Whilst nation states are faster than this all-threat-actor time, a detection opportunity remains. Even when using zero-day exploits for network access, attackers still need to move laterally, escalate privileges, exfiltrate files – within each step there are numerous possible detection and intervention points. **Browser isolation technologies** should also be considered. Nation states threats at their best are elite adversaries, but they are not beyond enterprise management.

1.3.2 Financial Gain

Nation states do not typically target enterprises for direct financial gain. This is for two reasons: first, all nations depend on the integrity of the global financial system and second, such attacks could result in international condemnation and sanctions. The exception to this rule is countries partially excluded from the international community, such as the Democratic People's Republic of Korea (DPRK [North Korea]). The DPRK is already in poor international standing and enduring crippling sanctions due to their missile programs, therefore, the typical consequences of financial gain operations are moot. The DPRK has stolen an estimated $2b using "widespread and increasingly sophisticated" cyber-attacks according to a 2019 UN assessment. At least 35 DPRK operations, many led by the Reconnaissance General Bureau, targeted financial institutions, crypto currency exchanges, and conducted mining activities to "raise money for its WMD (weapons of mass destruction) programs" [52]. In 2020, the US army estimated that around 1700 DPRK hackers focus on financial gain [53]. One well-known DPRK operation is their audacious 2016 attempt to steal $951m from Bangladesh's

Central Bank [54]. In this attack a DPRK threat group, known as Lazarus, breached the bank's network before spending months learning how to transfer funds using the SWIFT system, which was not segregated from its enterprise network [55].[7] The attackers harvested credentials before attempting to transfer $951m from the bank's accounts to cash-out mechanisms concluding in Filipino casinos. Fortunately, $850m of the transfers were flagged by the New York Federal Reserve, that held the bank's funds. Part of the recipient account's name tripped an automated Federal Reserve audit rule for a sanctioned entity, whilst the alert was a false positive, on closer inspection the Reserve's experts identified several transaction irregularities existed. Therefore, transfer re-confirmation was requested from the Bangladesh bank, thus enabling them to rescind the instruction. Another $20m of fraudulent transfers were stopped by Deutsche Bank, due to a misspelled word in the recipient account's name. $81m was successfully stolen [56]. Excluding the DPRK, theft is the preserve of criminals, Adrian Searle, former Deputy Director of the UK's National Cyber Security Centre comments, "It is unlikely major cyber players like Russia or China, would want to disrupt the operations of a bank other than at time of conflict" [57]. We have no precedent with which to assess what would likely happen during war, would interdependency inoculate global banks from attack but leave regional and local financial institutions vulnerable? There are no established norms – answers may only be revealed during conflict.

1.3.2.1 Countermeasures

Those at most risk are financial service operators. Such entities should utilize the most **advanced detection methods** available, as well as adhering to the guidance given earlier to counteract direct financial system attacks. **Detailed intelligence profiles of known threat actors should be mapped against controls to ensure defensive coverage.** Other high-revenue organizations associated with national power, and high-revenue enterprises, should **fortify defenses around financial transfer capabilities.**

1.3.3 Sabotage

Sabotage is up-trending in cyberspace. Many nations have avowed their cyber offensive capabilities. Sabotage typically occurs during declared conflict, however, it can also form part of hybrid warfare, and covert operations.[8] For example, Russia's 2015 sabotage of Ukrainian power plants during its hybrid warfare campaign resulted in a short-lived blackout across parts of Kiev [58]. Covert actions, such as Stuxnet, a likely US-Israeli operation against Iranian nuclear capability in 2009, represent another example of sabotage outside of declared conflict [59]. Stuxnet was likely intended to stall Iran's nuclear weapons program for long enough to allow international negotiations to reach an accord to permanently curtail its nuclear ambitions.

Cyber-sabotage was a less aggressive means than a missile strike to disrupt Iran's weapons program, and therefore less likely to cause a cycle of escalation or be considered an act of war – especially as Iran may not even have discovered the malware. Stuxnet is believed to have destroyed almost 1000 of Iran's 6000 centrifuges, the machines that enrich uranium for atomic bombs. It is highly likely that nations anticipating near to mid-term conflict are pre-positioning sabotage operations – in military parlance this is known "preparing the battlefield." For example, as early as 2011, the Russian-attributed Dragonfly campaign targeted the CPS of European and US power plants [60]. Symantec observed that Dragonfly was:

> interested in both learning how energy facilities operate and gaining access to operational systems themselves, to the extent that the group now potentially can sabotage or gain control of these systems should it decide to do so [61].

Campaigns like Dragonfly use a variety of methods to breach networks. The seeding of watering holes (referred to as strategic web compromises) is one vector. Seeding involves the adversary positioning "drive-by" malware exploitation, often achieved via a small HTML iframe, on websites their targets will likely visit. The enterprise's own website is a common watering hole target, as it is often set as the home page on corporate browsers. For those willing to take a more speculative approach, online help pages for a specific control system can be targeted. Another approach is targeting employees with recruitment-themed spear-phishing. It is often easy to find control system targets via LinkedIn. Adversaries can socially engineer targets to open trojanized attachments, or follow malicious links, when told by a purported recruiter that the resources are specifications for a high-paying job to which they are uniquely suited. Such vectors can yield rapid access to machines from which the control system is operated. Legacy CPS is often bespoke, with proprietary protocols and few security provisions. Such systems are designed to last for decades and cost millions of dollars, they are challenging and even impossible to update. Maynard comments of CPS security, "it's horrific [...] the required level of investment and maturity is not there [...] it's a nightmare" [33]. Maynard laments that, "enterprises don't have the OT [CPS] budget to attack the problem" [32]. One advantage of CPS is that their specialist nature means it can be hard for an adversary to achieve a specific outcome. For instance, causing an energy plant explosion may require the expertise of chemists, physicists, and CPS specialists – and even with such a skills array there may be further safety measures that can only be overridden at the equipment's physical location. Preparing such an operation often requires months of post-breach reconnaissance and planning. During this time the intruder must evade detection and ensure not to leave attribution-enabling artefacts – though, some threat actors may wish to make their identity known. CPS attacks typically require custom malware.

Sabotage is also used against non-CPS enterprise systems with capabilities via wiper malware. This was the case with the 2012 Shamoon campaign. The operation started with a spear phish against Saudi Aramco, a company providing around 10% of global oil. Shamoon destroyed 30,000+ hard drives causing Aramco to regress a generation to typewriters and fax machines [62]. A group called "Cutting Sword of Justice" claimed responsibility, stating that the, "Al-Saud corrupt regime [...] sponsors [...] oppressive measures by using Muslims oil resources [...] it's hands are infected with the blood of innocent children" [63]. Researchers and the US officials assess that the real culprit was the Iranian government, who used false flags in an attempt to prevent attribution [64], [65]. Shamoon was likely a proxy-retaliation for Stuxnet. Similar operations continue to occur, such as the Iranian-linked Dustman wiper sabotage against Bahrain's national oil company, Bapco, in December 2020 [66].

Additionally, nation states can use ransomware, operating under the guise of criminality, in order to add a layer of deniability to their activities. Iran has employed such methods against Israeli targets [11, p. 43].

1.3.3.1 Countermeasures

Countering nation state sabotage is perhaps the most severe challenge an enterprise confronts, in some cases failure can result in fatalities. Nation state threat actors have almost unlimited time and resources, and can employ a variety of technical and non-technical means to achieve their objectives. Non-technical enabling measures could include blackmailing employees, or even threatening violence against their loved ones. When confronting such a threat, there is a question as to whether even the best-resourced enterprise could indefinitely withstand such pressure. **Air-gapping** a CPS, that is segregating it from pathways to other networks such as the Internet, is a strong defensive measure, but is by no means a guarantee of security; air-gapped networks have been breached via methods such as removable drives, as the case in the Stuxnet operation. Research has also shown that many networks believed to be air-gapped are often not, this is due to poor architectural practices and employee actions to make their tasks easier (such as enabling remote access) [67]. There are other issues with air gaps. For instance, from a commercial perspective most enterprises operating CPS environments need to embrace cloud-based technologies to stay competitive. Active, over passive, security measures are often not advisable for legacy CPS, as even port scanning can cause older equipment to fail, which can result in cascading and escalating failures. Passive monitoring, employing **behavioral analysis** using technologies such as CyberX, Dragos, and MediGate can help detect attacks without risking CPS disruption. Other measures should include **strong authentication and authorization**, especially in geographically dispersed systems, and **extensive logging** to enable rapid forensics and response. Given the long post-breach time often required for attackers to prepare their end game, there is sufficient detection time if robust monitoring is implemented. **Zero trust** should also be embraced in CPS environments.

1.3.4 Influence

Nation states also use digital means to exert influence. Examples include micro-targeting advertisements to influence populations, such as in the case of Russia's attempted manipulation of the 2016 US presidential election, and the DPRK's 2014 attempt to deter Sony from publishing a satirical movie about its supreme leader. Such actions can employ the full spectrum of attack methodologies, from hacking and leaking confidential documents, to destructive actions, both of which occurred in the campaign against Sony. When leaking documents nation states may also seek to alter data in order to influence public opinion. For instance, in an operation against the World Anti-Doping Agency in 2016, after having stolen data the adversary, likely the Russian-State, changed unspecified data before leaking the files. Such modifications may often be minimal amongst vast data dumps, but their effect may be significant. Interspersing false information with true content makes the manipulated data much harder for the victim to refute, and for the public to discern [68]. During conflict, and in hybrid warfare, extensive disinformation campaigns as a core component of a broader information war will likely be waged in an attempt to confuse and disorient the enemy and its citizens.

1.3.4.1 Countermeasures

When considering the threat from nation state influence operations, enterprises should carefully consider their societal and political functions to inform their risk profile. For social media firms, or broadcasters, such threats are palpable, for retailers the threats are minimal. As well as **traditional defense-in-depth practices**, enterprises must consider **defenses unique to their business**, such as content moderation.

1.4 HACKTIVISTS

Hacktivism is a form of digital activism intended to support a political agenda such as human rights, environmentalism, or other issues of perceived social injustice. Whilst in the early 2010s hacktivism was prominent, a decade later incidents occur less frequently and are of lower impact.[9] Hacktivist operations are typically of low sophistication – DDoS attacks and website defacements are most common. Hacktivists also hijack social media accounts from which incendiary messages can be posted – often accounts are breached by password guessing, or by social-engineering operator employees. Another more aggressive tactic, which can potentially endanger lives, is doxing – the hack and leak of sensitive confidential information. For instance, during the 2020 Belarus protests against an allegedly fixed election, anti-government hacktivists released the names and dates of birth of more than 1000 Belarusian police officers [69]. Such information can include addresses, which could lead to physical attacks against victims. The reduction of hacktivism impact and frequency is likely due to advancing digital investigative capabilities, law enforcement prosecutorial tenacity, and corporate cyber security investment. Successful attacks now typically occur against sub-enterprise sized under-resourced entities, such as local public sector organizations. For example, during the 2020 protests following George Floyd's death, hacktivists launched a DDoS attack against Minneapolis government websites and systems, temporarily disabling them [70].

Contemporary disruptive digital activism is often non-hacking based. For instance, overwhelming opposition communities' hashtags can make their communications ineffectual. Such an attack occurred when LGBTQ Twitter users flooded a hashtag belonging to far-right group the Proud Boys with messages of love, in 2020 [71]. Such tactics allow a more communal form of activism, and avoid the prosecution risk.

1.4.1 Countermeasures

Basic security hygiene, DDoS protection, and the use of 2FA for high-profile employees will protect enterprises from hacktivism.

1.5 CYBER TERRORISM

If one considers terrorism the capability to physically harm people and property, with the aim to instill fear in pursuit of a political agenda, then cyber terrorism can be considered the equivalent enacted via digital networks. Based on this description, at time of writing cyber terrorism has not occurred. Terrorists have thus far used the Internet mostly for propaganda and recruitment, instead of intelligence gain and digital attacks. However, terrorists have expressed cyber terrorism ambitions since at least 2011 [72]. Where such groups have started to develop capabilities, they have proved ineffectual, and associated individuals were quickly killed by their would-be victims, such as in the case of Islamic State hacker Junaid Hussain, who died in a 2015 US drone strike [73]. In another case an Israeli missile killed Hamas cyber operators in 2019, before tweeting, "HamasCyberHQ.exe has been removed [...] Hamas no longer has cyber capabilities" [74]. The most likely short-term scenario is that terrorists will use intelligence acquired via breaching poorly protected organizations to identify symbolic targets for physical attack, such as military officers, as in the Hussain case [75].

Another risk is that terrorist cyber operations amplify traditional, physical attacks. For instance, if the communications of emergency services were incapacitated by a DDoS attack jeopardizing their response to a suicide bombing. Whilst terrorists are not presently demonstrating cyber-attack pedigree, their capabilities need to be closely monitored as they become more technologically literate.

1.5.1 Countermeasures

Enterprise threat assessments should explore whether terrorist attacks are likely against their organization, enacting calibrated risk reduction countermeasures where necessary. Most required controls will likely overlap with security protections against non-terrorists. Given the threat actors low sophistication, spear phishing, website vulnerability exploitation, and denial of services attacks are likely to be the adversaries preferred methods. Therefore, ensuring **mail filtering, web application firewalls,** and **secure coding practices,** as well as **DDoS attack mitigations** can help minimize risk.

1.6 INSIDER THREATS

Enterprises are particularly vulnerable to insider threats. Insiders operate at all seniority levels, from the cleaner to the executive, and include past and present employees, and third-party contractors. Insider breaches are not always due to malcontents, often insider's unintentional carelessness causes compromises. Insiders are an acute threat as they possess intimate knowledge of enterprise processes, and may have privileged accesses.

Assessing insider threat prevalence is challenging, as enterprises are reluctant to disclose embarrassing details of employees betraying them as Brutus did Caesar. Verizon estimate insiders caused 30% of compromises in 2019 [7, p. 7]. Ponemon found that 60% of enterprises have more than 20 insider-related breaches annually, however 63% of these cases were due to negligence, with only 23% being due to malicious intent [76, pp. 5–6]. In contrast, Mandiant found insiders involved in less than 1% of breaches they investigated in 2020 [11, p. 13].

Reducing employee carelessness requires increased education and a sound security strategy. Decreasing malicious insider risk is more complex. To calibrate defensive controls, we must first understand insider attacker motivation. The justifications insiders construct are as varied as the human condition itself. These motivations populate three broad categories: emotional, financial, and political [77].

Emotion-based motivations include a desire for retribution and demonstration of power or intellectual superiority – especially when an insider is disillusioned due to poor performance reviews or lack of corporate advancement. Another motivation is boredom, where an insider may be seeking entertainment, or "lulz." Romantic relationships, or lack thereof, may also be a motivator; in one case an insider cyber-stalked several colleagues, reading their emails, harvesting personal account credentials, and collecting their photos [19, p. 43].

Financially based motivations are self-explanatory. An insider may justify their actions by believing that their employer owes them a debt as a result of working unpaid hours, or as consequence of not receiving a perceivably deserved promotion. Other times motivation can include excessive debt, or the desire to win the approval of a third party. Sometimes the motivation is simply greed. An example of intellectual property theft for self-enrichment can be found in the case of a General Electric (GE) employee who, in 2019, was indicted for using steganography to embed proprietary GE files in pictures before sending them to his personal account. Prosecutors allege his plan was to use the intellectual property to manufacture GE's product cheaper in China, before selling the wares to the Chinese government [78]. Not all employees seek to harm their employer in malicious acts. For instance, an employee may seek to use digital corporate assets, or enterprise client data, for self-enrichment at the expense of a third party, or to exploit an opportunity that they believe will disadvantage nobody (a so-called "victimless crime"). Mandiant notes they are seeing an increasing number of insiders trying to extort their employers. In one case an attacker threatened to release corporate data unless a bitcoin ransom was paid. Stolen data samples were provided to verify the attacker's data possession claim. Investigators concluded that an external breach was unlikely – they assessed the attacker was probably a former employee. Subsequently, investigators identified large non-office hours file transfers over the enterprise's certificate-based VPN. The associated laptop was missing. However, correlating log-ons from the IP to which the VPN was connecting revealed the terminated employee responsible. Police recovered the stolen laptop, and no sensitive data was released. In another case, a Microsoft employee involved in testing his employer's online retail platform stole millions of dollars in digital gift cards, even framing his colleagues for the theft. The insider used a Bitcoin mixer to launder his $2.8m gains before routing the funds to his bank account. His tax returns claimed the bitcoin was a gift from a relative [79]. Dismissed or departing employees are data theft risks; data authors in particular may feel a sense of ownership over their work. Cyber security firm Securonix claims over 80% of flight-risk employees take data with them, anywhere from two to eight weeks before their exit [80, p. 2].

One particularly egregious case of an external threat actor attempting to enlist an insider for breach facilitation is that of Igor Kriuchkov. The Russian national offered a Tesla employee $1m to enable ransomware installation and to steal data for the purpose of extortion during 2020 [81, p. 4]. Kriuchkov had first met the potential insider years earlier, and obtained his phone number via a mutual acquaintance, enabling contact reestablishment via WhatsApp. Kriuchkov traveled to the potential insider's location in Nevada. The Russian began cultivation: he visited the target's home and treated him to multiple evenings of fine wine and dining. Once in the target's good graces, Kriuchkov invited him to participate in a "special project" [82, p. 4], [81, pp. 4–6]. Kriuchkov explained the "group" for which he worked had already successfully executed several such special projects. The insider would be required to provide intelligence on Tesla's network, and to deploy malware either via USB drive or by opening a malicious email. However, the potential insider was now working with the FBI, whose agents were surveilling their meetings. When the Tesla employee feigned concerns to the Russian that his act of sabotage may be discovered, he was informed that, "the oldest 'project' the 'group' had worked on took place three and a half years ago and the [...] co-optee still worked for the [victim] company." The potential insider was even told he could frame another Tesla employee if there were someone to whom he wanted to "teach a lesson" [81, pp. 4–9, 13]. A concurrent DDoS attack was planned to provide cover for the malware installation [82, p. 4]. Kriuchkov said a previous enterprise was extorted for $6m, of which $4m was paid – a similar sum was to be demanded from [81, pp. 10, 12]. Kriuchkov was arrested before he could flee to Russia [83]. Elon Musk commented, "this was a serious attack," and thanked the FBI for their assistance [84]. Tesla was a hard target for the likely criminal organization to breach via an insider attack. The manufacturer hires elite personnel, pays them well, and has a unique mission: contributing to the biosphere's salvation by developing cutting-edge technologies. Not all enterprises can offer staff such motivation to remain loyal, and with infrastructure sabotage occurring in 5.1% of insider cases, according to a 2020 Securonix study, a layered defensive approach is crucial to minimizing insider threats [80, p. 4].

Ideology-based motivations are more complex. The most famous case is that of Edward Snowden, an NSA contractor who stole classified files as he believed his agency was violating the US constitution [85]. Sometimes ideological insiders act because they are genuinely trying to right a perceived wrong, other times a hero complex or desire for attention are responsible. Enterprises involved in politically contentious or divisive issues, such as animal testing, are particularly vulnerable to ideological insiders. Nation states, who are ideological actors, may blackmail enterprise employees to facilitate their breach, thus creating an insider threat. Another approach uses their own nationals, who may already be serendipitously working for target enterprises, to enable compromise. In one case, a company hired Chinese PhD scientists to support a research project, the scientists were given access to sensitive research materials; however, they made few project contributions. Forensic analysis revealed the scientists had used a China-based cloud file storage application to upload the sensitive data [19, p. 42]. This breach was unlikely an isolated incident, a US Senate investigation reported that:

Launched in 2008, the Thousand Talents Plan incentivizes [Chinese] individuals engaged in research and development in the United States to transmit the knowledge and research they gain here to China in exchange for salaries, research funding, lab space, and other incentives. China unfairly uses the American research and expertise it obtains for its own economic and military gain [86, p. 1].

China is unlikely alone in using insiders to breach enterprises.

1.6.1 Countermeasures

Early detection is critical for minimizing insider-related damages. There are two approaches to uncovering insider threats: people-centric and technology-centric controls. However, such detection controls should recognize local ethical and cultural norms. Surveilling one's own staff can inculcate distrust which as well as being detrimental to moral, can foster disloyalty thus augmenting insider risk. Work-from-anywhere and bring-you-own-device (BYOD) introduce further ethical and legal issues. For instance, in some countries, such as Germany, it is illegal to monitor employees even on corporately owned assets. In BYOD cultures it is unlikely to be ethically acceptable to monitor an employee-owned device (however, the corporate provisioned services may be able to be monitored). To what degree employees should be made aware of surveillance should also be considered. Informing prospective employees of enterprise surveillance allows them to make an informed joining decision. However, enacting new surveillance measures directed towards existing employees is more complex, as they have not consented to such monitoring. Some enterprises may elect to fully advertise their measures, articulating the shared threat their community confronts, and tightly regulating the uses of such data. For instance, one confidence building measure may be to stipulate that only evidence of illegality would be shared beyond the security team – detection of minor infractions such as non-work browsing in office hours would be disregarded. This approach may win employee support and could disincentivize insider threats. Taking the opposite approach, an enterprise could keep their insider discovery program covert, which may improve its efficacy and negate the concerns of gaining employee consent. However, should the detection data ever be required in a prosecutorial scenario, the capability would be exposed potentially causing employee disgruntlement.

People-oriented, or persona, **controls focus on predictive analytics,** although they also contribute to **multi-tiered detection analytics**. Most employees do not join enterprises with the intent to cause harm, with the rare exception of nation state operatives, such as a suspected Russian intelligence officer who joined Microsoft likely in an attempt to steal corporate secrets [87,88, pp. 211–212]. **Psychological profiling** can be used in advance of hiring for sensitive roles, as well as **background checks,**

however, one should recognize this may deter potentially high-value employees. The motivation to become an insider threat usually form builds during an employee's tenure. Therefore, a window exists when enterprises can detect such motivation developing, and monitor or mitigate the risk. **Enterprises can use indicators to create models as to which employees may become insider threats.** For instance, a profile could be that of an employee who has become disillusioned due to a lack of career progression. Such a profile could be identified by monitoring appraisals, failed internal job applications, and role tenure length. There should also be an additional indicator on detection algorithms for employees who can cause the most damage (e.g., those with privileged access or in sensitive roles). Of course, these indicators are oftentimes shared by employees who simply tolerate their frustration or depart the enterprise; insider attacks are the exception, not the norm. **Predictive analytics can also be used to remedy grievances thus diminishing insider risk,** McKinsey advises that following insider risk profile creation enterprises:

> design changes in process, governance, hiring, compensation, and so on, specific to the identified risk areas [...] For example, if an employee group has a high prevalence of "flight risks" due to disgruntlement over a manager, the organization may require leadership coaching or even rotating the manager out of the group. If financial stress seems to be an issue, the organization may choose to [...] reevaluate its compensation model [89].

Threat-inducing factors, which also contribute to general poor moral and corporate performance, can further be identified through **satisfaction surveys.** Addressing these issues not only reduces threat levels, but increases employee performance, though one should recognize the cost of such measures.

Technically oriented detection controls are identical to those used to find external adversaries post-breach, making them easier to justify than people-oriented controls. Sequences of potentially malicious activity should be prioritized over individual suspicious acts to decrease false positives. Typically, such behavior patterns are drawn from a third-party-curated use-case library. Additionally, technologies such as **UEBA** can enable machine learning to **create individualized models of employee behavior enabling norm deviation detection** (assuming the model was not trained whilst malicious behavior was occurring). **Individualized models can also be compared to peer group models** as part of a tiered analytics process. The model can be continually refreshed, for instance the baseline could be created from a rolling 90-day window. The enterprise can configure the tolerable level of baseline deviation before triggering investigation. Indicators of suspicious activity include:

- Impossible travel analysis[10]: account usage from locations which are infeasible to traverse in the time between accesses (e.g., an account used in Perth, and then in Oslo two hours later). This may be indicative of unauthorized account sharing (or stolen credentials).
- Access to resources-groups (e.g., HR files) not typically accessed by peer group.
- High-volume uncharacteristic data transfers or printing.

A least privilege access model should also be used, as should multi-person authentication for sensitive operations, credential revocation on employee departure, and zero-touch engineering practices (safe proxies), to reduce the ability for an insider to execute a destructive act.

1.7 FUTURE THREATS

Whilst the future holds great uncertainty, particularly in the technology realm, one thing will persist, as articulated by KMPG Technical Director, Dimitrios Petropoulos, "The start position of the defender is to defend against everything, the attacker just needs to find one chink in the armor [...] that's not going to change" [90]. Therefore, we must scan the horizon and consider the scientific developments most likely to create new vulnerabilities in our defenses. Three areas with particularly acute growing risk implications are artificial intelligence, quantum computing, and CPS. Each will be briefly examined to understand the countermeasures we can today deploy to address tomorrow's threats.

1.7.1 Artificial Intelligence (AI)

AI is one of the twenty-first century's great disruptors; cyber security is not immune to such disruption. Whether AI will be a blessing, a curse, or of no comparative advantage to enterprise defenders is unknown. However, there is little doubt that maintaining pace with adversaries requires security professionals to embrace AI. Whilst the terms AI and ML are often used interchangeably, it should be noted that ML is a branch of AI, a branch that today is the dominant form of AI. This section briefly explores AI's offensive and defensive applications.

1.7.1.1 AI: Cyber Offensive Applications

Attackers dream of one day achieving fully autonomous attack systems able to intelligently adapt to complex target environments and evade associated countermeasures. However, Verizon comments that, "the promise of fully autonomous Artificial Hacking Intelligence is still at least 15 years away" [7, p. 19]. Limited applications of ML will benefit attackers in the nearer term. For instance, Nir Giller, co-founder of CPS security firm CyberX, comments that, "detecting zero days takes [attackers] a significant amount of time, if you can utilize AI to find a lot more zero days you can use it in a wide manner to pwn [compromise] that many more devices" [91]. Another offensive application will be using ML to create individualized social-engineering attacks. For instance, rather than sending out a million identical phishing emails, ML could help the attacker gather OSINT on each target to customize the phish, decreasing the chance of detection. ML can also help teach malware how to avoid AV detection engines. Intelligence on how much of this has already been achieved is severely limited as these offensive applications occur attacker-side. For instance, malware will unlikely retain artefacts of ML training during its development. However, given the potential operational gains it would be naive to think AI is not being enlisted to increase attacker capabilities. One AI development is evident today: Deepfakes.

1.7.1.1.1 Deepfakes (Synthetic Media)

Deepfakes are named for their reliance on deep neural networks, and are a form of "synthetic media."[11] Deepfakes are ML-generated audio, pictures, or videos of an entity. Early uses of deepfakes substituted celebrity's faces, typically women, onto the heads of pornographic actors. Synthetic media creation requires recording samples of the target. The quality of the deepfake is dependent on both the caliber of the generator's algorithm and the variety of the recordings – the best outputs result from a diverse sample set of the target in different environments, with varied lighting, and using a range of expressions. One of the few examples of deepfakes being used operationally was during a 2019 BEC attack against a UK-based energy firm [92]. The energy firm's CEO was called by the Chief Executive of its parent company who asked that he transfer €220,000 to a supplier within the hour. The funds were transferred. Rüdiger Kirsch, a fraud expert at the company's insurer Euler Hermes, comments that the CEO recognized his boss' slight German accent, and even the melody of his voice from the call. Kirsch believes commercial voice-generating software was used in the attack.

Deepfake technology will also enable new extortion attacks. Deepfake ransomware, or Ransomfake, attacks will use synthetically generated intimate or incriminatory videos of their prey, before demanding payment to destroy the content. Failure to submit to the attacker's will may result in the video being sent to the target's contacts, which could be obtained via endpoint breach or OSINT. Biometric authentication and authorization systems will also be targeted. Open-source tools such as DeepFaceLab and Faceswap allow any user with a little knowledge to create deepfakes. Given the potential applications of mastering such technologies these may not be the most advanced capabilities in existence, Petropoulos comments, "I'm sure the arsenals of nation states and organized criminals will be better than what is available publicly" [90]. The black market offers deepfake image creation for as little as $2.50, and video creation from $50 [93].

Countering synthetics is a significant cyber security research problem. Jovi Umawing, a malware intelligence analyst, advises users to, "watch what you post on social media in general: selfies, group pictures, TikTok videos, and other images are all up for grabs. You should think long and hard about who you're sharing your content with and where" [94]. Umawing's advice whilst appropriate for threat mitigation, conflicts with the reality of the digitized world. Camera phones are ubiquitous and enterprise employees, especially executives, are expected to represent their company externally, such as at conferences, which often results in recorded content being posted online. Whilst limiting one's digital footprint, and ensuring appropriate access settings is a good security practice for myriad reasons, such measures are often not feasible, and in isolation will not solve this problem. Counter-deepfake technologies are in their infancy. An early tool, Microsoft's video authenticator, was released to media agencies ahead of the 2020 US election in an attempt to disrupt disinformation campaigns. The tool works by, "detecting the blending boundary of the deepfake and subtle fading or greyscale elements that might not be detectable by the human eye." A percentage score is given of the likelihood the content is fake, an output which can be assigned to each video frame [95]. At present the tooling is exclusively available to media and political organizations. Government, industry, and academia continue to stimulate research in this area, and given the societal impact of the broader deepfake problem it is not unrealistic to expect at least some measure of progress [96].[12] However, for the immediate future, enterprises are reliant on using a spectrum of other defensive countermeasures. On assessing the threat from deepfakes Searle comments, "Deepfakes could be a significant challenge, but once we have got our heads around how they might be used and can counter them technically, my instinct is the impact won't be too bad" [57]. However, whether we will ever reach a point where deepfakes can be fully technically countered is an active research question. In 2021, close visual examination still betrays deepfakes. Deepfakes are particularly poor at reproducing fine facial details such as their subject's blinking patterns and teeth. These flaws enable most viewers to delineate between authentic and inauthentic content. However, an attacker may be able to disguise or explain inauthentic markers, such as by obscuring finer details with the use of a low-resolution video connection, the purported caller excusing the resolution by claiming they are traveling in a low-bandwidth area. Equally, an attack utilizing deepfake audio, a variant marginally more advanced than its picture and video equivalents, could purport to originate from a mobile phone whilst the caller is driving to explain the less-than-perfect audio facsimile. Where used in BEC attacks, enterprises can harden their processes as per the advice in Section 1.2.2.2, to include the requesting of information only the authorizer would know. Deepfake defense and offense will likely advance in near unity for years, perhaps even decades to come. Broader counter-measures require a combination of deepfake public education, developing embedded media verification tools, hardening business processes, and defense-in-depth practices.

1.7.1.2 AI: Cyber Security Applications

AI-infused security solutions permeate industry. Whether it is identity analytics, SOC automation, or AV software, security product marketing brochures seldom omit the phrases "artificial intelligence" or "machine learning." Whilst a detailed treatment of this topic is beyond this chapter's scope, a few brief notes on the subject are warranted as countering AI offensive tools will at least in some part require AI defensive developments. Whilst ML has flourished in some security domains, such as UEBA, often the promise of AI has not been realized in cyber defense applications.[13] For instance, AV technologies relying solely on ML have proved exploitable. [97] In many applications ML is most effective when used in concert with traditional technologies. For example, with regards AV, Sophos comments:

> By combining ML and signatures intelligently [...] users get the best of both worlds: the high specificity and rapid deployment of signatures, with the ability of ML to "plug the gaps" and discover novel malware variants that signature-based systems frequently miss [35, pp. 25–26].

Whilst improving tooling and aiding in automation, we must recognize the current limitations of ML's cyber applications. Often it is contextualization, creativity, and assessment where ML falls short, Petropoulos states ML has, "started converting information to knowledge, but [...] converting knowledge to wisdom is a quantum leap beyond that point" [90]. It is that wisdom, the type possessed by veteran security practitioners, which conveys trust in business-impacting breach response decisions such as the severing of an enterprise service. It will be a long time before there is sufficient confidence in the wisdom of AI to grant it the power to take similar response measures that could incur extortionate downtime costs. This is not to say we will not reach this point. ML advances are rapid. One day, perhaps like with autonomous vehicles, society will gasp in horror that humans, with their cognitive fallacies and lumbering reaction times, were ever trusted with control of these powerful systems. In the short to mid-term, wedding the rigor of a machine with the intuition of a human will offer optimum returns. Such an approach takes the strength of both entities to compensate for their counterpart's weaknesses, Petropoulos comments, "AI is still a way from being able to apply in every domain of security the higher cognitive functions that a human performs [...] AI is going to help a lot, but there will be lots AI cannot do, for instance architectural design - because design is where art and science overlap" [90]. In the longer-term, offensive

AI systems will likely be in conflict with defensive AI systems. Humans will be mostly, if not completely, out of the real-time loop, as reliance on their slow decisions could be a determinative handicap. Such a reality has dangerous consequences, Searle comments, "AI vs AI with no human involvement [...] could move towards unintended consequences" [57]. At a national level, such consequences may even lead to real-world military conflict. Enterprises have no choice but to embrace new AI defensive technologies as they prove their viability. However, cyber security generals must never forget that such tools have a critical dependence on their configuration and operation by human's possessing of context and intuition, or put another way, security wisdom.

1.7.2 Adversarial Machine Learning

Machine learning is creating new classes of vulnerability. Adversarial machine learning is the subversion of machine learning systems. Between 2016 and 2020 Microsoft observed a "notable increase" in attacks against ML systems [98]. A 2020 study found 25 of 28 enterprises lacked the tools to secure their ML systems [99]. There is no singular step to securing ML systems, as associated architectures require defense from a wide range of threats from supply-chain compromise, to the poisoning of training data and post-deployment attacks. Our common lexicon for this challenge is still under development, with helpful contributions including the articulation of ML failure modes by Microsoft and Harvard University, and MITRE's ML ATT&CK-style framework [100]. Tooling to address many aspects of these threats remains a challenge, with most defensive technologies still in research and development. Available capabilities include IBM and MIT's Cross Lipschitz Extreme Value for Network Robustness (CLEVER) tool, which measures the robustness of deep neural networks to adversarial machine learning attacks. IBM has also released an Adversarial Robustness Toolbox for machine learning to offer guidance and software to help guard against a wide spectrum of potential ML attacks [96,101]. Whist operations against ML in the wild remain rare; this will be a significant growth area in the coming years.

1.7.3 Quantum-Insecure Cryptography

Quantum computing (QC) represents a severe security threat as it can compromise some cryptographic functions upon which we rely. However, it is not known whether the promise of QC will be realized, how such realization would manifest, or when this could occur. What we do know, in the words of Cryptology Professor Keith Martin, is that "a quantum computer would render all our current asymmetric encryption and digital signature schemes ineffective" [102, p. 223]. Both asymmetric encryption and digital signatures rely primarily on two mathematical problems:

factoring and finding discrete logarithms. QC solves both problems more efficiently than conventional computing. Threat actors able to intercept enterprise communications could potentially break the asymmetric encryption using QC, compromising all associated traffic. State actors would develop this capability first, but, as Pereira comments, "The problem will really begin when Quantum services become accessible as-a-service from the cloud allowing criminal use" [13]. Such use will have broader than cryptanalysis scope, but that is the most urgent and tangible problem we must solve. *Postquantum* asymmetric algorithms and digital signatures that are able to withstand expected QC attacks are in development. The US' National Institute for Standards and Technology (NIST) is creating postquantum cryptography standards, with algorithms based on structured lattice schemes being the favored approach. NIST's intent is to release the first postquantum cryptography standard in 2022.

Thankfully, at present it is assessed that symmetric encryption algorithms, such as AES, will remain viable postquantum, as they rely on complex algorithmic and engineering computations, rather than on singular mathematical problems. Unless other flaws are found in symmetric algorithms, exhaustive searches to locate the decryption keys will remain the most feasible postquantum attack. Whilst not making symmetric algorithms unviable, QC will reduce the time required to conduct an exhaustive attack, and therefore enterprises will need to adapt [103, pp. 212–219]. It is estimated that the symmetric key lengths must double in order to offer security equivalent to todays in a post-quantum world. Some algorithms, such as TripleDES, are not designed to have their key sizes doubled, and will need replacing with other algorithms such as AES.

Given QC seems to be at least several years away, enterprises should be able to mitigate its cryptography impacts before risks mature, Professor Martin comments, "I am quietly confident that we will develop a suite of cryptographic algorithms suitable for protecting against quantum computers long before quantum computers become a reality" [102, p. 234]. This optimism is reassuring, as QC risks are not yet being considered by most enterprises, Petropoulos, comments, "today, most our clients are worried about regulations, Covid, and economic downturn, rather than quantum-safe cryptography" [90]. There are three actions enterprises must consider: First, conducting a crypto audit to understand the algorithms and associated ecosystems, such as APIs and accelerators, deployed in their enterprises; second, transitioning to symmetric algorithms with a minimum equivalent strength to that of AES128, but ideally AES192, or AES256; third, ensuring an employee owns the enterprise's postquantum asymmetric algorithm update program and that they are monitoring developments and preparing deployment plans [104]. QC will have many other security implications, but to explore each facet of this challenge is beyond the scope of this chapter.

1.7.4 Cyber-Physical Systems

The pandemic-accelerated digitization of our societies introduces a growing reliance on CPS. CPS Security trails vastly behind traditional IT security. The skills of machinery engineers and cyber security professionals seldom overlap. For a generation, older CPS have been isolated from the Internet. Now, remaining commercially competitive requires connectivity to exploit cloud technologies. Placing older CPS on the Internet absent robust security is akin to migrating a historically isolated tribe to bustling Tokyo – they would be overwhelmed by all the infections against which they have no developed immunity. Such a migration is occurring now, and legacy CPS equipment have few defenses. Giller comments, "Today I'm seeing it across the board, almost every manufacturer has a lot of problems" [95]. For example, medical connected devices that operate patient's life support systems mostly have little security provisions. Jonathan Langer, CEO of Medigate, a medical security firm, comments:

> What's stopping us from a second WannaCry? [a worming ransomware that disabled large swathes of hospital infrastructure] [...] nothing. Nothing has fundamentally changed since WannaCry [...] clinical infrastructure is still running on outdated software [...] patching is still not done in a timely manner [...] the only thing stopping another WannaCry is the will of attackers. That's the grim reality, that's where things are going. The Impact that can be inflicted at this point is unfathomable [105].

Giller offers another, more cinematic, example, "Today, there is a good chance you can exploit CPS security, and blow up a rocket" [91]. Giller notes that whilst in the realms of possibility, such attacks are not trivial to execute, and would require a dedicated and well-resourced attacker. Whilst such attacks are not easy, as CPS protocols, once proprietary and undocumented, become more broadly understood, as manufacturers transition to common protocols, and as malware such as Stuxnet escapes online and is studied by attackers, the barrier-to-entry will fall significantly. Commercial IoT technologies will become alluring prospects to criminals. For instance, one researcher compromised a connected coffee maker and caused hot water to be endlessly pumped out – a nearby child could easily have been scolded. The researcher could display a ransomware note on the device display. An attacker could rent a botnet of home routers to facilitate compromise, or could breach via the manufacturer's update mechanism (assuming one existed). If a million items were sold, such an operation could offer healthy returns. In another example, as early as 2013 researchers demonstrated the ability to compromise and disable the breaks of two cars manufactured in 2010 [106–108]. In the not too distant, with enough effort, remote assassinations could become feasible. Then there is the possibility of worming attacks inadvertently causing such effects all over the globe. Langer comments, "My biggest concern for the future is the level of sophistication attacks will reach with regards impact on people [...] you can only imagine how bad things can get" [105].

Whilst newer enterprise-oriented systems are generally adhering to secure-by-design and secure-by-default principles, there are still manufacturers who prioritize speed-to-market and profit margins over cyber security, especially for low-cost devices. Addressing this problem not only requires consumer awareness, but government regulatory intervention, Harvard's Bruce Schneier commented in 2019, "The internet is about to start killing people, and the government regulates things that kill people" [109]. Enterprises should not wait for regulation. Not only ethics but also corporate interests demand this issue to be addressed. Gartner, a research firm, predicts the financial impact to enterprises of CPS breaches will be $50 billion by 2023. Additionally, Gartner also expects that 75% of CEOs will be personally liable for CPS failures resulting in loss of life by 2024 [110]. Enterprises have many tools at their disposal to address this challenge as has already been articulated in this chapter. The critical dependency is executive sponsorship. Sadly, the catalyzing of such industry-wide sponsorship will likely require either a high-profile fatality-causing incident, or strict regulation.

1.8 CONCLUSION

Threat actors, present and future, will continue to flourish with their victories capable of destroying enterprises, and even human life. Defending business critical environments requires continued attention, investment, and innovation. To succeed we must place our faith in architectural principals and security doctrines such as defense-in-depth, zero trust, least privilege, secure-by-design/default, and assume compromise. This approach will reduce risks to manageable levels, and enable enterprises to thrive in the digital age.

NOTES

1 Prostitution is held as the oldest profession [111].
2 The CIS was formed as a coalition of former Soviet Union members after the 1991 dissolution of that entity. CIS members are: Russia, Armenia, Azerbaijan, Belarus, Kazakhstan, Kyrgyzstan, Moldova, Tajikistan, and Uzbekistan.
3 BEC is sometimes also known as Email Account Compromise (EAC).
4 The Onion Router (Tor) is a network of anonymised relays designed to obscure the source and destination of Internet communications, see http://www.torproject.org for further details.
5 Non-Ransomware breaches had a median dwell time of 45 days.

6 According to NIST, "Cyber-physical systems (CPS) are smart systems that include engineered interacting networks of physical and computational components." Similar concepts CPS are referred to as operational technology (OT), Industrial Internet, and Internet of Things (IoT). There is significant overlap, and contestation of definition, within these terms, which are often used interchangeably [112].

7 The SWIFT network is used to move funds between financial institutions.

8 Hybrid warfare is the Russian-pioneered doctrine of using proxies, disinformation, and measures short of war to achieve political objectives. Hybrid warfare has been most notably deployed in Ukraine.

9 For instance, see [108, p. 21].

10 Also known as land speed violations.

11 Synthetic media can have legitimate applications, such as voice-synthesis for a patient who has lost their voice due to illness.

12 For instance, on attempts to stimulate counter-Deepfake research see [113,114].

13 For instance, Exabeam are an established leader in this field.

REFERENCES

[1] Ponemon Institute, "*Cost of a Data Breach 2020*," Ponemon Institute, North Traverse City, Michigan, United States, 2020. [Online]. Access Date: 02/07/2021, Available: https://web.archive.org/web/20200920093651if_/https://www.ibm.com/security/digital-assets/cost-data-breach-report/%23/.

[2] Office of the Comptroller of the Currency, "*OCC Assesses $80 Million Civil Money Penalty Against Capital One*," 2020. [Online]. Access Date: 02/07/2021, Available: https://web.archive.org/web/20201207092238/https://www.occ.treas.gov/news-issuances/news-releases/2020/nr-occ-2020-101.html.

[3] Information Commissioner's Office, "*Intention to Fine British Airways £183.39m Under GDPR for Data Breach*," 2020. [Online]. Access Date: 02/07/2021, Available: https://web.archive.org/web/20200924174001/https://ico.org.uk/about-the-ico/news-and-events/news-and-blogs/2019/07/ico-announces-intention-to-fine-british-airways/.

[4] D. Baker, Interviewee, [Interview]. 9 September 2020.

[5] S. Tzu, *The Art of War*. New York: Oxford University Press, 1963.

[6] F. Cairncross, *The Death of Distance*. London: Texere, 2001.

[7] Verizon, "*2020 Data Breach Investigations Report*," 2020. [Online]. Access Date: 02/07/2021, Available: https://web.archive.org/web/20210428154758/https://enterprise.verizon.com/resources/reports/2020-data-breach-investigations-report.pdf.

[8] RSA Conference / Joel DeCapua, "*Feds Fighting Ransomware: How The FBI Investigates and How You Can Help*," 25 February 2020. [Online]. Access Date: 02/07/2021, Available: https://www.youtube.com/watch?v=LUxOcpIRxmg&feature=emb_title.

[9] M. Gomez, "*Dark Web Price Index 2020*," privacyaffairs.com, 2020. [Online]. Access Date: 02/07/2021, Available: https://web.archive.org/web/20201224185757/https://www.privacyaffairs.com/dark-web-price-index-2020/.

[10] Identity Theft Resource Center, "*Idtheftcenter.org*," 2020. [Online]. Identity Theft Resource Center Sees Data Compromises Drop 33 Percent in First Half of 2020.

[11] FireEye-Mandiant Services, "*M-Trends 2021: Special Report*," 2021. [Online]. Access Date: 02/07/2021, Available: https://web.archive.org/web/20210503202305/https://content.fireeye.com/m-trends/rpt-m-trends-2021.

[12] Checkpoint Software Technologies, "*2020: Cyber Security Report*," 2020. [Online]. Access Date: 02/07/2021, Available: https://web.archive.org/web/20200920161311/https://www.ntsc.org/assets/pdfs/cyber-security-report-2020.pdf.

[13] M. Pereira, Interviewee, [Interview]. 19 August 2020.

[14] A. source, Interviewee, [Interview]. August 2020.

[15] M. Philip, Interviewee, [Interview]. 14 September 2020.

[16] Agari Cyber Intelligence Division, "*Threat Actor Dossier: Cosmic Lynx*," 2020. [Online]. Access Date: 02/07/2021, Available: https://web.archive.org/web/20200928113504/https://www.agari.com/cyber-intelligence-research/whitepapers/acid-agari-cosmic-lynx.pdf.

[17] Federal Bureau of Investigation, "*Business Email Compromise: The $26 billion scam*," ic3.gov, 2019. [Online]. Access Date: 02/07/2021, Available: https://web.archive.org/web/20200923151924if_/https://www.ic3.gov/media/2019/190910.aspx.

[18] Anti-Phishing Working Group, "*Phishing Activity Trends Report, 4th Quarter 2020*," 2021. [Online]. Access Date: 02/07/2021, Available: https://web.archive.org/web/20210321122627/https://docs.apwg.org/reports/apwg_trends_report_q4_2020.pdf.

[19] FireEye-Mandiant Services, "M-Trends 2020: Special Report," 2020. [Online]. Access Date: 02/07/2021, Available: https://web.archive.org/web/20200920091836/https://content.fireeye.com/m-trends/rpt-m-trends-2020.

[20] Kaspersky Lab, "*The Great Bank Robbery: Carbanak Cybergang Steals $1bn from 100 Financial Institutions Worldwide*," 2015. [Online]. Access Date: 02/07/2021, Available: https://web.archive.org/web/20200414232401/https://www.kaspersky.com/about/press-releases/2015_the-great-bank-robbery-carbanak-cybergang-steals--1bn-from-100-financial-institutions-worldwide.

[21] R. McMillan, "*The Inside Story of mt. Gox, Bitcoin's $460 Million Disaster*," *Wired*, 2014. [Online]. Access Date: 02/07/2021, Available: https://web.archive.org/web/20201009151952/https://www.wired.com/2014/03/bitcoin-exchange/.

[22] CrowdStrike, "2020 Global Threat Report," 2020. [Online]. Access Date: 02/07/2021, Available: https://www.crowdstrike.com/resources/reports/2020-crowdstrike-global-threat-report/.

[23] Cambridge Centre for Alternative Finance, "*Cambridge Bitcoin Electricity Consumption Index*," 2020. [Online]. Access Date: 02/07/2021, Available: https://web.archive.org/web/20200901164753if_/https://www.cbeci.org/cbeci/comparisons.

[24] Checkpoint Software Technologies, "*2021: Cyber Security Report*," 2021. [Online]. Access Date: 02/07/2021, Available: https://web.archive.org/web/20210226190437/https://www.checkpoint.com/downloads/resources/cyber-security-report-2021.pdf.

[25] R. Hitzman, K. Goody, B. Wolcott and J. Kennelly, "How the rise of cryptocurrencies is shaping the cyber crime landscape: the growth of miners," *Fireye*, 2020. [Online]. Access Date: 02/07/2021, Available: https://web.archive.org/web/20201004152904/https://www.fireeye.com/blog/threat-research/2018/07/cryptocurrencies-cyber-crime-growth-of-miners.html.

[26] T. Greene, "How the Dyn DDoS attack unfolded," *Network World*, 2016. [Online]. Access Date: 02/07/2021, Available: https://web.archive.org/web/20200809141359/https://www.networkworld.com/article/3134057/how-the-dyn-ddos-attack-unfolded.html.

[27] D. Menscher, "Exponential growth in DDoS attack volumes," *Google*, 2020. [Online]. Access Date: 02/07/2021, Available: https://web.archive.org/web/20201217175414if_/https://cloud.google.com/blog/products/identity-security/identifying-and-protecting-against-the-largest-ddos-attacks.

[28] C. Cimpanu, "A DDoS gang is extorting businesses posing as Russian government hackers," *ZDNet*, 2019. [Online]. Access Date: 02/07/2021, Available: www.zdnet.com/article/a-ddos-gang-is-extorting-businesses-posing-as-russian-government-hackers/.

[29] D. Casciani, "Briton who knocked liberia offline with cyber attack jailed," *BBC*, 2019. [Online]. Access Date: 02/07/2021, Available: https://web.archive.org/web/20210112155338/https://www.bbc.com/news/uk-46840461.

[30] Kaspersky Lab, "*Businesses Blame Rivals for Staging DDoS Attacks*," 2017. [Online]. Access Date: 02/07/2021, Available: https://web.archive.org/web/20201228140110/https://www.kaspersky.co.uk/about/press-releases/2017_businesses-blame-rivals-for-staging-ddos-attacks.

[31] Sophos, "*The State of Ransomware 2020*," 2020. [Online]. Access Date: 02/07/2021, Available: https://web.archive.org/web/20200811225500/https://www.sophos.com/en-us/medialibrary/Gated-Assets/white-papers/sophos-the-state-of-ransomware-2020-wp.pdf.

[32] J. Maynard, Interviewee, [Interview]. 3 September 2020.

[33] Sophos, "*Sophos 2021 Threat Report*," 2021. [Online]. Access Date: 02/07/2021, Available: https://web.archive.org/web/20210104110158/https://www.sophos.com/en-us/medialibrary/pdfs/technical-papers/sophos-2021-threat-report.pdf.

[34] N. Mavis, "New snort, ClamAV coverage strikes back against cobalt strike," *Cisco*, 2020. [Online]. Access Date: 02/07/2021, Available: https://web.archive.org/web/20201008162416/https://blog.talosintelligence.com/2020/09/coverage-strikes-back-cobalt-strike-paper.html.

[35] Sophos, "*2020 Threat Report*," 2019. [Online]. Access Date: 02/07/2021, Available: https://web.archive.org/web/20200920162726/https://www.sophos.com/en-us/medialibrary/pdfs/technical-papers/sophoslabs-uncut-2020-threat-report.pd

[36] T. D. Overlord, "*Aesthetic Dentistry - Press Release*," 2016. [Online]. Access Date: 02/07/2021, Available: https://web.archive.org/web/20201007133102/https://pastebin.com/AE532KeP.

[37] University of Utah, "*University of Utah Update on Data Security Incident*," [Online]. Access Date: 02/07/2021, Available: https://web.archive.org/web/20201231105343/https://attheu.utah.edu/facultystaff/university-of-utah-update-on-data-security-incident/.

[38] McAfee, *"Take a "NetWalk" on The Wild Side,"* 2020. [Online]. Access Date: 02/07/2021, Available: https://web.archive.org/web/20201231105 801/https://www.mcafee.com/blogs/other-blogs/mcafee-labs/take-a-netwalk-on-the-wild-side.

[39] V. Marchive and A. Culafi, *"Cyberattaque: Une Rançon De 50 Millions De Dollars Demandée à Acer,"* 2021. [Online]. Access Date: 02/07/2021, Available: https://web.archive.org/web/20210510131304/https://www.lemagit.fr/actualites/252498175/Cyberattaque-une-rançon-de-50-millions-de-dollars-de-mandee-a-Acer.

[40] D. Voreacos, K. Chiglinsky and R. Griffin, *"Merck Cyberattack's $1.3 Billion Question: Was It an Act of War?,"* *Bloomberg*, 2019. [Online]. Access Date: 02/07/2021, Available: https://web.archive.org/web/20201 007102714/https://www.bloomberg.com/news/features/2019-12-03/merck-cyberattack-s-1-3-billion-question-was-it-an-act-of-war.

[41] R. Dudley, "The extortion economy: how insurance companies are fueling a rise in ransomware attacks," *ProPublica*, [Online]. Access Date: 02/07/2021, Available: https://web.archive.org/web/20201008153039/https://www.propublica.org/article/the-extortion-economy-how-insurance-compa-nies-are-fueling-a-rise-in-ransomware-attacks.

[42] Ponemon Institute, *"Costs and Consequences of Gaps in Vulnerability Response,"* 2019. [Online]. Access Date: 02/07/2021, Available: https://web.archive.org/web/20201215000039/https://www.servicenow.com/content/dam/servicenow-assets/public/en-us/doc-type/resource-center/analyst-report/ponemon-state-of-vulnerability-response.pdf.

[43] S. Caveza, S. Narang and M. King, "Tenable's 2020 threat landscape ret-rospective," *Tenable*, 2020. [Online]. Access Date: 02/07/2021, Available: https://web.archive.org/web/20210114155057/https://static.tenable.com/marketing/research-reports/Research-%20Report-Threat_Landscape_2020.pdf.

[44] J. A. Guerrero-Saade, D. Moore, C. Raiu and T. Rid, "Penquin's Moonlit Maze: The Dawn of Nation State Espionage," *Kaspersky Lab*, 2017. [Online]. Access Date: 02/07/2021, Available: https://web.archive.org/web/2 0201011162918/https://ridt.co/d/jags-moore-raiu-rid.pdf.

[45] J. Tidy, "How hackers extorted $1.14m from University of California, San Francisco," *BBC*, 2020. [Online]. Access Date: 02/07/2021, Available: https://web.archive.org/web/20201231112500/https://www.bbc.com/news/technology-53214783.

[46] University of California San Francisco, *"Update on IT security incident at UCSF,"* [Online]. Access Date: 02/07/2021, Available: https://web.archive.org/web/20201231113440/https://www.ucsf.edu/news/2020/06/417911/update-it-security-incident-ucsf.

[47] C. Stoll, *The Cuckoo's Egg*, New York: Pocket Books, 1989.

[48] Office of Personal Management, *"What Happened,"* no date. [Online]. Access Date: 02/07/2021, Available: https://web.archive.org/web/20210102 082854/https://www.opm.gov/cybersecurity/cybersecurity-incidents/.

[49] C. Wray, "The threat posed by the Chinese Government and the Chinese Communist Party to the Economic and National Security of the United States," *Federal Bureau of Investigation*, 2020. [Online]. Access Date: 02/07/2021, Available: https://web.archive.org/web/20210102083738/https://www.fbi.gov/

news/speeches/the-threat-posed-by-the-chinese-government-and-the-chinese-communist-party-to-the-economic-and-national-security-of-the-united-states.

[50] Cybereason, "Operation Soft Cell: A Worldwide Campaign Against Telecommunications Providers," 2019. [Online]. Access Date: 02/07/2021, Available: https://web.archive.org/web/20210102101544/https://www.cybereason.com/blog/operation-soft-cell-a-worldwide-campaign-against-telecommunications-providers.

[51] J. Rogin, "NSA Chief: Cybercrime Constitutes The 'Greatest Transfer of Wealth in History'," *Foreign Policy*, 2012. [Online]. Access Date: 02/07/2021, Available: https://web.archive.org/web/20210102131600/https://foreignpolicy.com/2012/07/09/nsa-chief-cybercrime-constitutes-the-greatest-transfer-of-wealth-in-history/.

[52] PWC, "*Uncovering A New Sustained Global Cyber Espionage Campaign,*" no date. [Online]. Access Date: 02/07/2021, Available: https://web.archive.org/web/20210102133138/https://www.pwc.co.uk/issues/cyber-security-services/insights/operation-cloud-hopper.html.

[53] M. Nichols, "North Korea took $2 Billion in Cyberattacks to Fund Weapons Program: U.N. Report," *Reuters*, 2019. [Online]. Access Date: 02/07/2021, Available: https://web.archive.org/web/20201011092832if_/https://www.reuters.com/article/us-northkorea-cyber-un-idUSKCN1UV1ZX.

[54] Army, United States of America, "*North Korean Tactics,*" 2020. [Online]. Access Date: 02/07/2021, Available: https://web.archive.org/web/2020081 8145855/https://assets.documentcloud.org/documents/7038686/US-Army-report-on-North-Korean-military.pdf E-1.

[55] United States District Court for the Central District of California, "*Criminal Complaint,*" 2018. [Online]. Access Date: 02/07/2021, Available: https://web.archive.org/web/20201217080532/https://www.justice.gov/opa/press-release/file/1092091/download.

[56] J. Hammer, "The billion-dollar bank job," *The New York Times*, 2018. [Online]. Access Date: 02/07/2021, Available: https://web.archive.org/web/2 0180512191034/https://www.nytimes.com/interactive/2018/05/03/magazine/money-issue-bangladesh-billion-dollar-bank-heist.html.

[57] A. Searle, Interviewee, [Interview]. 4 September 2020.

[58] A. Greenberg, "New clues show how Russia's grid hackers aimed for physical destruction," *Wired,* 2019. [Online]. Access Date: 02/07/2021, Available: https://web.archive.org/web/20201229183456/https://www.wired.com/story/russia-ukraine-cyberattack-power-grid-blackout-destruction/.

[59] J. Warrick and E. Nakashima, "Stuxnet was work of U.S. and Lsraeli Experts, Officials Say," *Washington Post*, 2012. [Online]. Access Date: 02/07/2021, Available: https://web.archive.org/web/20201230100545/https://www.washingtonpost.com/world/national-security/stuxnet-was-work-of-us-and-israeli-experts-officials-say/2012/06/01/gJQAlnEy6U_story.html.

[60] Cybersecurity and Infrastructure Security Agency, "*Alert (TA18-074A): Russian Government Cyber Activity Targeting Energy and Other Critical Infrastructure Sectors,*" 2018. [Online]. Access Date: 02/07/2021, Available: https://web.archive.org/web/20201227194614/https://us-cert.cisa.gov/ncas/alerts/TA18-074A.

[61] Symantec, "Dragonfly: Western Energy Sector Targeted by Sophisticated Attack Group," 2017. [Online]. Access Date: 02/07/2021, Available: https://web.archive.org/web/20201229110247if_/https://symantec-enterprise-blogs.security.com/blogs/threat-intelligence/dragonfly-energy-sector-cyber-attacks.

[62] J. Pagliery, "The inside story of the biggest hack in history," *CNN*, 2015. [Online]. Access Date: 02/07/2021, Available: https://web.archive.org/web/20201229141509/https://money.cnn.com/2015/08/05/technology/aramco-hack/.

[63] Cutting Sword of Justice, "Untitled," 2012. [Online]. Access Date: 02/07/2021, Available: https://web.archive.org/web/20201229140411/https://pastebin.com/HqAgaQRj.

[64] T. Roccia, J. Saavedra-Morales and C. Beek, "Shamoon attackers employ new tool kit to wipe infected systems," *McAfee*, 2018. [Online]. Access Date: 02/07/2021, Available: https://web.archive.org/web/20201229142817/https://www.mcafee.com/blogs/other-blogs/mcafee-labs/shamoon-attackers-employ-new-tool-kit-to-wipe-infected-systems/.

[65] N. Perlroth, "In cyberattack on Saudi Firm, U.S. sees Iran firing back," *Tehe New York Times*, 2012. [Online]. Access Date: 02/07/2021, Available: https://web.archive.org/web/20201219085807/https://www.nytimes.com/2012/10/24/business/global/cyberattack-on-saudi-oil-firm-disquiets-us.html.

[66] C. Cimpanu, "New Iranian data Wiper Malware Hits Bapco, Bahrain's National Oil Company," *ZDNet*, 2020. [Online]. Access Date: 02/07/2021, Available: https://web.archive.org/web/20201229135101/https://www.zdnet.com/article/new-iranian-data-wiper-malware-hits-bapco-bahrains-national-oil-company/.

[67] P. Neray, "New CyberX global ICS & IIoT risk report: ICS networks are soft targets," *CyberX*, 2018. [Online]. Access Date: 02/07/2021, Available: https://web.archive.org/web/20201230102258/https://cyberx-labs.com/blog/new-cyberx-global-ics-iiot-risk-report-ics-networks-are-soft-targets/.

[68] World Anti-Doping Agency, "*Cyber Security Update: WADA's Incident Response*," 2016. [Online]. Access Date: 02/07/2021, Available: https://web.archive.org/web/20210201172633/https://www.wada-ama.org/en/media/news/2016-10/cyber-security-update-wadas-incident-response.

[69] C. Cimpanu, "Hackers leak details of 1,000 high-ranking Belarus Police Officers," *ZDNet*, 2020. [Online]. Access Date: 02/07/2021, Available: https://web.archive.org/web/20201224034454/https://www.zdnet.com/article/hackers-leak-details-of-1000-high-ranking-belarus-police-officers/.

[70] M. Miller, "Minneapolis city systems temporarily brought down by cyber-attack," *The Hill*, 2020. [Online]. Access Date: 02/07/2021, Available: https://web.archive.org/web/20201230101737/https://thehill.com/policy/cybersecurity/500009-minneapolis-city-systems-temporarily-brought-down-by-cyberattack.

[71] M. Bryant, "LGBT twitter users tease far-right group by taking over proud boys hashtag," *The Guardian*, 2020. [Online]. Access Date: 02/07/2021, Available: https://web.archive.org/web/20201227151142/https://www.theguardian.com/world/2020/oct/05/proud-boys-hashtag-lgbt-twitter-users.

[72] J. Cloherty, "Virtual Terrorism: Al Qaeda video calls for 'Electronic Jihad'," *ABC News*, 2012. [Online]. Access Date: 02/07/2021, Available: https://web.archive.org/web/20210101122158/https://abcnews.go.com/Politics/cyber-terrorism-al-qaeda-video-calls-electronic-jihad/story?id=16407875.

[73] BBC, "*UK jihadist Junaid Hussain Killed in Syria Drone Strike, Says US*," 2015. [Online]. Access Date: 02/07/2021, Available: https://web.archive.org/web/20201213171032/https://www.bbc.com/news/uk-34078900.

[74] Israel Defense Forces, "*@IDF,*" 2019. [Online]. Access Date: 02/07/2021, Available: https://web.archive.org/web/20201228220045/https://twitter.com/idf/status/1125066395010699264.

[75] M. Coker, D. Yadron and D. Paletta, "Hacker Killed by Drone Was Islamic State's 'Secret Weapon'," *The Wall Street Journal*, 2015. [Online]. Access Date: 02/07/2021, Available: https://web.archive.org/web/20201230141538/https://www.wsj.com/articles/hacker-killed-by-drone-was-secret-weapon-1440718560.

[76] Ponemon Institute, "*Cost of Insider Threats: Global Report, 2020*," 2020. [Online]. Access Date: 02/07/2021, Available: https://web.archive.org/web/20200920164305/https://www.ibm.com/downloads/cas/LQZ4RONE.

[77] Team ObserveIT, "*The Primary Factors Motivating Insider Threats*," 2019. [Online]. Access Date: 02/07/2021, Available: https://web.archive.org/web/20200927083725/https://www.observeit.com/blog/primary-factors-motivating-insider-threats/.

[78] United States Department of Justice, "*United States of America V. Xiaoqing Zheng And Zhaoxi Zhang*," 2019. [Online]. Access Date: 02/07/2021, Available: https://web.archive.org/web/20210116174158/https://www.justice.gov/opa/press-release/file/1156521/download.

[79] United States Department of Justice, "*Former Microsoft Software Engineer Convicted of 18 Federal Felonies For Stealing More Than $10 Million In Digital Value Such As Gift Cards*," 2020. [Online]. Access Date: 02/07/2021, Available: https://web.archive.org/web/20201004141613/https://www.justice.gov/usao-wdwa/pr/former-microsoft-software-engineer-convicted-18-federal-felonies-stealing-more-10.

[80] S. Ben and A. Bhat, "2020 securonix insider threat report," *Securonix*, 2020. [Online]. Access Date: 02/07/2021, Available: https://web.archive.org/web/20200722002006/https://pages.securonix.com/rs/179-DJP-142/images/Insider-Threat-Report-May-2020-Securonix.pdf.

[81] M. J. Hughes, "Affidavit in support of arrest warrant and criminal complaint: United States District Court, District of Nevada: United States of America V. Egor Igorevich Kriuchkov (Case No: 3:20-mj-83-WGC)," *Federal Bureau of Investigation*, 2020. [Online]. Access Date: 02/07/2021, Available: https://web.archive.org/web/20200914212729/https://www.justice.gov/opa/press-release/file/1308766/download.

[82] N. Truanich, R. B. Casper and C. S. Heath, "United States District Court, District of Nevada: United States of America V. Egor Igorevich Kriuchkov (Case No: 3:20-mj-83-WGC)," *United States Department of Justice*, 2020. [Online]. Access Date: 02/07/2021, Available: https://web.archive.org/web/20200914212729/https://www.justice.gov/opa/press-release/file/1308766/download.

[83] United States Department of Justice, "*Russian National Arrested for Conspiracy to Introduce Malware Into A Nevada Company's Computer Network*," 2020. [Online]. Access Date: 02/07/2021, Available: https://web.archive.org/web/20200920093156/https://www.justice.gov/opa/pr/russian-national-arrested-conspiracy-introduce-malware-nevada-companys-computer-network.

[84] E. Musk, "Tesla employee turns down $1 million, works with FBI, and helps thwart a planned cybersecurity attack on Giga Nevada [Aug. 27, 2020]," *Twitter*, 2020. [Online]. Access Date: 02/07/2021, Available: https://web.archive.org/web/20200829103636/https://twitter.com/elonmusk/status/1299105277485088768?ref_src=twsrc%5Etfw.

[85] E. Snowden, "Edward Snowden Statement: 'It Was the Right Thing To Do and I Have No Regrets'," *The Guardian*, 2013. [Online]. Access Date: 02/07/2021, Available: https://web.archive.org/web/20200927085343/https://www.theguardian.com/world/2013/jul/12/edward-snowden-full-statement-moscow.

[86] United States Senate, "*Threats to the U.S. Research Enterprise: China's Talent Recruitment Plans*," 2019. [Online]. Access Date: 02/07/2021, Available: https://web.archive.org/web/20200919032809/https://www.hsgac.senate.gov/imo/media/doc/2019-11-18%20PSI%20Staff%20Report%20-%20China's%20Talent%20Recruitment%20Plans%20Updated.pdf.

[87] J. Markon, "U.S. Deports alleged 12th Russian Spy," *Washington Post*, 2010. [Online]. Access Date: 02/07/2021, Available: https://web.archive.org/web/20190907081559/http://www.washingtonpost.com/wp-dyn/content/article/2010/07/13/AR2010071302840.html.

[88] G. Corera, *Russians Among Us*, London: William Collins, 2019.

[89] T. Bailey, B. Kolo, K. Rajagopalan and D. Ware, "Insider threat: the human element of cyberrisk," *McKinsey*, no date. [Online]. Access Date: 02/07/2021, Available: https://web.archive.org/web/20200925162532if_/https://www.mckinsey.com/business-functions/risk/our-insights/insider-threat-the-human-element-of-cyberrisk.

[90] D. Petropoulos, Interviewee, [Interview]. 7 September 2020.

[91] N. Giller, Interviewee, [Interview]. 9 September 2020.

[92] C. Stupp, "Fraudsters Used AI to Mimic CEO's voice in unusual cybercrime case," *The Wall Street Journal*, 2019. [Online]. Access Date: 02/07/2021, Available: https://web.archive.org/web/20210128091454/https://www.wsj.com/articles/fraudsters-use-ai-to-mimic-ceos-voice-in-unusual-cybercrime-case-11567157402.

[94] J. Umawing, "The Face of Tomorrow's cybercrime: deepfake ransomware explained," *Malware Bytes*, 2020. [Online]. Access Date: 02/07/2021, Available: https://web.archive.org/web/20210128123010/https://blog.malwarebytes.com/ransomware/2020/06/the-face-of-tomorrows-cybercrime-deepfake-ransomware-explained/.

[93] M. R. Fuentes, "Trading in the dark: an investigation into the current condition of underground markets and cybercriminal forums," *Trend Micro*, 2020. [Online]. Access Date: 02/07/2021, Available: https://web.archive.org/web/20210128132202/https://www.trendmicro.com/vinfo/us/security/news/cybercrime-and-digital-threats/trading-in-the-dark.

[95] T. Burt and E. Horvitz, "New steps to combat disinformation," *Microsoft*, 2020. [Online]. Access Date: 02/07/2021, Available: https://web.archive.org/web/20210128151008/https://blogs.microsoft.com/on-the-issues/2020/09/01/disinformation-deepfakes-newsguard-video-authenticator/> [Accessed 28January2021.

[96] IBM, "*The Adversarial Robustness Toolbox: Securing AI Against Adversarial Threats*," 2018. [Online]. Access Date: 02/07/2021, Available:

https://web.archive.org/web/20210129160054/https://www.ibm.com/blogs/
research/2018/04/ai-adversarial-robustness-toolbox/.

[97] Skylight, *"Cylance, I Kill You!,"* 2019. [Online]. Access Date: 02/07/2021,
Available: https://web.archive.org/web/20210130103641/https://
skylightcyber.com/2019/07/18/cylance-i-kill-you/.

[98] R. S. S. Kumar and A. Johnson, "Cyberattacks against machine learning
systems are more common than you think," *Microsoft*, 2020. [Online]. Access
Date: 02/07/2021, Available: https://web.archive.org/web/20210129155118/
https://www.microsoft.com/security/blog/2020/10/22/cyberattacks-against-
machine-learning-systems-are-more-common-than-you-think/.

[99] R. S. S. K et al., *"Adversarial Machine Learning - Industry Perspectives,"*
2002. [Online]. Access Date: 02/07/2021, Available: https://arxiv.org/pdf/2
002.05646.pdf.

[100] MITRE, *"Adversarial ML Threat Matrix,"* 2020. [Online]. Access Date: 02/
07/2021, Available: https://web.archive.org/web/20210129155341/https://
github.com/mitre/advmlthreatmatrix.

[101] IBM, *"CLEVER: A Robustness Metric for Deep Neural Networks,"* 2018.
[Online]. Access Date: 02/07/2021, Available: https://web.archive.org/web/2
0210129160311/https://github.com/IBM/CLEVER-Robustness-Score.

[102] K. Martin, *Cryptography: The Key to Digital Security, How it Works, and
Why it Matters*, New York: W. W. Norton & Company, 2020.

[103] L. K. Grover, "A fast quantum mechanical algorithm for database search,"
in *Proceedings of the Twenty-Eighth Annual ACM Symposium on Theory of
Computing*, New York, 1996.

[104] ational Institute for Standards and Technology (NIST), *"Post-Quantum
Cryptography: FAQs,"* no date. [Online]. Access Date: 02/07/2021, Available:
https://web.archive.org/web/20201128165703/https://csrc.nist.gov/Projects/Post-
Quantum-Cryptography/faqs.

[105] J. Langer, Interviewee, [Interview]. 24 August 2020.

[106] A. Stanley, "This hacked coffee maker demands ransom and demonstrates a
terrifying implication about the IoT," *Gizmodo*, 2020. [Online]. Access
Date: 02/07/2021, Available: https://web.archive.org/web/2021011611243
6/https://gizmodo.com/this-hacked-coffee-maker-demands-ransom-and-
demonstrate-1845191662.

[107] A. Greenberg, "Hackers reveal nasty new car attacks - with me behind the
wheel," *Forbes*, 2013. [Online]. Access Date: 02/07/2021, Available: https://
web.archive.org/web/20210130160514/https://www.forbes.com/sites/
andygreenberg/2013/07/24/hackers-reveal-nasty-new-car-attacks-with-me-
behind-the-wheel-video/?sh=c8d4cb228c77.

[108] Federal Bureau of Investigation, *"2020 Internet Crime Report,"* 2021.
[Online]. Access Date: 02/07/2021, Available: https://web.archive.org/web/2
0210509095432/https://www.ic3.gov/Media/PDF/AnnualReport/2020_IC3
Report.pdf.

[109] B. Sussman, "How Bruce Schneier sees security in 2019," *Security World Expo*,
2019. [Online]. Access Date: 02/07/2021, Available: https://web.archive.org/
web/20210129161717/https://www.secureworldexpo.com/industry-news/bruce-
schneier-on-security.

[110] Gartner, *"Gartner Predicts 75% of CEOs Will be Personally Liable for
Cyber-Physical Security Incidents by 2024,"* 2020. [Online]. Access Date: 02/

07/2021, Available: https://web.archive.org/web/20210130160311/https://www.gartner.com/en/newsroom/press-releases/2020-09-01-gartner-predicts-75--of-ceos-will-be-personally-liabl.

[111] P. Knightley, *The Second Oldest Profession.* London: Pimlico, 2003.

[112] National Institute of Standards and Technology, "*NIST Special Publication 1500-201 Framework for Cyber-Physical Systems,*" 2017. [Online]. Access Date: 02/07/2021, Available: https://web.archive.org/web/202102011 63145/https://nvlpubs.nist.gov/nistpubs/SpecialPublications/NIST.SP.15 00-201.pdf.

[113] Partnership on AI's Media Integrity Steering Committee, "*Deepfake Detection Challenge: Identify Videos With Facial of Voice Manipulation,*" 2020. [Online]. Access Date: 02/07/2021, Available: https://web.archive.org/web/2 0210128124523/https://www.kaggle.com/c/deepfake-detection-challenge.

[114] M. Turek, " Media Forensics (MediFor)," *Defense Advanced Research Projects Agency*, no date. [Online]. Access Date: 02/07/2021, Available: https://www.darpa.mil/program/media-forensics.

Chapter 2

Enabling Corporate and Institutional Governance for Effective IT Governance

Munir Ahmad Saeed[1], Tahmina Rashid[2], and Mohiuddin Ahmed[3]

[1]Canberra Institute of Technology
[2]University of Canberra
[3]Edith Cowan University

CONTENTS

> Good IT governance is no longer a "nice to have", it is a "must have" [1,2]

2.1 INTRODUCTION

Corporate governance established itself as discipline in its own right a long ago, and the concept of governance has been extended to various other areas, such as information technology (IT) and project management [3]. Butler [4,5] states that the etymology of the word governance comes from the Latin words "guberbare" and "gubermator," which refer to steering of a ship and the steerer of a ship. The word governance also hails from a French word "gouvrernance," which means control and the state of being governed. UNESCO defines governance as structures and processes to ensure accountability, transparency, stability, and responsiveness, rule of law, equity, and inclusiveness. Governance and management are two different concepts, as governance is about how power is shared and distributed, and governance systems set the boundaries within which the management systems will operate (unesco.org). Management includes a number of arrangements, structures, and processes to effectively mobilize physical, financial, and human resources. Corporate governance provides structures enabling a company to identify and set up its objectives and means of attaining such objectives, as well as monitoring the performance [6]. ANAO [7] defines governance as "the way things get done, rather than just the things that are done." Governance in the public sector refers to practices and the arrangements that enable a public sector agency to identify its direction and manage its operations, to achieve expected outcomes and perform its accountability obligations [7]. IFAC [8] states, "governance in the public sector comprises the arrangements put in place to ensure that the intended outcomes for stakeholders are defined and achieved."

Butler [4] states the governance literature mainly discusses issues, such as governance from the board perspective, the roles and responsibilities of boards, policy frameworks, and responsible decision making. Referring to William [9], Miller and Hobbs (2004) assert that the governance literature identifies three streams of governance – corporate governance, institutional governance, and project governance. The corporate governance literature dilates on issues such as what structures should be put in place to govern an organization. Butler [4] states that corporate governance generally tends to focus on financial performance and legal compliance. Hollingsworth et al. [10] argue that the institutional governance is about markets, contracts, hierarchies, and regulations. Bekker and Steyn [3] define project governance as a set of management systems, rules, protocols, relationships, and structures that provide the framework within which the decisions are made for project development and implementation to achieve intended business or strategic motivations. We can see that quite similar principles of governance extend to IT governance as IT Governance Institute states,

> IT governance is the responsibility of the board of directors and executive management. It is an integral part of enterprise governance and consists of the leadership and organizational structures and processes that ensure that the organization's IT sustains and extends the organization's strategies and objectives (www.ITGI.org).

The IT governance enables the organization to realize it strategic objectives, as Grembergen [11], states:

> IT governance is the organizational capacity exercised by the board, executive management and the IT management to control the formulation and the implementation of IT strategy and in this way ensure the fusion of business and IT.

It will be interesting to explore how the corporate and institutional governance frameworks steer IT governance to protect and sustain IT assets and data from cyber threats and also employ IT governance to achieve the organizational strategic objectives. A recent doctoral study in project management has found that the senior executives in the major public sector organizations bring in their corporate management styles to the governance of major projects which include major reforms and IT systems roll out [12]. Therefore, we argue that there is a strong probability that the corporate governance frameworks and styles are applied for IT governance. But it raises an important question, whether the existing IT governance frameworks and structures provide the expected governance controls for the IT sector, particularly, for the management on cyber security and the emergence of data as most precious organizational asset.

This chapter explores the emergence and the evolution of governance and strategy and then discusses whether the current corporate and institutional governance styles are relevant to IT governance. It discusses major IT governance frameworks and how the organizations align their strategic objectives with IT goals, what challenges they encounter and how far these have been successful in their endeavors.

Chapter Roadmap:

- Introduction
- Governance as a concept and types of governance
- Governance and strategy
- Governance in various sectors
- Current IT governance frameworks
- Business goals and IT-investment alignment
- Chapter summary

2.2 GOVERNANCE AND STRATEGY

Organizations and businesses have their strategic goals and to achieve these they invest in technology through projects. Therefore, investments in technology become a part of strategy to achieve the organizational goals. The organizational managements build governance structures to implement an agreed strategy. Mintzberg [13] defines strategy as a set of deliberate conscious guidelines that steer the decision-making for the future. Referring to the definitions of strategy in various other disciplines such as military and game theory, Mintzberg identifies three important elements of strategy – strategy is explicit, consciously and purposefully developed, and is developed in advance to the decision-making. In simple terms, Mintzberg describes strategy as "a plan." However, it seems that describing strategy as a plan is an over simplification. Mintzberg argues that a strategy maker may formulate a strategy as a deliberate process; however, on the other hand, he argues that strategy can evolve unintentionally, as a decision maker makes decisions one by one and there is a pattern in this process. Mintzberg argues that strategy formulation process revolves around the interplay of three factors: environments, organizational operating system, and leadership. He argues that where environments change continually but irregularly, the organizational operating system endeavors to ensure stabilization, despite the ephemeral nature of the environments, the operating system tries to serve the environments. The role of the third factor, leadership, the author argues, is to mediate between two other players in an effort to ensure the stability of the operating system as well as ensuring the adaptation to the environments. Discussing the Volkswagen case study, Mintzberg states that despite the changed environments, bold actions were not taken by the leadership due to the inertia of bureaucratic constraints and when change did happen due to the dynamic leadership, it was too late. Thereby, Mintzberg seems to state that the momentum from all three factors is needed to effect changes in strategy. In this article Mintzberg introduces two key concepts about strategy formulation such as Intended strategies and Realized strategies. Intended strategies are those strategies that get realized and may be called as "deliberate" strategies. Realized strategies are those strategies which were in fact not intended as there may be no strategy intended at all.

In another article, Mintzberg [14] discusses three modes of strategy formulation in various businesses and organizations. These three modes are Entrepreneurial, Adaptive, and Planning, which are adopted by various organizations depending on the nature, size, and the leadership styles of the top management. Explaining the entrepreneurial mode, Mintzberg argues that a number of management writers are of the opinion that the entrepreneurial mode of strategy formulation is effective not only for starting new businesses but also useful for running businesses. This mode is predominantly associated with looking for new business opportunities. Businesses that potentially employ this mod are structured on centralized power in the hands of a CEO. Such organizations may not have any charted plan rather the strategy is driven by the vision of the entrepreneur and is based on finding new opportunities rather than being curtailed in solving problems. In an entrepreneurial organization, growth is the main goal. Organizations that often employ entrepreneur mode are small and young, where the authority lies with the powerful person [14].

The second mode of strategy formulation according to Mintzberg [14] is adaptive mode, in which the decisions are made in small steps without radically upsetting the status quo. Lindblom [15] terms adaptive mode as the "science of muddling through and 'disjointed incrementalism." The adaptive mode of policy-making is employed by the risk averse managements, that avoid uncertainty and tend to resolve immediate problems rather than pursuing new opportunities [14]. This adaptive mode is a contrast to entrepreneurial mode, where exploiting new opportunities are preferred over resolving existing problems. Writing about the nature of organizations that may employ adaptive mode of policy formulation, Mintzberg [14] argues that this could be a public sector organization, where power is distributed among the various members and has a complex matrix of stakeholders. In such an organization policy-making is reactive and directed to solve the existing problems as compared to entrepreneur mode, where policy-making is proactive. This policy-making mode is easier and not expensive and it enables the policy makers being flexible to adapt to the emerging challenges at will. Organizations that could opt for planning mode method must be big enough to defray the cost of formal analysis [14].

Mintzberg [14] states that the third mode of policy-making is planning mode in which analysts play a key role in strategy formulation. In this mode the analyst works in collaboration with the manager and applies some policy analysis and management science techniques. The planning mode is structured and systematic and is based on the understanding that formal analysis can offer the opportunity to comprehend the environment and influence as well. Mintzberg [14] argues that these modes of policy formulation are not mutually exclusive and can be applied in a combination, depending on the needs of a business/organization.

Vancil [16] defines strategy "as a glue that binds diverse activities of a complex organization together." The effectiveness of a strategy can be judged from two perspectives, namely whether or not the strategy is right for a particular organization in the given circumstances and does it provide a right fit between the available opportunities and the resources of the organization. The second perspective is whether strategy has been formulated to facilitate organizational processes.

McElroy [17–19] states that senior management allocate lot of effort and time to develop and implement strategy. But to its frustration top management discovers little progress in the areas where strategic change was expected to occur. He states that the force of strategic objectives mellows down as strategy cascades down through the middle management and the initial enthusiasm is lost even before the expected benefits are realized. McElroy [17] argues that in order to effectively implement strategic change within an organization, the management needs to overcome the existing organizational inertia. He argues that if management endeavors to implement strategy through the existing structures and cultures, the management is attempting to change the status quo with status quo. As we see later in this chapter that in order to make the right IT investment decisions and the implementation of information systems and assets management, appropriate and effective governance structures need to be established.

What is the relationship between governance and strategy, as Butler [4] states, where strategy literature predominantly deals with models, tools, and techniques of organizational strategy formulation, the governance literature mainly discusses issues, such as governance from the board's perspective, the roles and responsibilities of boards, policy frameworks and responsible decision making. Referring to William [9], Miller and Hobbs [20] assert that governance literature identifies three streams of governance – corporate governance, institutional governance, and project governance. The corporate governance literature dilates on issues such as what structures should be put in place to govern an organization. Butler [4] states that corporate governance generally tends to focus on financial performance and legal compliance. Governance Institute Australia states that corporate governance establishes relations between the management, board, shareholders, and the stakeholders of a company. It also builds the necessary structures to define the objectives of a company and provides the wherewithal to achieve those objectives (governanceinstitute.com.au). Hollingsworth et al. [10] argue that the institutional governance is about markets, contracts, hierarchies, and regulations. Bekker and Steyn [3] define project governance as a set of management systems, rules, protocols, relationships, and structures that provide the framework within which the decisions are made for project development and implementation to achieve intended business or strategic motivations. IT governance is a component of corporate governance, which aims to enhance the management of IT in order to increase the expected value from investments made in IT and its assets. This objective is achieved through the implementation of IT governance frameworks, so that the IT-related risks are managed effectively and the activities around technology are aligned to the overall business objectives (itgovernance.co.uk).

It is important that we understand the difference between corporate and project governance. Morgan and Gbedemah [21] state that the corporate governance deals with a set of relationships between the management of the organization, its board, owners, and stakeholders. Corporate governance provides structures that enable establishing of organization objectives and monitoring company performance against those objectives. Sir Adrian Cadbury, while defining corporate governance said, "Corporate governance framework is there to encourage the efficient use of resources and equally to require accountability for the stewardship of these resources" [21]. Turner [22] states that project governance enables structures, which define project objectives, provides means to monitor progress, and achieves agreed project objectives. Volden and Andersen [23] state that project governance ensures environments of adequate checks and balances to enable transparency and accountability, roles, and responsibilities as well as proving the project managers all the required support for successfully delivering project objectives. APM [24,25] states project governance:

> *"concerns those areas of corporate governance that are specifically related to project activities. Effective governance of project management ensures that an organization's project portfolio is aligned to the organization's objectives, is delivered efficiently, and is sustainable."*

Projects and programs are temporary organizations [26]; therefore, the governance arrangements last as long as the projects/programs exist. However, comparatively, the IT governance structures have longer life cycles and comprise a number of processes and elements. Symons [27] suggests that effective IT governance framework must comprise three main elements – such as structure, processes, and communication. Explaining these components, Symons [27] states:

Structure – addresses who makes decisions in the organization, the structure of the organization, and who will participate in the organization by assuming what responsibilities.

Process – covers how decisions about IT investment are made, what is the process for making decisions about IT investment, how the investments are reviewed, approved, and prioritize investment in IT.

Communication – deals with the communication of IT investment decisions with the senior executives, IT management, business management, and employees.

It is important to explore a number of major IT governance frameworks and see how these help organizations in their efforts to realize business goals in an era wherein businesses are increasingly relying on technology, particularly IT for survival and growth.

2.3 CURRENT IT GOVERNANCE FRAMEWORKS

Like frameworks in other disciplines such as project management and IT governance frameworks are not perfect. Larsen et al [28] identify 17 standards and tools for IT governance; however, this chapter focuses only on three main frameworks being employed by the majority of the organizations and businesses in the world [19,29]. These frameworks are Control Objectives for Information and related Technologies (COBIT), IT Infrastructure Library (ITIL), and ISO 270001. Symons [27] states there is no single comprehensive IT governance framework, and the existing major ones complement each other, therefore, requiring a mix and match approach to achieve effective IT governance.

2.3.1 COBIT

COBIT was developed by the Information Systems Audit and Control Association (ISACA) and is now managed as a framework by the IT Governance Institute (ITGI), which is in fact a component of ISACA. COBIT was first released in 1996, then versions 2, 3, and 4 were release by ISACA in 1998, 2000, and 2005, respectively. In the year 2018, a further improved version was released, which was rebranded as COBIT2019. This framework is used to set up and maintain control over the IT domain [30,31].

According to Compliance Council, the major theme of COBIT 2019 is to enable the organizations to align IT goals with their strategic business goals, with the aim to facilitate better access to key data before making business decisions (compliancecouncil.com.au). Lainhart [32] states that COBIT has generally been accepted as a standard for IT security and control practices. Larsen et al. [28] highlight three main components of this standard, such as (1) performance measurement elements for outcome measures, (2) critical success factors as best practices for each process, and (3) maturity model for benchmarking and decision-making for improvement of capabilities. According to Symons [27], COBIT has been strengthened with more action-oriented guideline to consolidate the monitoring the achievement of organizational goals and the performance in each IT process and for benchmarking organizational performance. Overall COBIT is a comprehensive framework for implementing IT governance with strong auditing and control emphasis. White [33] states that one major difference between COBIT and other frameworks is that it emphasizes on security, risk management, and governance. Quoting ISACA, White [33] states that COBIT2019 is a framework for the management and governance of the enterprise IT across the organization. COBIT2019 introduces Core Model, which comprises 40 governance and management objectives for setting up governance. Following are the six core principles of governance [34]:

- **Stakeholders' value:** The governance system must satisfy stakeholders' needs and generate value through an effective use of resources, managing risks, and develop actionable strategy.
- **Holistic approach:** The system may comprise different components, but it must be designed to work holistically.
- **Dynamic:** If one or more design factors change, the impact must be considered on the entire system.
- **Distinction between governance and management:** The governance structures and processes are different from management structures and activities.
- **Tailored to enterprise needs:** The system is based on design factors to enable governance systems for the needs of the enterprise.
- **End to end:** Governance covers all the functions of an enterprise including information technology.

Figure 2.1 shows how COBIT as IT governance framework aligns stakeholders' drivers through IT governance.

Overall COBIT is designed to enable the senior management to understand how to align technology to the enterprise strategic objectives. According to ISACA, the framework facilitates the top executives to see return on IT investment [33].

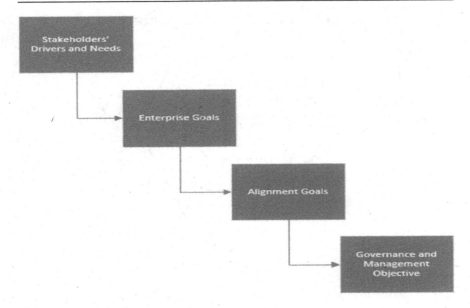

Figure 2.1 Goals cascading in COBIT 2019.

Source: Shiff [34].

2.3.2 ITIL

ITIL was developed in the 1980s by the British Government Central Computer and Telecommunication Agency (CCTA). Since 2013, ITIL is owned by Axelos and it issues licenses for the use of this framework and the current version ITIL4 was released in 2019 [35,36]. ITIL is another globally acknowledged framework that is employed for service management to guide businesses and organizations in the deployment of IT for realizing their business goals and respond to the changing nature of technology transformation. Shiff [34] states, ITIL has the following components:

ITIL Service Chain: comprises six activities such as Plan, Engage, Design and Transition, Obtain/Build, Deliver and Support, and Improve. Elaborating these components, Mathenge and Stevens-Hall [37,38] state:

- ITIL practices: consist of three main practices, namely general management practices, service management practices, and technical management practices.
- ITIL guiding principles: comprise seven principles – focus on value, start where you are, progress iteratively with feedback, collaborate and promote visibility, think and work holistically, keep it simple and practical, and optimize and automate
- Governance: consists of direct, monitor, and evaluate

ITIL Service Value System

Figure 2.2 ITIL Practices.

Source: Shiff [34].

- Continual improvement: comprises what is the vision, where are we now, where do we want to be, how do we get there, take action, did we get there.

Figure 2.2 shows ITIL practices listed above.

Referring to Axelos, White and Greiner [35] argue ITIL4 can help organizations in the following ways:

- Helps organizations manage risk, failure, and disruptions
- Improved customers' relations by meeting their needs through effective service delivery
- Establishing cost-effective practice
- Setting up stable environment and yet enabling growth and change

Axelos claims that ITIL is the best practice framework provides a common language and tools that promotes collaboration between the IT teams to be able to deliver value across the organization (axelos.org). Nyhuis [36] states that ITIL4 offers the following benefits:

- Modular structure that enables continuous improvements
- Service value chain integrates the ITIL framework across the entire organization
- Global standard for the delivery of quality IT service
- Provides new avenues to improve efficiency of service

Nyhyis [36] states the implementation of ITIL takes longer time, if it is implemented in its entirety, and it may involve significant change management of the current working practices. Most organizations introduce ITIL in stages and due to its modular structure and staged implementation is a less risky strategy. Due to the very nature of ITIL, continuous improvements will become a norm in the organization, where ITIL will be implemented [36].

As noted previously that the existing major Information Technology Governance (ITG) frameworks complement each other in many ways; therefore, most of the organizations employ the hybrid framework model. Shiff [34] states that COBIT and ITIL4 have the potential to join forces to transform stakeholders' desires into value. If COBIT2019 answers the "what" question, the ITIL provides the "how" answer. The latest versions of both the frameworks continue to complement each other. ITIL4 guides how to carry out many COBIT processes [34]. We argue that using the hybrid framework for IT governance is not unusual as in Project Management (PM), it is a common practice to employ PM Body of Knowledge (PMBOK) and PRINCE2 methodologies and PRINCE2 and Agile in the public sector in Australia.

Both frameworks claim to help align business and IT goals by facilitating linkages between the two and encourage closer understanding between IT and other components of the organization [33]. According to Sarah [37,38] where COBIT endeavors to govern all the processes in an organization ITIL strives to provide value to all stakeholders. COBIT seeks to manage end-to-end governance and ITIL4 seeks value creation. Therefore, we argue that both frameworks can co-exist to manage process governance and value creation. However, Sarah [39] warns that these frameworks should be employed by the organizations with mature processes in place, as COBIT is more effective for supplier management, security, and business continuity. ITIL stands out in "general management practices" such as architecture management, service financial management, relationship management, strategy management, workforce and talent management, continual management, and change management [39]. Figure 2.3 shows the complementary nature of ITIL and COBIT for IT governance.

Where ITIL lacks in control, COBIT prides in robust control (governance) regime, and ITIL demonstrates strength in promoting relationships, collaboration with stakeholders, complements COBIT which is more inward looking [39]. Ozdemir et al. [29] state that ITIL can be implemented rather easily than its competitors such as COBIT and ISO 27001. Further, ITIL practices can be deployed stage over a period of time, whereas COBIT and ISO27001 cannot be implemented partially. Therefore, we argue that as organizations work through the maturity journey, they can start with ITIL, taking the baby steps, managing change slowly and less risky manner. Ozdemir et al. [29] state that COBIT practices are usually implemented from the audit budget but ITIL and ISO27001 are generally implemented using IT budget.

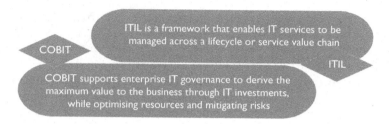

Figure 2.3 ITIL Vs COBIT.

Source: Sarah [39].

2.3.3 ISO/IEC27001

According to ISO, ISO/IEC 27001 is a standard for information security of the information assets. The current standard was release in 2018 and has been designed for any size and type of organizations. ISO/IEC27001 is a vendor and technology neutral standard and offers a number of features for enhanced security of the information system (iso.org). In the Europe, the organizations seeking business with governments and large corporates are increasing finding ISO27001 a prerequisite. A large body of legislation has been enacted during the last 20 years around information and data security, which includes personal data and corporate financial data (itgovernance.-co.uk). Ozdemir [29] states that ISO/IEC 27001 is considerably different from COBIT and ITIL, as this standard narrowly focuses on the information security aspect, whereas the other two cover a wide spectrum of IT governance and management including information security, but not as comprehensively as the ISO/IEC20071 does. Therefore, we argue that currently when cyber threats have become so widespread and imperiling not only the information systems and IT assets but have also caused political repercussions at the global levels between major world powers, the ISO/IEC27001 has become more relevant. Hall [40] argues that information system security, under ISO27001 is achieved through a systematic analysis of the risks to the organization's IT assets. The following table shows the key security areas and the high-level security objectives of each area Table 2.1.

Following are the salient principles of ISO27001: (Compliance Council 2019)

- Risk assessment
- Establishing strategies to manage the identified risks
- Identifying the objectives of security controls
- Implementing adequate security controls
- Regularly reviewing the security system performance and making improvements as needed

Highlighting the weaknesses of the ISO27001 standard, Hall [41] states the focus of the standard on three key principles of the information management

Table 2.1 Security Areas and High-Level Objectives

Security Area	High-Level Objectives
Access control	To control access to information
Asset management	To achieve and maintain appropriate protection of organizational assets
Business continuity management	To counteract interruptions to business activities and to protect critical business processes from the effects of major failures of information systems or disasters and to ensure their timely resumption
Communications and operations management	To ensure the correct and secure operation of information processing facilities
Compliance	To avoid breaches of any law, statutory, and regulatory or contractual obligations, and of any security requirements.
Human resources security	To ensure that employees, contractors, and third-party users: • Understand their responsibilities and liabilities before during and after employment • Are aware of security issues facing the organization and are equipped to deal with them in their normal duties • Reduce the risk of theft, fraud, misuse of facilities, and human error
Information security incident management	To ensure information security events and weaknesses associated with information systems are: • Communicated in a manner allowing timely corrective action to be taken • Dealt with in a consistent and effective manner
Information systems acquisition, development and maintenance	To ensure that security is an integral part of installed information systems technology base
Organizing information security	To manage information security within the organization
Security policy	To provide management direction and support for information security in accordance with business requirements and relevant laws and regulations

Source: Hall [41].

system security, such as confidentiality, integrity, and availability, is quite limiting in the light of the nature of the modern computing environment. The focus on these factors necessitates that all the assets in an organization should be assessed for information security needs, which is not always possible. After discussing three major IT governance frameworks, it will be interesting to have a brief comparison to present common, complementing, and distinct features of these frameworks. Table 2.2 below shows a brief comparison of three IT governance frameworks.

Table 2.2 Comparison of COBIT, ITIL, and ISO270001

Area	COBIT	ITIL	ISO270001
Description	Business framework for IT governance and management of enterprise IT	Best practice for IT service management	International standard for IT service management and requirements
Market view	Main focus is on IT governance and IT compliance. The latest version focuses on enterprise IT which has wider scope than previous versions	Main focus on internal IT processes. Latest version focuses on customer service and value	Focused on certification achievement in order to demonstrate the compliance of international standard
User groups	IT audit and compliance Personnel	Internal IT operations personnel	External IT service provider
Purpose	Defining the audit and compliance requirements for IT	Defines internal IT service management processes	Demonstrating the organization meets international standard
Scope	More scope coverage than ITIL	ITIL is a framework of best practices for service management and is complementary to ISO27001	Complementary to ITIL
Flexibility	Flexible implementation particularly in organizations requiring IT governance and audits can be implement partially	ITIL is quite flexible as only required practices and processes can be implemented	Requires complete implementation to get certified

Peng, Thomas [42] and Novel Vista [43].

As pointed out above that ITIL, COBIT, and ISO/IEC27001 are not mutually exclusive; rather these complement each other. The best strategy would be to employ a mix of these frameworks, as Peng [42] states ITIL offers comprehensive guidance on implementing processes for IT operation but it is weaker on governance. However, where COBIT lacks in process implementation, COBIT shows great prowess in governance and integration with other frameworks. Therefore, COBIT has been recommended for IT audit and compliance purposes [42]. We argue that with an increase in cyber security concerns, for ensuring the continuity, integrity, and availability of IT operations, ISO27001 offers a robust IT security framework, which can be implemented to ensure the security of IT assets along with ITIL for operations and COBIT for governance and audit purposes. However, we argue that these three major frameworks discussed above, guide us in implementing processes for IT operations, governance, and audit as well as information system security, but these frameworks do not guide the management how to make decisions about IT investments to realize business objectives. We argue, on the basis of a recently concluded doctoral study, that when the IT project proposals are developed, the business cases do not tightly link the project outcomes/benefits with the business objectives. This research also informs that during the project implementation, instead of IT governance frameworks, the project/program governance frameworks are applied. Therefore, it is important to explore how the businesses/organizations align the business goals with the goals of investments in IT assets and operations in the Australian public sector.

2.4 BUSINESS GOALS AND IT INVESTMENT ALIGNMENT

The alignment of strategic business objectives with the IT investments goals is one of the major challenges facing the organizations. The challenge of aligning the organizational strategic objectives with the investment goals has been highlighted in the PM literature as well. Young et al. [43] investigated the success of the Australian public sector investment projects by the Victorian government from 1999–2012. This research explored whether the targeted strategic goals were achieved by the projects implemented in various state government agencies. While analyzing annual reports of the agencies under study, the authors discovered that performance measures were selectively picked to demonstrate that the agency has made improvements during the reporting period. The authors found that strategic goals were not consistently reported during the period of study. In the education department, the authors found that literacy rate has largely remained static, except improvements in early childhood and the numeracy rates have nose-dived across all age groups. A similar scenario has been exposed in the health department as well, where over a decade an amount of $25 billion was spent on various projects. In the health sector, the authors state that despite the availability of performance data, no systematic data was available to demonstrate, whether the waiting period for access to health services improved or not. On the basis of various other data, the authors conclude that the waiting period for health services has either remained unchanged or deteriorated. Young et al. state that despite the fact that the State of Victoria is a leader in New Public Management (NPM) and its investment frameworks matched best practices, but still the program management and governance practices are not geared towards achieving the strategic goals. The authors conclude that projects made insignificant contribution towards organization strategy of the two agencies and a systematic weakness has been identified in the manner projects are selected and governed. Identifying the deficiencies in the program management practices of the Victorian government, Young et al. argue that project selection methods are inherently deficient and provide no guarantee that strategic objectives will be achieved. A similar research into the public sector projects in NSW paint a resembling picture to Victoria. Young and Grant [44] analyzed projects of the five agencies of the NSW government, consuming 67% of the state budget between 2001–2010. The authors divided this study in two components, such as 2001–2006 and 2007–2010. The reasons for this compartmentalization of the study periods may be that 2001–2007 was the period when NPM was in force in the state and from 2007 to 2010 the Whole of Government (WoG) approach was adopted by the state government. Young and Grant state that during 2001–2006 under NPM; the agencies frequently changed their strategic objectives; therefore, strategic instability characterizes this period. The authors identified that nearly 34% of projects strategic objectives changed during this period. Therefore, the authors argue, that even in ideal conditions, wherein, even if the entire project was aligned to strategic goals, one in three projects would become irrelevant in the following year due to the fluid nature of strategic objectives. The authors state that in comparison to NPM, during the 2007–2010 period, when WoG was introduced, provided much needed strategic stability, wherein strategic objectives were set at the state level rather than at the agency level. Presenting the comparison of projects implemented under NPM and WoG, Young and Grant, state that under NPM policy environment, only 22/115 metrics (19%) showed improvement and the remaining were either negative or statistically insignificant. Whereas, under WoG policy environment, 41/121 metrics (34%) had improved and the remaining 66% did not show any marked improvement. The authors add that there was no evidence of the impact of global financial crisis or any other factors such as technological changes and other external influences may have had any impact on project performance.

The above two case studies of the state governments demonstrate that aligning the organizational strategic objectives and project goals have been a persistent challenge in the Australian public sector organizations. We argue that similar challenges would be encountered by organizations to align their strategic goals with the IT investment projects. Therefore, it is important to explore what factors impact on the formation business-IT alignment. Because organizations make hefty investments in IT applications and assets to achieve the business goals. Briefly, we will discuss what factors impact on achieving the business objectives and the IT investment goals. Jonathon et al. [45] argue that the organization structures play a role in the alignment of business and IT alignment. [46] states "applying IT in an appropriate and timely way, in harmony with business strategies, goals and needs," has remained an elusive objective for the practitioners and the information system researchers. Kappelman et al. [47] state that surveys with the IT executives across all industries, in many countries, highlight that the business IT alignment has been a key area of concern over the years.

We argue that first of all the businesses and organizations should have clearly define strategic goals, which would remain stable for a considerable time, then decisions to make investments in IT technologies and assets be made to achieve the organizational strategic goals. Effort should be made that when the IT investment business cases are prepared, these should be thoroughly contested and scrutinized for watertight alignment with the business goals. However, we further argue that mere alignment at the initial phase is not the end itself, rather it should be the responsibility of the management through governance arrangements that when the IT technology and assets are operationalized, there should be a process to evaluate whether the promised technological goals have been achieved and how these goals contributed towards achieving the organizational strategic objectives. In order to achieve this objective Selig [48] argues for integrated framework for effective IT governance. Selig [49] elaborate that effective governance should be based on three critical pillars (shown in Table 2.3):

- Leadership, organization, and decisions rights – define organization structure, roles and responsibilities, shared vision, and decision rights
- Flexible and scalable processes – for effective project/program management, IT management, service management, and alignment
- Enabling technology – leverage leading major tools and technologies that supporting major IT governance components.

We conclude that effective Portfolio/Program/Project Management (P3M) is missing the link between the management and IT governance. The integrated IT governance is expected to fill this gap by guiding the management how to ensure alignment between the business objectives and IT goals. We suggest that the gap between business management and IT governance be bridged through the implementation of IT portfolio and program management structures as a component of integrated IT governance, so that decisions on IT investment projects and programs are made to realize the organizational strategic goals. We recommend there should be a process of impartial

Table 2.3 Integrated IT Governance Framework and Roadmap

Areas of Work	Description/Components	Deliverables/References
Business plan/ objectives (Demand management & alignment)	• Strategic business plan – vision, objectives, financials, operations, SWOT, imperatives (must do's), initiatives • Capital planning • Business performance management • Executive and other steering review committees, organization structure	• Plan document and process • Financials • Balanced scoreboard metrics
IT plan, objectives, portfolio investment and approvals (Demand management & alignment)	• IT plan is aligned with business plan • IT portfolio investment (portfolio management model) • IT performance management	• IT strategic/tactical plan metrics • Portfolio management Engagement model (roles)
IT plan execution & delivery (Resources & execution management)	• Program, project and operating plans (capital plans, project plans, and budget) • Policies, standards, guidelines and processes (PMO, ITIL, enterprise architecture, security, data management) • Resource management • Financial, program, project, and maintenance	Assess implications of methodologies, standards, frameworks (PMBOK, Agile, ITIL, etc.) Infrastructure and operational integrity, continuity, and security
Performance management, controls, risk, compliance, and vendor management (Execution management)	• Manage and measure plans, budget programs, projects, operations & risks • Define and track KPIs • Compare plans to actuals and take corrective actions • Outsourcing and vendor management	Performance management • Management controls/COBIT • Contract management

(*Continued*)

TABLE 2.3 (*Continued*)

Areas of Work	Description/Components	Deliverables/References
People development, talent management/ succession, continuous improvement, & learning)	• Business and IT continuity, security, privacy, contingency, disaster recovery • Human capital development • Organizational, projects, and operational maturity model • Managing change and transformation • Training and certification	• Adopt current and emerging industry and government best practices standards and guidelines • Career development, succession planning, and certification

Source: Selig [49].

contestability to scrutinize IT investment proposals, where the business cases are assessed to confirm whether the proposed technologies will help achieve business objectives of the organization.

2.5 CHAPTER SUMMARY

This chapter discussed governance as a concept and its evolution into difference branches such corporate, institutional, project, and IT governance. We highlighted the conceptual difference between management and governance. Three major IT governance frameworks, COBIT, ITIL, and ISO27001, were discussed and compared with each other. This chapter also analyzed how governance and strategy can work together and it briefly discussed the challenges associated with aligning the organizational strategic objectives with investments goals. This chapter proposes program/project management structures as component of an integrated IT governance framework to enable making sound investment decisions, effective governance of investments in technology, and processes for deriving value from the IT systems and assets.

REFERENCES

[1] P. Webb, C. Pollard, and G. Ridley, "Attempting to define IT governance: wisdom or folly." Proceedings of the 39th Hawaii International Conference on System Science, 2006.

[2] M. Bekker and H. Steyn, "Project governance: definition and framework." *Journal of Contemporary Management*, vol. 6, pp. 214–228, 2009.

[3] M. C. Bekker and H. Steyn, "(2009). The impact of project governance principles on project performance," Portland International Conference on Management of Engineering and Technology. July 27-31, 2008. doi: 10.1109/PICMET.2008.4599744.

[4] Y. Butler, "*Governance in the Boardroom: How Project Management Can Deliver Organizational Strategy*," 2008. Accessed on: Janauary 26, 2017. Available: http://docplayer.net/5908187-Governance-in-the-boardroom-how-project-management-can-deliver-organisational-strategy.html.

[5] UNESCO, (N.D). "Concepts of Governance." accessed on Janauary 28, 2017. Available: http://www.unesco.org/new/en/education/themes/strengthening-education-systems/quality-framework/technical-notes/concept-of-governance/

[6] OECD, *G20/OECD Principles of Corporate Governance*. Paris: OECD Publishing, 2015. Accessed on: Janauary 27, 2017. Available: 10.1787/9789264236882-en

[7] ANAO, "*Public Sector Governance: Strengthening Performance Through Good Governance*." 2014. Accessed on: February 4, 2017. Available: www.anao.gov.au

[8] IFAC (International Federation of Accountants, "*International Framework: Good Governance in the Public Sector*," 2014. Accessed on: February 4, 2017. Available: www.ifac.org

[9] O. E. William, "The mechanism of governance, Oxford, UK, OUP, In miller and hobbs (2004) governance regime for large complex projects." *PMJ*, vol. 36, no. 3, pp. 42–50, 1996.

[10] J. R. Hollingsworth and R. Boyer, Eds. *Contemporary Capitalism: The embeddedness of institutions*. England: Cambridge University Press, 1997.

[11] W. Van Grembergen, "Introduction to the minitrack IT governance and It's mechanisms." Proceedings of the 35th Hawaii International Conference on System Sciences (HICSS), 2002.

[12] M. A. Saeed, A. Abbasi and R. Tahmina, "Project benefits realization – Academics' dream or practitioners' nightmare," *Project Governance and Controls Annual Review (PGCAR)*, vol. 2, no. 1, pp. 1–12, 2019.

[13] H. Mintzberg, "Patterns in strategy formation," *Management Science*, vol. 24, no. 9, pp. 3097–3097, 1978.

[14] H. Mintzberg, "Strategy-making in three modes," *California Management Review*, Winter vol. 1973, p. 16, 1973.

[15] C. E. Lindblom, "The science of muddling through," *Public Administration Review*, vol. 19, no. 2, pp. 44–53, 1959.

[16] R. F. Vancil, "Strategy formulation in complex organizations," *Sloan Management Review*, vol. 17, no. 2, pp. 67–86, 1976.

[17] W. McElroy, "Implementing strategic change through projects," *IJPM*, vol. 14, pp. 79–88, 1996.

[18] https://www.governanceinstitute.com.au/search-results/?Keyword=corporate++governance&ResultType=All&SortBy=Relevance&pageNo=2

[19] "*IT Governance Institute: Definition of IT Governance*." Accessed on: June 13, 2021. Available: https://www.itgovernance.co.uk/it_governance

[20] R. Miller and B. Hobbs, "Governance regimes for large complex projects," *PMJ*, vol. 36, no. 3, Website Accessed on June 2, 2021, 2005.

[21] A. Morgan and S. Gbedemah, *"How Poor Governance of Projects Causes Delays?"* 2010. Accessed on: February 01, 2017. Available: http://www.pwc.co.uk/assets/pdf/society-of-construction-law-oct10.pdf.

[22] J. R. Turner, "Towards a theory of project management: The nature of project governance and project management." pp. 22–24, 2006.

[23] G. H. Volden and B. Anderson, "The hierarchy of public project governance frameworks: An empirical study of principles and practices in Norwegian ministries and agencies," *IJMPB*, vol. 11, no. 1, pp. 93–95, 2018.

[24] Association for Project Management, *Directing change: A guide to governance of project management.* High Wycombe, UK: Association for Project Management, 2004.

[25] E. W. Larson, B. Honig, C. F. Gray, U. Dantin, and D. Baccarini, *Project Management: The Managerial Process.* NSW: McGraw Hill Education, 2014.

[26] as quoted in E. W. Larson, B. Honig, C. F. Gray, U. Dantin, and D. Baccarini, *Project Management: The Managerial Process.* NSW: McGraw Hill Education, 2014. Available: www.ITGI.org

[27] C. Symons, *"IT Governance Framework, Forrester Best Practices."* 2005. Accessed on: May 25, 2021. Available: https://www.scirp.org/(S(i43dyn45teexjx455qlt3d2q))/reference/ReferencesPapers.aspx?ReferenceID=1301066

[28] M. H. Larsen, M. K. Pedersen, and K. V. Andersen, "IT governance: reviewing 17 IT governance tools and analysing the case of novozynmes A/S." Proceedings of the 39th Hawaii International Conference on System Sciences, 2006.

[29] Y. Ozdemir, H. Basligil, P. Alcan, and B. M. Kandemirli, "Evaluation and comparison of COBIT, ITIL, and Iso27k1/2 standards within the framework of information security," *International Journal of technical Research and Applications*, no. 11, 2014.

[30] C. Kidd, *"What is COBIT? COBIT Explained."* 2019. Accessed on: May 31, 2021. Available: https://www.isaca.org/resources/cobit

[31] Compliance Council, compliancecouncil.com.au. Accessed on: May 31, 2021.

[32] J. W. Lainhart IV, "A Methodology for managing and controlling information and information technology risks and vulnerabilities," *Journal of Information Systems*, vol. 14, no. 1, 2000.

[33] S. White, *"What is COBIT? A Framework for Alignment and Governance."* 2019. Accessed on: May 27, 2021. Available: https://www.cio.com/article/3243684

[34] L. Shiff, *"COBIT Vs ITIL: Comparing IT Governance Frameworks."* 2021. Accessed on: May 31, 2021. Available: https://www.bmc.com/blogs/cobit-vs-itil-understanding-governance-frameworks

[35] S. White, and L. Greiner, 2019. Accessed on: May 31, 2020. Available: https://www.cio.com/article/2439501/infrastructure-it-infrastructure-library-itil-definition-and-solutions.htm

[36] M. Nyhuis, *"What is the ITIL Framework."* 2020. Accessed on: June 1, 2021. Available: https://insights.diligent.com/compliance/what-is-the-itil-framework/.

[37] J. Mathenge and J. Steven-Hall, *"The ITIL4 Service Value Chain."* 2019.

Accessed on: May 31, 2021. Available: https://www.bmc.com/blogs/itil-service-value-chain/.

[38] "Benefits of ITIL." Accessed on: May 31, 2021. Available: https://www.axelos.com/best-practice-solutions/itil/benefits-of-itil.

[39] Sarah, "*ITIL Vs Cobit – Differences Between Two IT Governance Frameworks.*" 2019. Accessed on: May 31, 2021. Available: https://www.itil-docs.com/itil-vs-cobit-differences-between-two-it-governance-framework.

[40] "ISO/IEC27001" Accessed on: May 31, 2021. Available: https://www.iso.org/isoiec-27001-information-security.html.

[41] J. Hall, *ISO27001 Frameworks for IT Management.* Amersfort NL: Van Haren Publishing, 2006.

[42] T. Peng, "*Choosing ITIL, COBIT or ISO 20000.*" 2016. Accessed on: June 2, 2021. Available: https://www.linkedin.com/pulse/choosing-itil-cobit-iso-20000-thomas-peng/.

[43] Novel Vista, "*COBIT, ITIL and ISO20000, The Main Differences.*" 2020. Accessed on: June 2, 2021. Available: https://www.novelvista.com/blogs/it-service-management/difference-between-cobit-itil-iso20000.

[44] R. Young, M. Young, E. Jordan, and P. O'Connor, "Is strategy being implemented through projects? Contrary evidence from a leader in New public management," *International Journal of Project Management*, vol. 30, no. 8, Website Accessed on June 2, 2021, 2012.

[45] R. Young and J. Grant, "Is strategy implemented by projects? Disturbing evidence in the State of NSW," *International Journal of Project Management*, vol. 33, no. 1, pp. 887–900, 2015.

[46] G. M. Jonathon, L. Rusu, and E. Perjons, "Organizational structure's influence on business IT alignment: looking back to look forward," *International Journal of IT/Business Alignment and Governance*, vol. 9, no. 2, pp. 15–28, 2018.

[47] J. Luftman, "Assessing business-IT alignment maturity," *Communications of the association for Information Systems*, vol. 4, no. 1, pp. 15–29, 2000.

[48] L. Kappelman, V. Johnson, E. Mclean, and C. Maurer, "The 2017 SIM IT issues and trends study," *MIS Quarterly Executive*, vol. 17, no. 1, pp. 1–50, 2018.

[49] G. J. Selig, "IT Governance – An integrated framework and roadmap: How to plan, Deploy, and sfor improved effectiveness," *Journal of International Technology and Information Management*, vol. 25, no. 1, pp. 1–45, 2016.

Chapter 3

The Non-Malicious Risky Behavior in the Enterprise Information System Security

Saiyidi Mat Roni[1], Hadrian Geri Djajadikerta[1], and Terri Trireksani[2]

[1]School of Business and Law, Edith Cowan University, Australia
[2]Murdoch Business School, Murdoch University, Australia

CONTENTS

3.1 INTRODUCTION

Most studies in information system (IS) security emphasize malicious external attacks on the enterprise system. The recent cyberattack on Channel 9 News in Australia [1], for example, highlights the vulnerabilities of IS, prompting organizations to reassess and fortify their defense against such threat. However, in many cases, an external attack is accomplished with an "assistance" from within the organization itself, either intentional or caused by naïvety. Perpetrators of an attack not only need the information technology skill to execute a cyberattack but also require a good understanding of the mechanics of the system's inner working. The latter is typically obtained through social engineering [2,3] and security lapses surrounding the operators of the IS. This is where the human element in IS security domain plays a pivotal role in security perimeter of an organization IS assets.

Employees or users of an IS are generally considered as one of the weakest links [4] in the IS security blanket. A study by Nobles [5] concluded that around 90% of security incidents were attributable to human errors. What is more interesting in the study was that the more ill informed the employees are about IS security, the more risks they pose to the organization. Therefore, it comes to no surprise that research in this area has gained some tractions to assist organizations in protecting their IS assets through a good understanding of the motivations and triggers of risky behavior among the insiders.

Despite being the weakest link in the IS security measure, the insiders are also the greatest asset an organization can have for the IS defense [6] when the issue of policies of compliance and non-compliance are unrooted, investigated, and pre-emptively addressed. This study, therefore, extends existing work on insider threats in the IS security field by investigating the non-malicious dysfunctional behaviors of employees.

3.2 FRAUD TRIANGLE AND DYSFUNCTIONAL BEHAVIOR IN INFORMATION SYSTEM

Fraud triangle [7] is one of the widely used theories to explain fraudulent behaviors. The theory has three colluding facets that enable a perpetrator to commit fraud. These are *pressure*, *opportunity*, and *rationalization,* which all must be present. An absence of one of these elements usually hinders a fraudulent act. We illustrate the fraud triangle in Figure 3.1 and discuss each facet in the paragraphs that follow.

Pressure can be originated from many sources. While in a white-collar crime, *pressure* typically comes from an urge to sustain an exorbitant lifestyle or companies facing financial distress, in the act of non-malicious

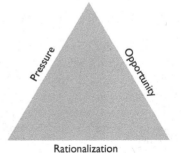

Figure 3.1 Fraud triangle. Adapted from Cressey (1953).

intent, *pressure* can originate from the work environment itself. For example, the performance-linked incentive was identified as a contributing factor for bad lending practices among banks in Australia [8]. The idea behind the reward was good to promote a healthy work culture, but it also carried a bad repercussion by putting vulnerable customers into a heavy debt burden that they cannot afford to service. In a study on corporate fraud in the United States and Europe, Brennan and McGrath [9] found that the pressure to meet forecast was the fraud's primary motivation. Other sources of work-related non-financial pressures were highlighted in Lokanan's [10] work that includes employee's dissatisfaction and perceived inequities in the workplace.

Although pressure arguably triggers dysfunctional behavior, the mischievous act is notional until an opportunity exists. Such opportunity is typically a product of security lapses or management oversight. Schuchter and Levi [11] found that *opportunity* is a universal precondition of fraudulent acts despite perceived pressure is salient to most frauds. This is not unexpected as the very presence of IS security policies and other defenses effectively removes or limits the exposure to threats of the enterprise system. User access privilege, for example, is a common practice to eliminate opportunities for unauthorized access, thus limiting the risks the organization is exposed to.

The third and final facet of the fraud triangle is *rationalization*, which can be viewed as a *white-wash* of dysfunctional behavior. Rationalization defines behavior as "appropriate" in a given situation [12] even when the action is clearly contradictory to generally accepted practices. Farshadkhah et al. [13] argue that a feeling of guilt motivates a high sense of personal responsibility, compliance, and constructive efforts. However, if an employee can rationalize their negative act, that removes the guilt, which is a potential deterrent against insider threats.

3.2.1 Explaining the Psychological Dimensions of Dysfunctional Behavior

3.2.1.1 The Organizational Factors

An organizational work environment helps shape the way its members act. It defines what action is customary and what behavior is deemed unacceptable. Scholars in organizational culture [e.g., 14–16] appreciate the influence of the organizational psychological facets on one's behavior. In some cases, a seemingly unacceptable practice can be viewed as a tolerable routine if the act is widely and regularly exercised. From an employee's point of view, actions by significant others help normalize one's assessment of risky behavior. For example, opening a doubtful attachment of an unsolicited email in a company's computer can be viewed as harmless and will not put the enterprise system at risk when an employee perceived that others would have done the same, even when there is a clear policy against such action. In the absence of IS security policies, insiders' perceptual assessment of what action is considered required, permitted, allowed, not recommended, and forbidden can differ from what is internalized by individual employees [17].

Peer influence is not the only factor fashioning one's action at the workplace. In some cases, an organization remuneration scheme can also promote risky behavior despite the fact that the scheme was designed for the betterment of the organization. The performance-based reward has been found to be an impetus for good job performance [18,19] by having an agreed target to achieve and also a trigger for questionable actions [see 8,20]. This is because some performance indicators can be too ambitious or when the performance is benchmarked against peers creating pressure to work above others to reap the reward. While the pressure is good to promote healthy competition, excessive work pressure can potentially be counterproductive and even dangerous to the organization. Employees unwittingly circumvent security policy to achieve the performance target or improve the quality of their job outputs even if the means to secure the end puts the organization IS at risk.

3.2.1.2 Information System Characteristics

User-friendliness has become a staple in IS design to promote the use of an enterprise system and improve productivity. The well-known *Technology Acceptance Model* (TAM) by Davis [21] demonstrates how uptakes of IS is contingent to user's *perceived ease of use* [22]. An easy and intuitive user interface promotes healthy interaction between operators and a computerized system and therefore encourages its significant use. On the other hand, a complex system can deter users from meaningful use of the enterprise system (Figure 3.2).

IS, in general, is designed to simplify job tasks by taking the complexity away from the users. As such, in an enterprise-wide system, IS can be extremely large with a myriad of complex architecture. That complexity happens at the backend and is typically hidden from the end user. However, a complex system is not fundamentally bad. Complexity is a by-product of or a

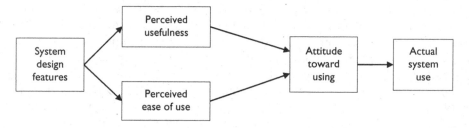

Figure 3.2 Technology acceptance model. Adapted from Davis [21].

necessity to ensure that a system caters to the needs of the users and aligns with organization goals. System complexity can be a defensive measure in its own right. Cybercriminals, either external or within an organization, need to have advanced knowledge of the inner workings of an IS to have a mental picture of how the system processes operate, to enable them anticipating how output would look like for any given input, and to erase their track after an attack. In this regard, a convoluted human–computer interaction can be a barrier, while a well-defined and predictable IS can present an opportunity for insiders to sidestep the IS security.

3.3 METHODOLOGY

3.3.1 Sample and Instrument

This study uses a quasi-experimental research method to solicit responses from the respondents. Two scenarios were designed to fit two behavioral types [see 23] that can have security implications. The respondents were middle managers from small- and medium-sized enterprises located in industrial estates in Malaysian Peninsular. We selected the middle managers as this managerial position allows them to work closely with the organization's information system but not to the extent of having super-user privilege.

Each respondent was assigned with only one of the two scenarios. We chose this quasi-experimental approach to encourage responses by putting a psychological distance between the subjects in the scenario and the behaviors being investigated, which can be viewed as a potential threat to organization's information system. We summarize scenario one and two in Table 3.1.

Following each scenario, we presented the questions as listed in Table 3.2 to the respondents. These questions ask the respondents to estimate their likelihood of carrying a similar action (LK1) and measure other variables that intertwined with the respondents' workplace. These include the organizational climate and system-specific influences. Each of these questions was anchored on a seven-point Likert scale type ranging from *extremely likely* (1) to *extremely unlikely* (7) for the single-item measure of likelihood, and *strongly disagree* (1) to *strongly agree* (7) for other questions.

A total of 85 useable responses were collected, of which 49 were presented with scenario 1 (i.e., unauthorized software installation) and the remaining 36 were given scenario 2 (i.e., password sharing). We summarize the combined scale descriptive statistics for each latent variable and their reliability estimates as well as their factor loadings in Table 3.3, with the exception of the likelihood as this is a single-item measure.

As indicated in Table 3.3, Cronbach's alphas for all latent constructs are higher than 0.70 (Nunnally, 1975), which supports the notion of their internal consistency.

Table 3.1 Scenario and Behavioral Types

Vignette	Theme	Behavioral Taxonomy/Type
Scenario 1 Lee is given a laptop by the company that he can use while in the office as well as on the move. However, the laptop does not have software that allows him to tap into the production planning system that he is authorized to access through other computer terminals. He believes that a particular software will make his work more efficient and effective. A request to the IT department to purchase the software is denied because it is too expensive. To solve the problem, Lee obtains an unlicensed copy of the software and personally installed it into the laptop.	Unauthorized software installation	Dangerous tinkering
Scenario 2 Linda works in the marketing department and therefore has access to the company's customer account database. One day at the office, Linda's co-worker in the same department asked to borrow her password in order to access the customer database because she forgot her password. The system administrator who was in charge of resetting the password was on sick leave. Linda gave her password to the co-worker for her to access the customer account database.	Password sharing	Naive mistake

3.3.2 Analysis

We analyzed the survey data using *t*-test to compare the magnitude of the likelihood of engaging in two dysfunctional behaviors scoped in the scenarios 1 and 2 of the study. Multiple regression analysis was later performed on the dataset to examine the effect of organizational factors and system characteristic on the likelihood of sharing password and installing unauthorized software into an organization IS asset. We also ran a partial correlation between seemingly correlated latent variables (performance and job quality) to ensure that the regression model is not compromised. All analyses were conducted with 2000 bootstrap sample [see 27] with *bias-corrected accelerated* (BCa) to correct data distribution for bias and non-constant variance [28]. We explain the analysis and the results in the result and findings section.

Table 3.2 Question Items

Question Item	Note/Source
Likelihood LK1: If you are in X's situation, how likely are you to perform a similar action?	The likelihood of oneself to take a similar action.
Peer PE1: People who influence my behavior think that I should carry out such action. PE2: People who are important to me think that I should carry out such action. PE3: My fellow colleagues would themselves have carried out this action if they had been in my place.	Organizational setting. Ayaz and Yanartaş [24] Venkatesh, Morris [25].
Job quality JQ1: Carrying out such action can decrease the time needed for my important job responsibilities. JQ2: Carrying out such action can significantly increase the quality of output of my job. JQ3: Carrying out such action can significantly increase the quantity of output of my job.	A basis for *rationalization* of the fraud triangle theory. Venkatesh, Morris [25].
Performance PF1: is individual appraisal directly related to the attainment of goals? PF2: does management specify the targets to be attained? PF3: is it clear how performance will be evaluated? PF4: are there hard criteria against which job performance is measured? PF5: is reward dependent on performance?	A proxy for *pressure* of the fraud triangle theory. van Muijen and al [26].
System complexity CX1: My interaction with the system is clear and understandable. CX2: I find the system is easy to use.	A proxy for *opportunity* of the fraud triangle theory. Venkatesh, Morris [25].

Table 3.3 Descriptive Statistics and Reliability Estimates

Variables	Mean	Std. Deviation	N	Cronbach's Alpha (N of items)	Factor Loadings
Likelihood	3.92	1.999	85		
Peer	4.1035	1.72868	85	0.951 (3)	0.859 to 0.910
System	5.6412	0.96859	85	0.826 (2)	0.909 to 0.914
Job quality	4.6636	1.71061	85	0.950 (3)	0.892 to 0.903
Performance	5.3129	1.11716	85	0.875 (5)	0.756 to 0.864

Factor loadings were extracted from Principal Component Analysis with varimax rotation.

3.4 RESULTS AND FINDINGS

3.4.1 Behavioral Difference

We analyzed two types of behavior in this study. These were the password sharing and the unauthorized software installation on the organization IS assets. We mapped these two behaviors on Stanton's [23] behavior taxonomy making the former as *naïve mistake* category while the latter fits the *dangerous tinkering* action.

In order to test if these two behaviors are statistically different from each other, we ran a bootstrap t-test with 2000 bootstrap sample and the bias-corrected accelerated (BCa) method on the likelihood variable. The shows that these two behaviors are statistically different, $t(83) = 3.68, p < 0.001$. A Levene's test for the between-group equality of variances indicates that the variances between naïve mistake and dangerous tinkering groups are similar, $F(1, 84) = 0.35, p = 0.56$, therefore satisfying the equality of variance assumption required by t-test [29].

3.4.2 The Effect of Organizational Factors and Information System Characteristics

We ran bootstrapped stepwise multiple regression to investigate the organizational factors and system characteristic on the employees' likelihood of risky behavior. Similar to the t-test, the regression was bootstrapped with 2000 bootstrap sample and BCa. The result shows that the model accounts for 56% variations in the likelihood of dysfunctional behavior practices, $R^2 = 0.56$, *adj.* $R^2 = 0.54$, $F(2, 80) = 49.36, p < 0.001$.

The regression analysis also shows that only peer and job quality are significant predictors of the likelihood. Performance and system were found to be statistically non-significant. The result is summarized in Table 3.4.

Table 3.4 Regression Analysis Result

Model	B		Bootstrap			
		Bias	Std. Error	Sig. (2-tailed)	BCa 95% Confidence Interval	
					Lower	Upper
1 (Constant)	3.409	.203	1.710	.044	.772	7.466
Performance	.218	−.004	.230	.359	−.213	.662
System	−.139	−.030	.241	.551	−.629	.231
2 (Constant)	.530	.075	.911	.545	−.826	2.809
Performance	−.092	.004	.147	.540	−.357	.206
System	−.025	−.011	.140	.853	−.319	.216
Peer	.464	−.001	.145	.003	.140	.739
Job quality	.424	−.004	.130	.002	.186	.683

We also ran a partial correlation test to check if the performance and job quality is correlated. This is because performance-linked reward (performance) and the expected quality of output (job quality) can be thought of as two dimensions of the same construct. If these variables are correlated, then there is a possibility that a higher-order latent construct was measured by the instrument of this study, which could raise a concern over the regression model's validity. The partial correlation was chosen to partial out any potential effect embedded in each type of behavior under the investigation. The partial correlation test shows that performance and job quality are not correlated, $r(82) = 0.11$, $p = 0.34$.

3.5 DISCUSSION AND IMPLICATIONS

3.5.1 Dysfunctional Behavior

Dysfunctional insider behavior in the information system varies in many facets. At one side of the spectrum is the maliciously intentional act requiring a high-level technical IS skill to execute that makes headline when takes place, while at the other end is simple conducts which, in some cases, are performed in good faith. Existing studies on insider threats, therefore, are largely motivated by the intentional sophisticated inside attacks. Hence the tone of a majority of the policies is designed primarily to address these issues.

Nevertheless, some malicious intentional attacks are products of seemingly innocent security non-compliance behavior of employees. For example, delayed software updates can cost a company millions of dollars, as demonstrated in the case of several retail banks in Malaysia [30] and in the United States [31]. The banks chose to "postpone" an update of the Windows operating system (OS) that was the backbone of their nationwide ATMs. The OS update contained security patches for known vulnerabilities. Had this update been made, it would have denied the perpetrator (s) the chance to exploit this vulnerability to drain the cash from the ATMs.

While many studies focus on addressing and promoting security compliance, non-compliance behavior has always been thought to come naturally. However, security compliance and non-compliance are two sides of different coins. Factors affecting the compliance to the organization security policy can be different from those influencing the non-compliance. In this study, therefore, we examine the non-malicious insider threats. We investigate the phenomenon from the organizational settings and IS features that define the interaction between the system and its operator. Pivoted on the fraud triangle theory, we assessed the influence of the climate within organizations, IS features, and the job tasks, which can be the seeds for the opportunity, pressure, and rationalization of the IS security non-compliance.

The results of our study show that naïve mistake, which was based on sharing a password to gain access to the organization's IS, and dangerous tinkering that was pinned on an unauthorized software installation are two distinct behaviors. Both behaviors in our study situate the respondents in conditions primed to get a job done. Our result reveals that the likelihood of oneself to action the unauthorized software installation is higher compared to sharing their password, although password sharing is a simple, straightforward act and requires virtually no IT skill. We speculate that password sharing is more personal to oneself. Given that a vast majority of users use the same password or a similar password structure for other accesses, sharing a work-access password can compromise other non-job-related platforms such as personal social media accounts.

On the other hand, the unauthorized software installation is related to the needs of completing a job task. Although some degree of IT skill is required to execute this action, the respondents of this study were middle managers who mostly worked with a computerized system daily. Therefore, installing a software is not relatively difficult to do. Factoring the need to complete an assigned task, an employee, therefore, feels compelled to do what it takes to ensure a tick on the checkbox.

The result from the bootstrapped regression also shows peers and quality of job outputs are two influential factors shaping the non-malicious insider security non-compliance. The quality of the job output becomes a statistically significant underpinning to rationalize the risky behavior. This is parallel to the result and explanation we offer in the preceding paragraph.

From the fraud triangle perspective, we do not find evidence to support pressure as contributing factor to prompt employees to negate IS security policy. Pressure was proxied by the performance-linked reward system. An explanation for this non-significance result rests in the rationalization of the non-compliance act. It was likely that the employees rationalize the risky behavior by producing high-quality outputs for the organizations. This in turn benefits the organization as a whole, justifying the wrong mean to reach the right end. Although we do not find any statistically meaningful correlation between performance and job output quality, it is reasonable to assume that high-quality output helps the employees reap a better reward. The situation, therefore, alleviates the influence of pressure emanating from the performance-based remuneration scheme, as shown in the results of this study.

Our study also does not find the human–computer interaction as an enabling factor for the security non-compliance behavior. We posit that a well-understood interaction between an operator and IS could have provided an opportunity for the actor to exploit the organization's IS asset. This is because the operator can accurately anticipate how a system behaves for any input giving them a sense of control over the output. However, the data from our sample does not support this notion.

3.5.2 Implications for Organizations

The findings of our study provide insights into the weakest link in the information system security domain. We examine the organizational factors and system characteristic from the perspective of fraud triangle theory to provide a clear understanding of these facets on the dysfunctional behavior of insiders.

As evidence shows, promoting a culture of security compliance is necessary to reduce the likelihood of insider security incidence. Although this is not something new, the result of the study re-emphasizes the importance of this action given that an employee relies heavily on their perceptions of others' *"approval"* of a given action even when such action can weaken the enterprise system defenses. This is consistent with Schuchter and Levi [11], where rationalization (of security non-compliance behavior) is a major driving factor.

In conjunction with the rationalization facet of the fraud triangle theory, the expectation of the quality of outputs expected from the employees also needs to be assessed. The organization not only needs to provide sufficient supporting infrastructure for the employee to complete assigned tasks, there should also be room to negotiate a performance expectation. These two actions effectively remove the rationalization which can overshadow the guilt that typically hinders oneself from performing a security risk action.

3.6 CONCLUSION

Human actor is always seen as the weakest link in the IS security chain. This study, therefore, investigates the human element in enterprise information system security. We focus on the relatively less-explored types of non-malicious security non-compliance behavior, which presents exploitable lapses in the IS security. Using the fraud triangle theory as a guiding lens, we explore pressure stemming from the performance-based reward system, opportunity presented by familiarity with the IS mechanics, and rationalization of the non-compliance behavior that is pegged on completion of assigned tasks and perception of approval from colleagues.

Our study shows that perception of approval from the peers and anticipated good outputs of assigned tasks are two contributing factors that drive an employee to circumvent IS security. The findings emphasize the need for organization to promote a strong security culture in the workplace as the employee relies on the assumption that others will agree to their non-compliance action. Also intuitively, we find that an organization needs to provide sufficient support infrastructure-wise, to enable an employee to perform well in their work.

This study only looks at two non-malicious behaviors and was based on a sample drawn from a certain population. We do not factor in an extensive organizational culture and climate or a performance-reward system into our research model. We believe these factors play a non-negligible role in shaping the employee's security behavior. Therefore, we call for future research to investigate these elements to shed more lights into the needs to address the insider threats.

REFERENCES

[1] E. Manfield, "How did the cyber attack on Nine and Parliament House happen?," in *ABC News*. Sydney: ABC News, 2021. Access Date: 18/12/2021. Accessible from: https://www.thestar.com.my/news/nation/2014/09/29/police-launch-nationwide-manhunt-for-at m-hackers

[2] T. Li, X. Wang, and Y. Ni, "Aligning social concerns with information system security: A fundamental ontology for social engineering," *Information Systems*, vol. 104, p. 101699, 2020.

[3] J. M. Hatfield, "Social engineering in cybersecurity: the evolution of a concept," *Computers & Security*, vol. 73, pp. 102–113, 2018.

[4] A. Urueña López, et al., "Analysis of computer user behavior, security incidents and fraud using self-organizing maps," *Computers & Security*, vol. 83, pp. 38–51, 2019.

[5] C. Nobles, "Shifting the human factors paradigm in cybersecurity," *Viitattu*, vol. 23, p. 2019, 2018.

[6] J. Fielding, "The people problem: how cyber security's weakest link can become a formidable asset," *Computer Fraud & Security*, vol. 2020, no. 1, pp. 6–9, 2020.

[7] D. R. Cressey, "Other people's money; a study of the social psychology of embezzlement." 1953.

[8] K. M. Hayne, "Final report of the royal commission into misconduct in the banking, Superannuation and financial services industry," *S.a.F.S.I. Royal Commission into Misconduct in the Banking*, Canberra: Commonwealth of Australia, 2019.

[9] N. M. Brennan and M. McGrath, "Financial statement fraud: Some lessons from US and European case studies." *Australian Accounting Review*, vol. 17, no. 42, pp. 49–61, 2007.

[10] M. E. Lokanan, "Challenges to the fraud triangle: questions on its usefulness," *Accounting Forum*, vol. 39, no. 3, pp. 201–224, 2015.

[11] A. Schuchter and M. Levi, "Beyond the fraud triangle: Swiss and Austrian elite fraudsters," *Accounting Forum*, vol. 39, no. 3, pp. 176–187, 2015.

[12] S. Albrecht and W. S. Albrecht, *How to Detect and Prevent Business Fraud*. NJ: Prentice-Hall Englewood Cliffs, 1982.

[13] S. Farshadkhah, C. Van Slyke, and B. Fuller, "Onlooker effect and affective responses in information security violation mitigation," *Computers & Security*, vol. 100, p. 102082, 2021.

[14] A. Da Veiga and J. H. Eloff, "A framework and assessment instrument for information security culture," *Computers & Security*, vol. 29, no. 2, pp. 196–207, 2010.

[15] A. Martins and J. Elofe, "Information security culture," in *Security in the Information Society: Visions and Perspectives*, M. A. Ghonaimy, M. T. El-Hadidi, and H. K. Aslan, Eds. Boston, MA: Springer US, 2002, pp. 203–214.

[16] E. H. Schein, "Culture: the missing concept in organization studies," *Administrative Science Quarterly*, vol. 41, no. 2, pp. 229–240, 1996.

[17] C. Posey and R. Folger, "An exploratory examination of organizational insiders' descriptive and normative perceptions of cyber-relevant rights and responsibilities," *Computers & Security*, vol. 99, p. 102038, 2020.

[18] B. W. Schay and S. F. Fisher, "The challenge of making performance-based pay systems work in the public sector," *Public Personnel Management*, vol. 42, no. 3, pp. 359–384, 2013.

[19] B. Larsson, Y. Ulfsdotter Eriksson, and P. Adolfsson, "Motivating and demotivating effects of performance-related pay in Swedish public sector organizations," *Review of Public Personnel Administration*, vol. 0, no. 0, p. 0734371X21990836, 2021.

[20] L. M. Roth, "Because I'm worth It? Understanding inequality in a performance-based Pay system*," *Sociological Inquiry*, vol. 76, no. 1, pp. 116–139, 2006.

[21] F. D. Davis, R. P. Bagozzi, and P. R. Warshaw, "User acceptance of computer technology: a comparison of two theoretical models," *Management Science*, vol. 35, no. 8, pp. 982–1003, 1989.

[22] F. D. Davis, "A technology acceptance model for empirically testing new end-user information systems: Theory and results," *Massachusetts Institute of Technology*, 1985.

[23] J. M. Stanton, et al., "Analysis of end user security behaviors," *Computers & Security*, vol. 24, no. 2, pp. 124–133, 2005.

[24] A. Ayaz and M. Yanartaş, "An analysis on the unified theory of acceptance and use of technology theory (UTAUT): acceptance of electronic document management system (EDMS)," *Computers in Human Behavior Reports*, vol. 2, p. 100032, 2020.

[25] V. Venkatesh, et al., "User acceptance of information technology: toward a unified view," *MIS Quarterly*, vol. 27, no. 3, pp. 425–478, 2003.

[26] J. J. van Muijen, et al., "Organizational culture: the focus questionnaire," *European Journal of Work and Organizational Psychology*, vol. 8, no. 4, pp. 551–568, 1999.

[27] A. Field, "Discovering statistics using IBM SPSS statistics: North American edition," California: Sage, 2017.

[28] S. Mason, et al., "The internationality of published higher education scholarship: how do the 'top' journals compare?," *Journal of Informetrics*, vol. 15, no. 2, p. 101155, 2021.

[29] S. Mat Roni and H. G. Djajadikerta, *Data Analysis with SPSS for Survey-based Research*. Singapore: Springer, 2021.

[30] Online mainstream news. "Police launch nationwide hunt for ATM hackers," in *The Star*. The Star: Kuala Lumpur, 2014. Access Date: 18/12/2021. Accessible from: https://www.abc.net.au/news/2021-03-30/how-did-the-cyber-attack-on-nine-and-parliament-ho use-happen/100035414.

[31] D. Volz, *Jackpotting' Hackers Steal over $1 million from ATMs across U.S.: Secret Service*. Washington: Reuters, 2018.

Chapter 4

Cybersecurity Incident Response in the Enterprise

Nickson M. Karie[1,2] and Leslie F. Sikos[2]
[1]Cyber Security Cooperative Research Centre, Perth, Australia
[2]School of Science, Edith Cowan University, Perth, Australia

CONTENTS

DOI: 10.1201/9781003121541-4

4.1 INTRODUCTION TO CYBERSECURITY INCIDENCE RESPONSE

The Fourth Industrial Revolution (Industry 4.0) has made organizations and individuals more security-aware. This is because the ongoing shift toward modern enterprise-grade architectures by many organizations globally has not changed the fact that every system or technology infrastructure deployed into an organization is a potential target for cyber-attacks [1]. At the same time, technological advancements and, in particular, developments in the field of data science and machine learning make it practically infeasible to implement countermeasures for all types of cyber-attacks, let alone in (near-)real-time [2]. Automated malicious actions can now be conducted by software agents, as seen with adversarial machine learning. However, security professionals can also utilize other areas of artificial intelligence, such as formal knowledge representation to automate honeypot data analysis [3], and automated reasoning to stay on top of cybersecurity incidents via cyber-situational awareness [4]. For these reasons, the ability to quickly detect and effectively mitigate any attack or data breach can, for example, minimize damage, disruption, as well as save on cost for organizations. However, how quickly an organization can detect attacks or data breaches in its systems and mitigate them depends heavily on its incident response strategies and preparedness. We begin this chapter by introducing terminologies, concepts, and definitions used by cybersecurity incident response teams in the enterprise.

4.1.1 Cybersecurity Incidents

A cybersecurity incident may be defined as a security event that could compromise business systems, damage data, disrupt operations, and jeopardize information security [5]. For example, when an employee gives out confidential business information via a phishing email, this can negatively impact the business; thus, should be treated as a security incident. Security incidents, however, vary depending on the nature and operation environment of an organization. This implies that what one organization may consider as a security incident might not be as critical for another. One common thing across all security incidents though is that they all negatively impact an organization.

4.1.2 Security Events

Every time something happens in an organization's infrastructure, whether good or bad, it can be considered an event. However, if the event impacts security or is relevant to information security, it becomes a security event (information security event). Downloading software to a company device, for example, whether authorized or unauthorized, can be considered a security event. According to the ISO/IEC 27000:2018 standard [6], which deals with information technology, security techniques, and information security management systems, a security event may refer to any "detected, identified occurrence or change in the normal behavior of a system, process, IT infrastructure, workflow, service or network state indicating a possible breach of information security policy or failure of controls, or a previously unknown situation that can impact security or is relevant to information security." Note that not all security events can be considered security incidents, but all security incidents are security events.

4.1.3 Responders

The risks associated with security incidents vary greatly due to technological advances, and the ever-changing attack vectors used by perpetrators. For an organization to protect its systems and improve security, skilled incidence responders have become a necessity in preventing, averting, and mitigating security threats. An incident responder is any individual who can create security plans, policies, protocols, and training that prepare an organization to respond efficiently and effectively to security incidents [7], which are inevitable (this makes cyber-resilience crucial). Many incident responders work as part of a Security Operations Center (SOC) team.

4.1.4 Cyber-Resilience

The ability for an organization to manage a cyber-attack or data breach while continuing to operate its business effectively is called cyber-resilience. A good cyber resilient program means that an organization can detect, manage, and recover from cybersecurity incidents with minimum impact on its business operations. Different types of security tools can be used in a SOC environment to achieve cyber-resilience, including Security Information and Event Management (SIEM) systems.

4.1.5 Security Operations Centers (SOCs)

The advances in technology constantly introduce new, advanced security threats for organizations. To continuously monitor the cybersecurity posture and prevent security threats and data breaches in near real-time, many organizations make use of a SOC. According to McAfee [8], "a Security Operations Center (SOC) is a centralized function within an organization employing people, processes, and technology to continuously monitor and improve an organization's security posture while preventing, detecting, analyzing, and responding to cybersecurity incidents." Many SOCs utilize

Security Information and Event Management (SIEM) to have a holistic view of an organization's information security [9].

4.1.6 Security Information and Event Management (SIEM)

For a SOC to be able to provide an organization with real-time analysis of security alerts as well as continuously monitor and improve an organization's security posture, SIEM products are used. Ideally, SIEM is a set of tools, products, software, and services offering a holistic view of an organization's IT security environment. The tools, products, software, and services work by collecting log and event data generated by different or multiple applications, security devices and host systems then forward it into a single centralized platform for analysis. The analyzed data then provide insights into the events or incidences taking place within the IT environment or help to catch abnormal behavior or potential cyber-attacks.

4.1.7 Security as a Service (SECaaS)

Many organizations require skilled personnel to maintain, and ensure the effectiveness of, a SOC or SIEM. This causes cost overhead to an organization. For organizations that want to utilize SIEM and other security products against security issues yet cannot meet the cost of buying and implementing SIEM products, or do not have a clear understanding of how to do it on their own, Security as a Service (SECaaS) offers an alternative. With SECaaS organizations can outsource all their cybersecurity services from third-party companies on a subscription basis, thereby avoiding all the upfront costs for buying hardware as well as the continuing costs for security software licenses. SECaaS allows organizations to use strong and powerful security tools, including SIEM products from third-party companies (mostly cloud providers) using only a web browser, making the use of SIEM functions easy and affordable. SECaaS is therefore considered a new way of delivering cybersecurity technologies to different organizations as a cloud service.

Many other terminologies, concepts, and definitions used by cybersecurity incident response teams in the enterprise exist besides the ones discussed in Section 4.1, however, the remaining part of this chapter examines existing literature and highlights different areas impacting cybersecurity incident response teams in the enterprise. In Section 4.2, cybersecurity incident concepts are discussed, while Section 4.3 explains the challenges of cybersecurity incidents. Section 4.4 handles how to prepare for cybersecurity incidents, followed by an explanation of hacking techniques and countermeasures in Section 4.5. Section 4.6 presents detecting network events, and Section 4.7 discusses how to respond to cybersecurity incidents. Finally, the chapter is concluded in Section 4.8.

4.2 UNDERSTANDING CYBERSECURITY INCIDENTS

According to the Australian Cyber Security Centre [5], a cybersecurity incident is defined as any "unwanted or unexpected cybersecurity event, or a series of such events, that have a significant probability of compromising business operations." Different types of cybersecurity incidents exist, as detailed in the next sub-section.

4.2.1 Different Types of Cybersecurity Incidents

Many types of cybersecurity incidents exist, the common ones include: Malware attacks (e.g., ransomware), illegal encryption of data, phishing attacks delivered mostly via emails, insider threats (e.g., theft of data and trade secrets), unauthorized access to systems or data, illegal deletion or corruption of data, privilege escalation attacks, password attacks, eavesdropping attacks, man-in-the-middle (MITM) attacks, brute-force and dictionary network attacks, denial-of-service (DoS) attacks leading to disruption of services, AI-powered attacks, web application attacks, cyberfraud or theft (e.g., illegal financial transfer), advanced persistent threat (APT), side-channel attacks, and botnet attacks.

Regardless of the motives behind any incidence affecting an organization, the language of the attackers can be similar. Understanding the cyber-attack lifecycle and the terminologies used by attackers can help the incidence response (IR) team and organizations become well aware of how different attacks are carried out and further help in mitigating the risk of having systems and data being compromised and manipulated. To commit a crime, attackers must first gain access to a computer or a network to deliver a payload or malicious outcome. Some of the common terminologies used are briefly explained below.

- **Reconnaissance:** This occurs when an attacker gathers information about a target system or network using active or passive means.
  - *Active reconnaissance* is when the intruder engages with the targeted system or network to gather vulnerability information.
  - *Passive reconnaissance*, on the other hand, is an attempt to gather information about targeted systems and networks without actively interacting with them.
- **Attack Vector:** This is usually any method, path, or means that attackers use to breach or infiltrate a computer or network and deliver a payload or malicious outcome. Common examples of attack vectors that can be used to exploit system vulnerabilities or launch cyberattacks include malware and ransomware, man-in-the-middle attacks, compromised credentials, and phishing. Note that attack vectors can contain one or more malicious payloads.

- **Exploit:** Any software, data, or commands that can take advantage of a vulnerability in an operating system, software, computer system, or other security flaws to cause unintended behavior or to gain unauthorized access to computers, networks, and sensitive data is considered an exploit.
- **Payload:** A payload is a component of an attack vector that causes harm to a victim's computer or network such as deleting or modifying files, data theft, encrypting data, activity monitoring, sending spam, running background processes, displaying advertisements, and downloading new files. Malicious payloads can be found in different areas including email attachments with many ways to execute them such as opening executable files, setting off specific sets of behavioral conditions as well as opening certain non-executable files.
- **Enumeration:** When an attacker finally creates an active connection to the victims' system or network, he or she can then perform directed queries to extract more information from the target, such as users, usernames and groups, machine names, network resource and shares, routing tables, auditing and service settings, applications and banners, as well as Simple Network Management Protocol (SNMP), and Domain Name System (DNS) details. This process is called enumeration and helps the attacker to identify more vulnerabilities or weak points in the system or network.
- **Vulnerability and Exploit:** A security vulnerability is a weakness or any entry point that hackers make use of to gain access to a website, a system that connects to a website, operating systems, web applications, software, networks, and other IT systems [10] to compromise the confidentiality, availability, or integrity of a resource [11]. Once a vulnerability is identified, an exploit (which is a specific code or attack technique) is crafted and used by an attacker to take advantage of the discovered vulnerability in a target system or software to carry out an attack, compromise a resource or gain unauthorized access. Irrespective of the vulnerability discovered, to infiltrate a network or a system, many attackers make use of different attack frameworks such as the "cyber kill chain" to exfiltrate sensitive data. Other frameworks, like the MITRE ATT&CK framework and Microsoft STRIDE, may also be used, depending on the attackers' objectives. The Cyber Kill Chain, the MITRE ATT&CK, and the Microsoft STRIDE frameworks are briefly explained in the next sections.

4.2.2 The Lockheed Martin Cyber Kill Chain

The Lockheed Martin Cyber Kill Chain [12], sometimes referred to as the Cyber Attack Chain, was developed by Lockheed Martin to help in the identification and prevention of cyber-intrusion activities. The Cyber Kill Chain framework specifies the path or all the steps that an adversary must take to penetrate systems and achieve their objectives on the target. It can also be used as a model to develop incident response and analysis capabilities. Figure 4.1 shows the seven steps of the Cyber Kill Chain: Reconnaissance, Weaponization, Delivery, Exploitation, Installation, Command & Control, and Actions on Objectives. Each of these steps is briefly explained in the subsections below.

4.2.2.1 Reconnaissance

As a first step in understanding a target, attackers will always carry out reconnaissance. In this pre-attack step, like a detective, an attacker gains as much information about a target system or network as possible using active or passive means before launching cyber-attacks. Active reconnaissance occurs when the intruder engages with the targeted system or network to gather vulnerability information. In contrast, passive reconnaissance is an attempt to gather information about the targeted systems or networks without actively engaging them or alerting them of any surveillance activity.

4.2.2.2 Weaponization

To exploit any vulnerabilities of a target discovered during the reconnaissance phase, the intruders must create weapons, hence the need for the weaponization phase. The threat actors craft or tailor their weapons to meet the specific requirements of the target system or network. Some of the well-known cyber-weapons include botnets, malware, distributed denial of service (DDoS), among other things. Malware weapons like viruses and worms, as well as packet sniffers, can be injected into a system or network to do things the owner would not want [13]. Depending on the targeted system or network as well as the motive of the attacker, the weapons developed can be used to exploit new, undetected vulnerabilities or can focus on a combination of different vulnerabilities [14]. Weaponization is therefore the phase during which attackers develop malware weapons (sometimes with the help of automated tools) to exploit the specific vulnerabilities discovered in a target.

4.2.2.3 Delivery

Once a weapon has been crafted or developed, it must be delivered to the target system or network. This phase deals with the transmission of the weaponized payloads to the intended victims. Intruders have many ways of transmitting these payloads, however, some of the most prevalent delivery vectors are email attachments delivered via a phishing email, websites, and USB drives.

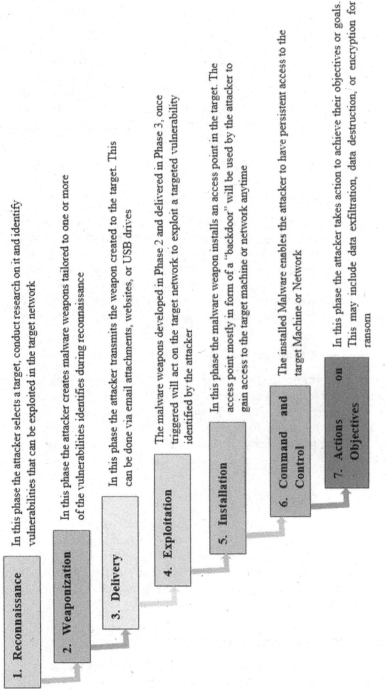

1. **Reconnaissance** — In this phase the attacker selects a target, conduct research on it and identify vulnerabilities that can be exploited in the target network

2. **Weaponization** — In this phase the attacker creates malware weapons tailored to one or more of the vulnerabilities identifies during reconnaissance

3. **Delivery** — In this phase the attacker transmits the weapon created to the target. This can be done via email attachments, websites, or USB drives

4. **Exploitation** — The malware weapons developed in Phase 2 and delivered in Phase 3, once triggered will act on the target network to exploit a targeted vulnerability identified by the attacker

5. **Installation** — In this phase the malware weapon installs an access point in the target. The access point mostly in form of a "backdoor" will be used by the attacker to gain access to the target machine or network anytime

6. **Command and Control** — The installed Malware enables the attacker to have persistent access to the target Machine or Network

7. **Actions on Objectives** — In this phase the attacker takes action to achieve their objectives or goals. This may include data exfiltration, data destruction, or encryption for ransom

Figure 4.1 The Cyber Kill Chain[1].

4.2.2.4 Exploitation

When the weaponized payload is delivered on the target system or network, exploitation triggers the execution of the intruders' code to exploit the target's vulnerabilities. Depending on how it was programmed, it may target an application or operating system vulnerability but can also exploit the victim or leverage an operating system feature that auto-executes code [15]. During this phase, intruders usually exploit discovered vulnerabilities to gain superuser access or attempt privilege escalation, download additional tools, extract password hashes, among other things on the targeted system or network.

4.2.2.5 Installation

Successful exploitation can lead to the installation of malware, a backdoor or other ingress accessible to the attackers on the target systems. With an active exploit running on the target system, intruders may search for additional vulnerabilities or use privilege escalation to gain additional access to the system. Acquired privileges can then be used to install backdoors or remote access trojans that allow for persistence within the environment. Some malware may use obfuscation to conceal their presence and mask activities to avoid detection as well as thwart digital forensic investigation processes.

4.2.2.6 Command & Control (C&C or C2)

A compromised system or network, most of the time, will communicate with external servers to establish a command & control channel. Remote-access Trojans, for example, may be used to open a command-and-control connection to allow remote access to the victims' system or network. This further allows the intruders to gain persistent access to the victim's systems or network, exfiltrate data, and conduct destruction or denial of service operations.

4.2.2.7 Actions on Objectives

Once the attacker has managed to move through all the steps described above and gained persistent access, the last step is to take action to achieve their original objectives. This may include data theft, encryption for ransom, data corruption, data exfiltration, or even data destruction. Typically, most attackers aim to violate either confidentiality, integrity, or availability or at times a combination of these.

4.2.3 The MITRE ATT&CK Framework

Developed by the MITRE Corporation, the MITRE ATT&CK framework [16], which stands for MITRE Adversarial Tactics, Techniques, and Common

Knowledge (ATT&CK), "is a globally accessible knowledge base and model of adversary tactics and techniques based on real-world observations." The MITRE ATT&CK framework shows the various phases of an adversary's attack lifecycle and the platforms they are known to target. It is also used as a foundation for the development of specific threat models and methodologies in the private sector, government, and the cybersecurity product and service community. Unlike the Cyber Kill Chain, the MITRE ATT&CK framework has 14 phases, namely: Reconnaissance, Resource Development, Initial Access, Execution, Persistence, Privilege Escalation, Defense Evasion, Credential Access, Discovery, Lateral Movement, Collection, Command and Control, Exfiltration, and Impact.

Together, the 14 phases of the MITRE ATT&CK framework play a key role in assessing the effectiveness of security operations center processes and defensive measures to identify areas for improvement as well as to improve post-compromise detection of adversaries in enterprises by illustrating the actions an attacker may have taken.

4.2.4 Microsoft STRIDE

Developed by Microsoft, STRIDE [17], which is derived from an acronym of six different threat categories ("Spoofing, Tampering, Repudiation, Information Disclosure, Denial of Service, Elevation of Privilege"), primarily aims to identify and classify computer security threats. Each security threat has an associated violation of desirable properties in a system, as shown in Table 4.1.

4.3 CHALLENGES OF CYBERSECURITY INCIDENTS

The rapid developments in new technologies, such as artificial intelligence, the Internet of Things, ubiquitous Internet access, and cellular connectivity, have brought about many challenges in dealing with cybersecurity incidents. Some of the challenges faced by modern organizations when dealing with cybersecurity incidents are discussed in the following sub-sections.

4.3.1 Identifying a Suspected Incident

With the continued technological evolution and the dynamic nature of attack vectors, being able to accurately identify and classify a suspected incident is becoming a big challenge to organizations with many attacks going unnoticed for a long time. To minimize the impact on organizations' operations and respond effectively, accurate incident detection and identification is crucial.

Table 4.1 Security Threat vs. Desired Property

Security Threat	Description	Desired Property
Spoofing	Using another user credentials without their knowledge. Spoofing target weak authentication mechanisms [18].	Authenticity
Tampering	Only authorized users should be able to modify a system or the data it uses. Tampering with the system or data can have some consequences on the usage of the system itself.	Integrity
Repudiation	This is when attackers try to hide their malicious activities to avoid detection or being blocked by erasing them from the logs, or by spoofing the credentials of another user	Non-Repudiability
Information disclosure	Attackers most often want to get hold of confidential information and then disclose it to unauthorized parties.	Confidentiality
Denial of Service	This occurs when attackers have some hidden interest in preventing regular users from accessing a particular system.	Availability
Elevation of Privilege	Every user in a system has some sort of privileges. Attackers try to acquire additional user privileges by spoofing a user with higher privileges, or by tampering with the system to change their privileges.	Authorization

4.3.2 Establishing Objectives

It is always challenging to establish the objectives of an attack or an incident. However, most of the incidents have criminal or malicious intent driven by fraud, financial gains, or reputational harm to an individual, group, or entity. Similarly, different types of cyber-attacks have different motivations. Some of the most common reasons include theft, espionage, spamming, control, disruption, vulnerability testing, fun, and many others.

4.3.3 Analyzing All Available Information

To understand security incidents and find ways of reacting and responding to them, network data needs to be thoroughly analyzed constantly. This is becoming a big challenge with the introduction of cloud-based services and big data, where massive volumes of data arrive from different data sources and in different formats.

4.3.4 Identifying What Has Been Compromised

Another challenge of dealing with cybersecurity incidents lies in the identification of what has been compromised. With almost every process appearing to be legitimate, it can be challenging to identify what has been compromised. However, some of the common indicators are suspicious behavior and unusual system resource utilization. An important factor to consider when analyzing the scope of compromise is the inbound and outbound network connections available at the time of the incident, the devices and software the IT infrastructure consists of, and whether network segmentation is in place.

4.3.5 Identifying What Information Has Been Accessed or Stolen

Beyond knowing what has been compromised, it can also be challenging to know what information has been accessed, stolen, deleted, or corrupted by unauthorized parties.

4.3.6 Cyber-Attribution

Cyber-attribution, which is the process of tracking, identifying, and laying blame on the perpetrator of a cyber-attack, is a very challenging task. Finding out who is responsible for an attack has never been easy. As noted by [19], depending on the tools and processes, it can be a long and laborious process, often taking months or even years of investigation to learn anything of value.

4.3.7 Determining Business Impact

Determining the impact and criticality of a security incident on business activities and associated resource requirements to ensure operational resilience and continuity of operations during and after a disruption can be challenging. Any findings arising from a Business Impact Analysis (BIA) should be accurate as BIA findings are used to make critical business decisions [20]; this is why the accuracy of the information contained in the BIA is crucial.

To deal with the above challenges and reduce their impact on the business operations, several tools can be used to help organizations in incident detection and response. Choosing the right tool to use can also be challenging as technology keeps changing where old tools become obsolete and new ones emerge. The next sub-section presents a brief review of some of the commonly used incident detection and response tools.

4.3.8 Incident Detection and Response Tools

Incident detection and response tools can be used to improve visibility across an organization's network as well as help find intruders earlier in the attack chain to alleviate some of the above-mentioned challenges. Using the right incident detection and response tools, the IR team can be alerted of suspicious activities as soon as they happen and initiate investigations and responses before critical data or system is compromised.

4.3.8.1 Live Detection Tools

The live detection tools are divided into private SIEMs and public SIEMs.

4.3.8.1.1 Private SIEMs

- **IBM QRadar:**[2] Developed by IBM, this tool is meant to help security teams accurately detect and prioritize threats across the enterprise as well as provide intelligent insights that enable teams to respond quickly to reduce the impact of incidents.
- **Microsoft Azure Sentinel:**[3] Azure Sentinel, a product of Microsoft, is a cloud-native (SIEM) platform that uses built-in AI to help analyze large volumes of data across an enterprise.
- **RSA NetWitness:**[4] This tool collects and analyzes network data in real-time to enhance a security team's capabilities to detect and respond to advanced threats.
- **Rapid7:**[5] Rapid7 was developed to help in reducing risks across an organization's entire connected environment. This includes vulnerability management, malicious behavior monitoring, investigating, and shutdown attacks, or automating operations.
- **SolarWinds:**[6] This tool was developed primarily for network, systems, and information technology infrastructure management.
- **Splunk Enterprise Security:**[7] Splunk is used to collect, analyze, and act upon the big data generated by technology infrastructure, security systems, and business applications. It can also analyze trends, correlate different data streams, identify patterns, anomalies, and exceptions. Splunk's Enterprise Security edition provides analytics-driven security with continuous monitoring of modern threats.

4.3.8.1.2 Public SIEMs

- **ELK Stack (Elasticsearch, Logstash, and Kibana):**[8] This free and open-source toolkit provides users with a platform that collects and processes data from multiple data sources, stores it in one centralized data store that can scale as data grows, and provides a set of tools to analyze the data.
- **Snort:**[9] Snort is a free open-source network intrusion detection and prevention system. It uses a series of rules that help define malicious network activity and uses those rules to find packets that match against them and generate alerts for users.

4.3.8.2 Intelligence Gathering Tools

- **AbuseIPDB:**[10] This is a project dedicated to help combat the spread of hackers, spammers, and abusive activity on the Internet. Its primary aim is to help make the Web safer by providing a central blacklist for webmasters, system administrators, and other interested parties to report and find IP addresses that have been associated with malicious activity online.

- **IP and Domain Reputation Center:**[11] This is a real-time threat detection network meant to collect daily security intelligence across millions of deployed web, email, firewall, and IPS appliances.
- **URLScan.io:**[12] URLScan.io is a website scanner for suspicious and malicious URLs focusing on analyzing all possible details about any established HTTP connection, site content, and relations with other sites.
- **Shodan:**[13] This is a search engine that lets the user find specific types of computers connected to the Internet using a variety of filters.
- **VirusTotal:**[14] This is a tool developed to inspect items with over 70 antivirus scanners and URL/domain blacklisting services, in addition to a myriad of tools to extract signals from the studied content.

4.3.8.3 Forensic Tools

Forensic tools are used to collect data, network packets [21], as well as analyze security breaches or analyze software to see how it performs the attack and can fall into many different categories. Some of the commonly used tools are:

- **ANY.RUN:**[15] This is an interactive cloud-based malware analysis sandbox used to detect, analyze, and monitor cybersecurity threats.
- **Autopsy:**[16] Autopsy is an end-to-end open-source digital forensics platform that is a fast, thorough, and efficient hard drive investigation solution.
- **Aid4Mail:**[17] This tool is used for email analysis, email data mining and extraction, long-term email archiving, conversion to custom formats.
- **Burb Suite:**[18] This is a penetration testing and vulnerability finder tool that can also be used for examining web application security. The enterprise edition enables automated scanning.
- **Cuckoo Sandbox:**[19] This is open-source software for automating the analysis of suspicious files that provide a detailed report outlining the behavior of the file when executed inside a realistic but isolated environment.
- **NetworkMiner:**[20] This is an open-source Network Forensic Analysis Tool (NFAT) for Windows, but it also works in Linux/Mac OS X/ FreeBSD. The tool can be used as a passive network sniffer/packet capturing tool to detect operating systems, sessions, hostnames, open ports among others without putting any traffic on the network.
- **TCPdump:**[21] This is a data-network packet analyzer that prints out a description of the contents of packets on a network interface that matches the Boolean expression preceded by a timestamp.

- **Wireshark:**[22] This is a free and open-source packet sniffer and ana-lysis tool used for network troubleshooting, analysis, software and communications protocol development, and education.

4.3.8.4 Threat Maps

- **Live Cyber Threat Map:**[23] Developed by Check Point Software Technologies, this platform shows live statistics of recent attacks, display the total amount of attack data, including new attacks, the source of the attacks, and their destinations.
- **FireEye Cyber Threat Map:**[24] This tool shows the origin, destination, total number of attacks, and other statistics for the previous 30 days, such as top attacker countries and topmost attacked industries.
- **Kaspersky Cyberthreat Real-Time Map:**[25] is considered one among the best tools with on-demand scans, email and web antivirus detec-tions, type of malicious objects as well as intrusion detection sub-systems and a list of information captured by security vulnerabilities.
- **NETSCOUT Cyber Threat Horizon:**[26] This is a cybersecurity situa-tional awareness platform that provides highly contextualized visibi-lity into the global threat landscape.
- **Darktrace Antigena:**[27] This is an autonomous response solution that responds to cyber-threats in real-time and offers cybersecurity in-telligence by utilizing machine learning to detect breaches in the net-work. Darktrace Antigena adopts a rare type of unsupervised machine learning algorithm that does not require humans to specify what to look for.
- **Arbor Networks DDoS Attack Map:**[28] This tool is dedicated to tracking all incidents related to DDoS attacks around the world. The data gathered by this system comes from a worldwide analysis of over 300 ISPs with over 130 Terabytes per second of live traffic.

Other common monitoring tools that are also present in the industry in-clude Bitdefender Threat Map[29] SonicWall Worldwide Attacks,[30] Fortinet Threat Map,[31] Cisco Talos Threat Map,[32] Akamai Real-Time Web Attack Monitor,[33] LookingGlass Phishing/Malicious URL Map,[34] Threat Butt Hacking Attack Map,[35] Deteque Live Botnet Threats Worldwide,[36] and the Sophos Threat Tracking Map.[37]

4.3.9 Risk Management

To further help an organization deal with different challenges of cyberse-curity incidents, the risk matrix can also be used to minimize the probability of potential risk and optimize performance. A risk matrix helps to show the risks affecting a project to enable organizations to develop a mitigation strategy. To prepare a project risk assessment matrix, several steps have

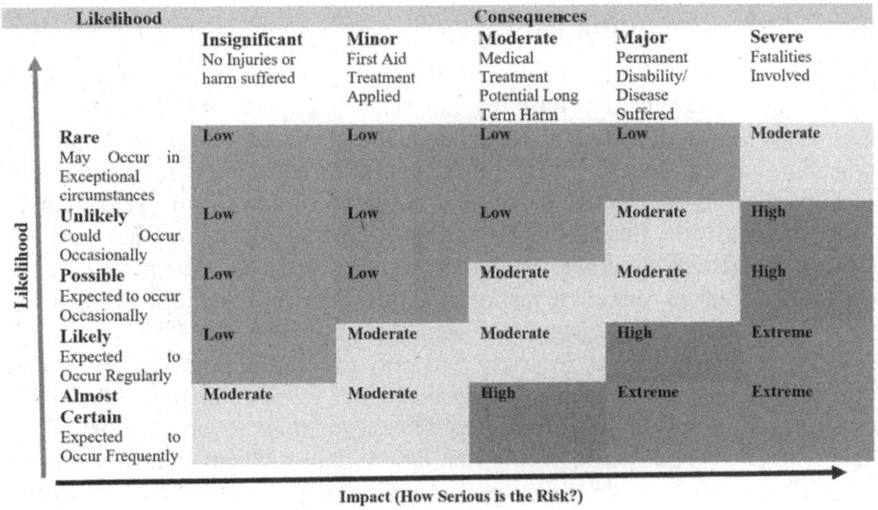

Likelihood	Consequences				
	Insignificant No Injuries or harm suffered	**Minor** First Aid Treatment Applied	**Moderate** Medical Treatment Potential Long Term Harm	**Major** Permanent Disability/ Disease Suffered	**Severe** Fatalities Involved
Rare May Occur in Exceptional circumstances	Low	Low	Low	Low	Moderate
Unlikely Could Occur Occasionally	Low	Low	Low	Moderate	High
Possible Expected to occur Occasionally	Low	Low	Moderate	Moderate	High
Likely Expected to Occur Regularly	Low	Moderate	Moderate	High	Extreme
Almost Certain Expected to Occur Frequently	Moderate	Moderate	High	Extreme	Extreme

Impact (How Serious is the Risk?)

Figure 4.2 Example of a risk matrix [24].

been identified [22] to help organizations in developing a risk matrix. These are enumerating the risks, rating for probability and impact, classifying risks, and deciding on mitigation planning.

By developing a risk matrix, organizations can [23] identify event outcomes that should be prioritized or grouped for further investigation, provide a good graphical portrayal of risks across a project/task, simplify the risk management process, help identify areas for risk reduction, provide a quick and relatively inexpensive risk analysis, and enable more detailed analysis to be focused on high-risk areas. Figure 4.2 shows an example of a risk matrix by oac.chris21 [24].

Beyond having a risk matrix, organizations can also make use of risk registers to track and measure risks. Risk registers, like the CyberSaint Security's [25] risk register, can help the IR team align to initiatives that matter, thereby saving an organization valuable resources, time, and person-hour. The next section discusses how to prepare for cyber security incidents.

4.4 PREPARING FOR CYBERSECURITY INCIDENTS

When dealing with cybersecurity incidents, the Cyber Security Incident Response Teams (CSIRTs) together with cybersecurity analysts, should comprehensively structure their incident response strategy to cover modern enterprise architectures and the complex needs of modern organizations. A well-prepared organization can recover its systems more quickly from cybersecurity incidents, minimize the impact of the attack, instill confidence in its customers, and even save money in the long term.

4.4.1 Understanding CSIRTs

A CSIRT is a group of professionals tasked with the responsibility of providing an organization with the capability to expose, avert, and respond to cyber-attacks or cybersecurity-related incidents targeting an organization. Fundamentally, the CSIRT is a part of the incident response team responsible for the detection, control, and extermination of cybersecurity incidents. Besides, the CSIRT is also responsible for recovering and restoring the systems that are affected by security incidents. The three distinct components of any incident response team, therefore, are [26] the CSIRT, the PR expert or advisor, and the legal expert or advisor.

The CSIRT team must be active and fully functional before, during, and after cybersecurity incidents. During this time, they are responsible for incidents' data analysis and provide feedback on how to prevent breaches. The CSIRT feedback and recommendations can also be shared with the organization to provide awareness. As part of preparedness, the CSIRT should be able to do a criticality assessment of key assets, conduct threat analysis, consider the implications of people, process, technology, create a controlled environment to provide an appropriate level of protection, and also review the state of readiness in incidence response. Some of the things an organization should consider and have in place are briefly explained in the following sub-sections.

4.4.1.1 Criticality Assessment for the Organization

Criticality assessment involves identifying an organization's critical assets and determining where they are located in the organization, recording important details about their level of criticality, and also assigning responsibility for protecting the assets to capable, named individuals.

4.4.1.2 Threat Analysis

Cybersecurity threat analysis helps organizations to understand the different types of cybersecurity incidents and their level of threat to the organization.

4.4.1.3 Implications of People, Process, and Technology

The organization should have in place people responsible for dealing with cybersecurity incidents equipped with adequate processes or methodologies to help them deal with cybersecurity incidents in a fast, effective, and consistent manner. Existing systems should be configured with adequate monitoring processes in place to help the IR team identify or respond to cybersecurity incidents. And finally, information should always be made readily available to the IR team to help them respond quickly and effectively.

4.4.1.4 Create a Controlled Environment

Creating a controlled environment can help an organization reduce the likelihood of a cybersecurity incident. Some of the common control measures used include access control, firewalls, demilitarized zone (DMZ), malware protection, and backups. Even though these controls do not prevent cybersecurity attacks from happening, they can, however, frustrate a determined attacker giving more time to the organization to detect the attack before it gets to a critical point.

4.4.1.5 Review the State of Readiness in Incidence Response

A review process helps the organization maintain an appropriate cybersecurity incident response capability equipped with appropriately skilled people. This also ensures that the organization is guided by well-designed processes that enable the effective use of relevant technologies. Having the right capability can help an organization conduct a thorough investigation and successfully eradicate adversaries.

4.5 HACKING TECHNIQUES AND COUNTERMEASURES

Hacking is defined by the Australian Cyber Security Centre (ACSC) [27] as the unauthorized access of a system or network, often to exploit a system's data or manipulate its normal behavior. Irrespective of the motives, the common phases of hacking are Reconnaissance, Scanning, Gaining Access, Maintaining Access, and Covering Tracks [28].

4.5.1 Reconnaissance

This is usually the first step of hacking also known as foot printing and information gathering. This is the phase where hackers prepare to collect as much information as possible about the target. Some of the data collected include, but are not limited to, information about a computer network, weaknesses, and security vulnerabilities in host computers and the people involved. The steps of reconnaissance include [29] accumulating inceptive data, deciding the range of the network, recognizing all active machines, getting hold of the operating system being used, uniquely marking the working framework, revealing services used on ports, and understanding the network layout. There are two types of reconnaissance: active reconnaissance and passive reconnaissance.

4.5.1.1 Active Reconnaissance

Active reconnaissance allows the hacker to directly interact with the target to gather information about the target. One of the tools that can be used for active reconnaissance is Nmap, which scans the target for specified information.

4.5.1.2 Passive Reconnaissance

In passive reconnaissance, the hacker collects information about the target without directly accessing the target. Some of the information may be publicly available through social media, public websites, among many other online sources.

4.5.1.3 Tools for Reconnaissance

- **Nmap:**[38] Nmap is a free and open-source network scanner used to discover hosts and services on a computer network by sending packets and analyzing the responses. It has several features for probing computer networks, including host discovery and service and operating system detection.
- **Google:**[39] This well-known search engine can be used for passive reconnaissance. With the help of the Google Hacking Database, hackers can find publicly available information, intended for penetration testing and security loopholes.
- **OpenVAS:**[40] This is a full-featured vulnerability scanner primarily used for vulnerability scanning and vulnerability management.
- **Nessus:**[41] This is a proprietary vulnerability scanner used to distinguish weak applications running in the network and gives an assortment of insights regarding possibly exploitable weaknesses.
- **Metasploit:**[42] Metasploit provides information about security vulnerabilities and aids in penetration testing and IDS signature development.
- **Shodan:**[43] This is a search engine for security and Internet-connected devices. It is primarily used to find specific types of computers connected to the internet using a variety of filters.
- **Nikto:**[44] It is a vulnerability scanner that scans web servers for dangerous files or CGIs, outdated server software, and other problems.
- **Cyr3con:**[45] This is an intelligence-driven machine learning technology to predict exploits. The tool predicts cyber exploits by combining machine learning and threat intelligence to drive vulnerability management. Cyr3con pr1ority[46] is a feature that helps predict which vulnerabilities hackers will exploit using artificial intelligence and real threat intelligence mined from hacker communities.

4.5.1.4 Detecting Reconnaissance

Any unprotected device on an organizations network presents an entry point for hackers and other malicious intruders. To protect an organization from hackers many tools have been developed to scan and filter all incoming and outgoing traffic. Some of the tools that can be used to detect reconnaissance are briefly discussed below.

- **Zeek:**[47] Zeek is an open-source network security monitoring tool that supports several network protocols like HTTP, SMB, Kerberos, etc.
- **Splunk Add-on for Zeek:**[48] This tool allows a Splunk software administrator to analyze packet capture data directly or use it as a contextual data feed to correlate with other vulnerability related data in the Splunk platform.
- Other tools include InsightIDR[49] and Attivo ThreatDefend Detection and Response Platform.[50]

4.5.2 Scanning

Scanning is used to find services that can be used to misuse existing frameworks. With scanning, hackers can know what services are executed in different clients as well as what clients own administrative rights. They can know if incognito logins are upheld regardless of whether certain organization administrations require validation among other vulnerabilities. There are three types of scanning, as discussed in the following sections.

4.5.2.1 Port Scanning

This involves scanning the target for information like open ports, live systems, live frameworks, and various services and administrations running on the host.

4.5.2.2 Vulnerability Scanning

This involves checking the target for weaknesses or vulnerabilities, which can be exploited mostly with the help of automated tools.

4.5.2.3 Network Mapping

This helps in finding the topology of the network, switches, routers, firewalls, servers if any, and host information and drawing a network diagram with the available information.

4.5.3 Gaining Access

In this phase, the attacker breaks into the system or network using various tools or methods and can also increase his privilege to the administrator level so he can install application, modify data, or hide data.

4.5.4 Maintaining Access

Once the hacker gains access to the system or network he may want to maintain access or persist the connection in the background without the knowledge of the user. This phase aims to maintain access to the target until the hacker accomplishes his planned objectives in that target. Tools like Trojans, Rootkits, or other malicious files may be used to achieve this state.

4.5.5 Covering Tracks

Once all the objectives have been achieved, this phase helps the hacker to clear all evidence so that no one will find any traces leading to his identity. Hacker will do this by modifying/corrupting/deleting log files, modifying registry values, and uninstalling all applications used and deleting all folders created. The next section explains how to detect network events.

4.6 DETECTING NETWORK EVENTS

Detection is the process of finding intruder events or incidents in an organization network infrastructure, retracing activities, containing the threat, and removing any foothold. Successful cybersecurity incidents detection and investigation are dependent on the availability of appropriate data sources [30], which can be extracted from existing systems without requiring specialized capabilities. The table below extracted from the Australian Cyber Security Centre shows some of the data sources that organizations can use for detecting and investigating cybersecurity incidents Table 4.2.

4.6.1 Endpoint and Network Traffic Monitoring

Endpoint and network traffic monitoring continue to attract a lot of attention from the industry as well as researchers. This section reviews existing work in traffic monitoring and highlight existing research works and techniques that have been proposed. Categorized techniques and solutions together with their research advances are elaborated in the following subsections.

- **Firewalls:** Firewalls are computer network security systems designed either as hardware or software or a combination of both to prevent unauthorized access or restricts internet traffic to or from a private network. Depending on the application environment, several types of firewalls exist, such as Web application firewall, Packet Filters, Stateful Inspection and Proxy Server Firewalls. With the advancement in technology, it has become common for cybercriminals to hack firewalls.

Table 4.2 Sample Data Sources for Detecting and Investigating Cybersecurity Incidents

Data Source	Description
Domain Name System Logs	Can assist in identifying attempts to resolve malicious domains or Internet Protocol (IP) addresses, which can indicate an exploitation attempt or successful compromise.
Email Server Logs	Can assist in identifying users targeted with spear-phishing emails. Can also assist in identifying the initial vector of a compromise.
Operating System Event Logs	Can assist in tracking process execution, file/registry/network activity, authentication events, operating system created security alerts, and other activities.
Security Software and Appliance Logs	Can assist in the identification of anomalous or malicious activity which can indicate an exploitation attempt or successful compromise.
Virtual Private Network and Remote Access Logs	Can assist in identifying unusual source addresses, times of access, and logon/logoff times associated with malicious activity.
Web Proxy Logs	Can assist in identifying Hypertext Transfer Protocol-based vectors and malware communication traffic.

- **Syslog:**[51] Syslog refers to System Logging Protocol. It is a standard protocol used to collect various device logs or event messages from several different machines and send them to a central location Syslog server. The Syslog server then sends diagnostic and monitoring data that can be analyzed for system monitoring, network maintenance, and review.
- **Windows Event Logs:** As shown in Figure 4.3, this is a detailed record of system, security, and application notifications stored by Windows

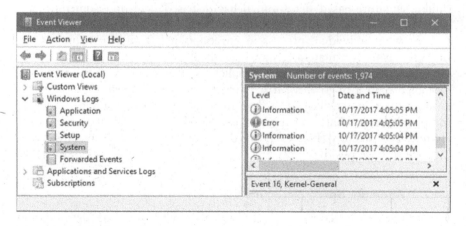

Figure 4.3 Windows event logs.

and used by administrators to troubleshoot, diagnose system problems, and predict future issues. To view the event, application logs, system messages including errors, information messages, and warnings on a local or remote machine, EventViewer[52] is used.

4.6.2 Anomaly Detection

This section highlights some of the existing anomaly detection techniques that organizations can use.

4.6.2.1 Signature-Based Detection

A signature is a unique identifier or characteristic used to detect a known threat. Different signatures may be used for different types of threats [31]. In the case of a virus, it may be a unique pattern of code that attaches itself to a file, or it may be as simple as the hash of a known bad file. In a network environment, intrusion detection systems may be configured to look for specific characteristics within network traffic. The process where such unique identifiers or characteristics are used to established known threat using detection software such as anti-viruses or intrusion detection systems forms part of a signature-based detection mechanism. Every time a specific pattern, signature, or characteristic is discovered in a file or network traffic, the file or the network traffic can be flagged as being infected or malicious [32]. The biggest limitation of signature-based detection is that they are always reactive and can only detect threats that are already known. Signatures cannot identify unknown and emerging threats because no signature may have been written to detect them.

4.6.2.2 Complex Behavior Matching

Unlike signature-based detection, behavior-based detection sometimes referred to as complex behavior matching is designed to look for specific results such as what individual process in an endpoint is trying to achieve [32]. Complex behavior matching monitors the behaviors of a program or a process to determine whether it is malicious or not [31]. Regardless of the type of program or process, if it is trying to gain privilege escalation, for example, it may be flagged as being malicious. The advantage of using complex behavior matching approaches is that it has the potential to discover unknown threats [33]. However, one disadvantage of this approach is that it is prone to false positives [32].

4.6.2.3 Anomaly-Based Detection

Anomaly-based detection approaches specifically focus on the identification of unexpected events, observations, or items that differ significantly from the norm and generate alerts based on unknown suspicious behaviors [34]. Anomaly-based detection systems can detect both network and endpoints intrusions and misuse by monitoring their activities and classifying them as either normal or anomalous. Different types of anomalies exist. Some of the common ones include network anomalies, application performance anomalies, and web application security anomalies [35]. Different anomaly detection techniques also exist with some employing machine learning detection algorithms, such as clustering-based anomaly detection, density-based anomaly detection, support vector machine-based anomaly detection, supervised machine learning for anomaly detection, unsupervised machine learning for anomaly detection, and semi-supervised anomaly detection [35]. The next section discusses how to respond to cybersecurity incidents.

4.7 RESPONDING TO CYBERSECURITY INCIDENTS

Although it is a well-known fact that "there is no such thing as perfect security," when it comes to responding and managing cyber-attacks, having a good methodology or incidence response plan ensures that a structured investigation process can be done in an organization and targeted responses to contain and remediate security threats can be provided. If an organization suffers an unlikely data breach, the incidence response and disaster recovery plans should help address it quickly. This is because no organization, regardless of size, business, industry, technology infrastructure, type of data handled, and geographic location, is free from cybersecurity threats. This section of the chapter, therefore, discusses briefly how to prepare an incidence response plan (IRP), prioritization as well as disaster recovery plan, and offer insights on how to use the IRP to proactively respond and recover from cybersecurity incidents.

4.7.1 Preparing an Incidence Response Plan

In preparing an IRP, organizations should consider the following: its purpose which answers the "why" question behind the plan, the scope which highlights all the areas of authorization, roles, and responsibilities, which dictates who is to be on the IRP team and how he or she is expected to act when events are investigated, definitions which must highlight what an event, incident, or breach is, among other IRP elements [36]. During the IRP preparation process, some of the key elements and basic steps [37] to consider are ensuring that all stakeholders are involved, assigning alternate members with decision-making authority, establishing communications procedures and responsibilities, scheduling incident response plan reviews and testing, ensuring that contact information is updated for the IRP team members and outside resources, and scheduling regular tests plan to identify any gaps.

4.7.2 Incident Response Plan (IRP) Phases

An IRP is an essential blueprint and strategy for responding to cybersecurity events and incidents [36]. It helps organizations handle cybersecurity events and incidents that might impact or impede critical operations [38]. A good incident response plan will also help organizations follow a step-by-step process in identifying the roles and responsibilities of teams across the organization [39]. This is important in stopping undesired actions, mitigate their impact, and start the recovery process using international acceptable best practices. To effectively address any security incidents that an organization could experience a good IRP should follow the following six important steps.

- **Preparation:** This is one of the most important steps in an incident response plan. Preparation determines how the Incidence Response (IR) team will respond to any incident that may affect the organization. It is in this phase that security policies are developed that specify what a security incident is, how data breaches will be handled, and end users' policies throughout the organization [40], including training of staff, software, and hardware resources that will be used, approved, and funded in advance [41], execution strategies and developing incident response drill scenarios. Also, organizations should establish policies and procedures for incident response management and enable efficient communication methods both before and after the incident [42]. The more prepared the IR team is, the less likely they'll make critical mistakes.
- **Identification:** This phase is used to determine whether an organization has been breached or not and further finding out the depth of the breach or compromise, its source, and its success or failure. According to [43], this step also involves "detecting deviations from normal operations in the organization, understanding if a deviation represents a security incident, and determining how important the incident is."
- **Containment:** Limiting the damage from any identified security incident and preventing any further damage is the goal of this phase. Containment actions must be done quickly to avoid damage escalation. This includes isolating compromised devices within the organization as well as backing up any critical data on an infected system.
- **Eradication:** The eradication process begins after an incident has been successfully contained. This phase aims to fully restore all affected systems and includes actions like patching devices, disarming malware, disabling compromised accounts, changing passwords of compromised accounts, or removing all other artefacts that may have been introduced by the attack.
- **Recovery:** Once all systems have been verified to be clean and all threats eradicated, the recovery phase aims to restore normal service

to the business and bring all systems back to full operation. However, additional monitoring of affected systems can also be implemented to check for malicious activities.

- **Lessons Learned:** This phase aims to help with future incident response activities by answering the "how do we stop this from happening again?" question. A detailed report that reviews the entire incident response process including incident investigation and remediation should be produced and supplied to all the relevant stakeholders. Recommendations on improving the IR process and how threats can be contained and eradicated in the future may be given at this stage.

4.7.3 Incident Prioritization

When developing an IRP, it is important to consider incident prioritization to help organizations focus on which incidents to address first by assessing both the urgency of the incident and the level of impact it is causing. Urgency deals with how quickly a resolution of an incident is required, while impact handles the extent of the incident and of the potential damage caused by the incident before it can be resolved.[53] Many organizations use the incident prioritization matrix to determine the priority of an incident, based on business needs. Table 4.3 is an example of how incident priority levels are determined.

It can be inferred from Table 4.3 that an incident with both high impact and high urgency will always have the highest priority, while an incident with low impact and low urgency will get the lowest priority. According to [44], many organizations use the guidelines shown in Table 4.4 to categorize incident urgency as well as determining incident impact.

4.7.4 Disaster Recovery Plan

A disaster recovery plan (DRP) is a formal written document [45], a plan [46], or a set of tools and procedures [47] created by an organization and contains detailed instructions describing the steps that the organization will use to respond to unplanned incidents or disasters and restore operations after major disruption to its information technology assets. The primary

Table 4.3 Basic Impact, Urgency, and Priority Matrix

		IMPACT		
	PRIORITY	*High*	*Medium*	*Low*
URGENCY	High	1 – Critical	2 – High	3 – Moderate
	Medium	2 – High	3 – Moderate	4 – Low
	Low	3 – Moderate	4 – Low	5 – Low

Table 4.4 Guidelines to Categorize Incident Urgency and Determining Incident Impact

High Urgency	• Mission-critical for daily operations (a service that is critical for day-to-day operations is unavailable) • Extremely time-sensitive (time-sensitive work or customer actions are affected) • Propagation rate rapidly expanding in scope (the incident's sphere of impact is expanding rapidly, or quick action may make it possible to limit its scope) • Visibility to business stakeholders or C-suite – The incident affects high-status individuals or organizations (i.e., upper management or major clients).
Low Urgency	• Optional services (i.e., "nice to have, but not essential") – Affected services are optional and used infrequently • The issue affects only a small section of the IT environment – not expanding (the effects of the incident appear to be stable) • Low visibility in terms of affecting the business (important or time-sensitive work is not affected)
High Impact	• A critical system is down • One or more departments are affected • A significant number of staff members are not able to perform their functions • The incident affects many customers • The incident has the potential for major financial loss or damage to the organization's reputation • Other criteria, depending on the function of the organization and the affected systems, could include such things as a threat to public safety, potential loss of life, or major property damage
Moderate Impact	• Some staff members or customers are affected • None of the services lost is critical • Financial loss and damage to the organization's reputation are possible, but are limited in scope • There is no threat to life, public safety, or physical property
Low Impact	• Only a small number of users are affected • No critical services are involved, and there is little or no potential for financial loss or loss of reputation

aim of a DRP is to get over or minimize the effects of a disaster and restore normal operations quickly. The major components of a disaster recovery plan are the emergency plan, backup plan, recovery plan, and test plan.

- **The Emergency Plan:** This plan specifies the steps to be taken immediately after a disaster strikes and usually organized by types of disaster, such as fire, flood, or earthquake. The procedures followed in the case of an emergency differs depending on the nature and extent of the disaster.

- **The Backup Plan:** Following the emergency plan is the backup plan which specifies how an organization uses backup files and equipment to resume information processing. This plan specifies the location of an alternate computer facility in the event the organization's normal location is destroyed or unusable following a disaster.
- **The Recovery Plan:** This plan specifies the actions to be taken to restore full information processing operations. Like the emergency plan, the recovery plan also differs depending on the type, nature, and extent of the disaster. Planning committees responsible for different forms of recovery are key for disaster recovery and should be established beforehand in preparation for disaster recovery processes.
- **The Test Plan:** Every DRP must be tested for its completeness. The Test Plan should have information for simulating various levels of disasters and recording an organization's ability to recover from such disasters. During simulation, staff must follow all the steps outlined in the DRP. Modification can be done after every test.

4.7.5 Following up a Cybersecurity Incident

Like any other incident, many important activities should be undertaken after a cybersecurity incident has been detected, reported, and investigated. However, it is common to find that some organizations not following-up some incidents because of one of the following reasons:

- Insufficient resources to support the follow-up process;
- Higher priorities on some incidents than others;
- Lack of awareness or the pressing need to get the organization back on track.

Lessons must be learned from each incident to help evaluate future improvements. Following up on a cybersecurity incident helps to show what exactly happened and the impacts on the organization. It also helps the organization review and evaluate the existing cybersecurity incident response plan and budget. Besides, a follow-up can help verify if more security mechanisms or mitigating controls need to be put in place or adapted to prevent similar incidents in the future [48]. The next section briefly explains the concept of carrying out a post-incident analysis.

4.7.6 Carrying Out a Post-Incident Analysis

Having encountered a cybersecurity incident in the organization could mean that there are some shortcomings in the security strategy or practice of the organization which needs improvement. For this reason, every incident needs to be properly analyzed to help in future improvements. During this phase, every previous discussions or decision made should be well documented and a report should be produced and presented to all relevant stakeholders.

4.7.7 Containment and Eradication

Once an incident is detected and its source established, the organization should act fast to contain it to reduce its impact on the operations. Some of the things that can be done to contain and manage an incident include disabling network access for infected computers, reset passwords for any accounts that were breached, block accounts suspected to have caused the incident, back up all affected systems to preserve their state for future forensics, and installing security patches. The containment strategy should aim to return all systems to production, lockdown, or purge user accounts and backdoors that enabled the intrusion [49].

4.7.8 Recovery and Post-Incident Measures

To support a smooth recovery, it is important to document every incident, the actions taken, and the time spent on each incident and each action. The best way to manage this is by using incident metrics. For this reason, it is important for organizations to quantify and track metrics around uptime, downtime, and how quickly and effectively the IR team resolves any of the incidents reported. This is because every organization at some point will experience equipment failures. Some of the most common incident metrics as described by [50] are MTBF, MTTR, MTTF, and MTTA.

- **MTBF**: *Mean Time Between Failure* is the average time between repairable failures of a technology product calculated using an arithmetic mean and measured in hours.
  To calculate MTBF, the total number of operational hours in a period is divide by the number of failures that occurred in that period.

$$MTBF = \frac{Number\ of\ operational\ hours}{Number\ of\ failures}$$

- **MTTR**: *Mean Time to Repair* is the time it takes to repair a system after the occurrence of the failure.

$$MTTR = \frac{Number\ of\ downtime\ hours\ caused\ by\ system\ failures}{Number\ of\ failures}$$

- **MTTR**: *Mean Time to Recover* is the average time it takes to recover from a product or system failure.

MTTR: *Mean Time to Respond* is the average time it takes to recover from a product or system failure from the time when you are first alerted to that failure.

- **MTTR:** *Mean Time to Resolve* is the average time it takes to fully resolve a failure.
- **MTTF:** *Mean Time to Failure* is a maintenance metric that measures the average amount of time a non-repairable asset operates before it fails.

$$MTTF = \frac{Number\ hours\ of\ operation}{Total\ assets\ in\ use}$$

- **MTTA:** *Mean Time to Acknowledge* is the average time it takes from when an alert is triggered to when work begins on the issue. A summary of the above metrics is shown in Figure 4.4.

4.7.9 Cybersecurity Incident Reports

A good security management program keeps accurate records or reposts of security incidents other types of security events that occur at an organization. Some tools like Splunk can be used to create reports that show statistics and visualizations of events. Once created Splunk reports can be run anytime, and each time they fetch and display fresh results. It is also possible to drill down and see the underlying events that create the final statistics. The next section concludes this chapter.

4.8 CONCLUSIONS

Incident response is becoming increasingly complex with the constantly evolving network infrastructures, computing devices, and usage trends. For this reason, security measures in the enterprise can and should be implemented at many different levels locally, in the data center, and in the cloud to mitigate the possibility of catastrophic security incidents. Security frameworks, such as MITRE ATT&CK and the Lockheed Martin Cyber Kill Chain, can also be utilized by security professionals to prepare for, detect, and mitigate cybersecurity incidents effectively. A wide range of software tools and best practices are also available, and some have been discussed in this chapter, which can be used for network monitoring, detecting cyber-attacks, and responding to security incidents promptly. However, as a constantly evolving field where instant action is often imperative, incident response needs continuous research and development so that cost-effective and efficient security countermeasures can be implemented in enterprise environments.

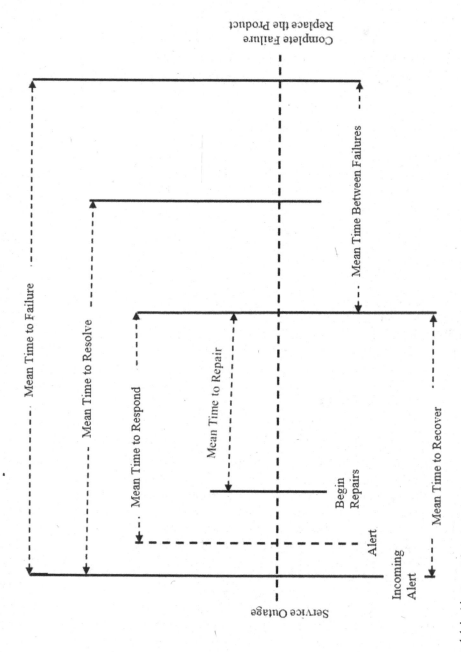

Figure 4.4 Incident metrics summary.

ACKNOWLEDGMENTS

The work has been supported by the Cyber Security Research Centre Limited whose activities are partially funded by the Australian Government's Cooperative Research Centres Programme.

NOTES

1 https://www.lockheedmartin.com/content/dam/lockheed-martin/rms/photo/cyber/THE-CYBER-KILL-CHAIN-body.png.pc-adaptive.1280. medium.png
2 https://www.ibm.com/be-en/products/qradar-siem
3 https://azure.microsoft.com/en-us/services/azure-sentinel/
4 https://www.rsa.com/content/dam/en/solution-brief/rsa-netwitness-platform.pdf
5 https://www.rapid7.com
6 https://www.solarwinds.com
7 https://www.splunk.com/en_us/resources/videos/splunk-enterprise-overview-turning-machine-data-into-operational-intelligence.h tml
8 https://www.elastic.co/what-is/elk-stack
9 https://www.snort.org
10 https://www.abuseipdb.com
11 https://talosintelligence.com/reputation_center/
12 https://urlscan.io
13 https://www.shodan.io
14 https://www.virustotal.com
15 https://any.run
16 https://www.autopsy.com
17 https://www.aid4mail.com
18 https://portswigger.net/solutions
19 https://cuckoosandbox.org
20 https://www.netresec.com/?page=networkminer
21 https://www.tcpdump.org/manpages/tcpdump.1.html
22 https://www.wireshark.org
23 https://threatmap.checkpoint.com
24 https://www.fireeye.com/cyber-map/threat-map.html
25 https://cybermap.kaspersky.com
26 https://horizon.netscout.com
27 https://www.darktrace.com/en/products/antigena-network/
28 https://www.digitalattackmap.com
29 https://threatmap.bitdefender.com
30 https://attackmap.sonicwall.com/live-attack-map/
31 https://threatmap.fortiguard.com
32 https://talosintelligence.com
33 https://www.akamai.com/us/en/resources/visualizing-akamai/enterprise-threat-monitor.jsp
34 https://map.lookingglasscyber.com
35 https://threatbutt.com/map/
36 https://www.spamhaus.com/threat-map/

37 https://www.sophos.com/en-us/threat-center/threat-monitoring/threatdashboard.aspx
38 https://nmap.org
39 https://www.exploit-db.com/google-hacking-database
40 https://www.openvas.org
41 https://www.tenable.com/products/nessus
42 https://www.metasploit.com
43 https://www.shodan.io
44 https://tools.kali.org/information-gathering/nikto
45 https://www.cyr3con.ai
46 https://www.cyr3con.ai/pr1ority
47 https://zeek.org
48 https://splunkbase.splunk.com/app/1617/
49 https://blog.rapid7.com/2018/04/24/how-to-identify-attacker-reconnaissance-on-your-internal-network/
50 https://attivonetworks.com/solutions/recon-exploit/
51 https://www.paessler.com/it-explained/syslog
52 https://www.howtogeek.com/123646/htg-explains-what-the-windows-event-viewer-is-and-how-you-can-use-it/
53 https://wiki.en.it-processmaps.com/index.php/Checklist_Incident_Priority

REFERENCES

[1] L. Shi, X. Chen, S. Wen and Y. Xiang, "Main Enabling Technologies in Industry 4.0 and Cybersecurity Threats," In J. Vaidya, X. Zhang, and J. Li. (eds) *Cyberspace Safety and Security. CSS 2019. Lecture Notes in Computer Science*, vol: 11983, Cham.: Springer, 2019. https://doi.org/10.1007/978-3-03037352-8_53

[2] L. F. Sikos and K.-K. R. Choo, *Data Science in Cybersecurity and Cyberthreat Intelligence*. Switzerland: Springer, Cham, 2020. DOI: 10.1007/978-3-030-3 8788-4.

[3] L. F. Sikos, "Knowledge representation to support partially automated honeypot analysis based on wireshark packet capture files." in *Intelligent Decision Technologies*, I. Czarnowski, R. J. Howlett, and L. C. Jain, Eds. Singapore: Springer, pp. 345–351, 2019. DOI: 10.1007/978-981-13-8311-3_30.

[4] L. F. Sikos, M. Stumptner, W. Mayer, C. Howard, S. Voigt, and D. Philp, "Automated reasoning over provenance-aware communication network knowledge in support of cyber-situational awareness," in *Knowledge Science, Engineering and Management*, W. Liu, F. Giunchiglia, and B. Yang, Eds. Switzerland: Springer, Cham, pp. 132–143, 2018. DOI: 10.1007/978-3-319-99247-1_12.

[5] ACSC, "Guidelines for Cyber Security Incidents," *ACSC*, 4 November 2020. Accessed on: May 20, 2021. [Online]. Available: https://www.cyber.gov.au/acsc/view-all-content/advice/guidelines-cyber-security-incidents

[6] ISO/IEC, "ISO/IEC 27000:2018(en) Information Technology – Security Techniques – Information Security Management Systems – Overview and Vocabulary," *ISO*, 2018. Accessed on: May 20, 2021. [Online]. Available: https://www.iso.org/obp/ui/#iso:std:iso-iec:27000:ed-5:v1:en

[7] Cyberdegrees, "How to become an incident responder," *Cyberdegrees*, 29 April 2021. Accessed on: May 20, 2021. [Online]. Available: https://www. cyberdegrees.org/jobs/incident-responder/

[8] McAfee, "What Is a Security Operations Center (SOC)?," *Mcafee*. Accessed on: May 20, 2021. [Online]. Available: https://www.mcafee.com/enterprise/ en-us/security-awareness/operations/what-is-soc.html

[9] M. N., "Analysis of SIEM systems and Their usage in security operations and security intelligence centers," in *Biologically Inspired Cognitive Architectures (BICA) for Young Scientists. BICA 2017. Advances in Intelligent Systems and Computing*, A. Samsonovich and V. Klimov, Eds. Cham: Springer, 2018. 10.1 007/978-3-319-63940-6_40.

[10] D. Lewis, "Exploit vs vulnerability: what's the difference?," *Sectigostore*, 25 September 2020. Accessed on: May 20, 2021. [Online]. Available: https:// sectigostore.com/blog/exploit-vs-vulnerability-whats-the-difference/

[11] Enisa, "Vulnerabilities and exploits," *European Union Agency for Cybersecurity (ENISA)*. Accessed on: May 20, 2021. [Online]. Available: https://www.enisa. europa.eu/topics/csirts-in-europe/glossary/vulnerabilities-and-exploits

[12] Lockheed Martin, "The cyber kill chain," *Lockheed Martin Corporation*. Accessed on: May 20, 2021. [Online]. Available: https://www.lockheedmartin. com/en-us/capabilities/cyber/cyber-kill-chain.html

[13] Deloitte, "7 stages of cyber kill chain supplementary reading," 2017. Accessed on: May 20, 2021. [Online]. Available: https://www2.deloitte.com/ content/dam/Deloitte/sg/Documents/risk/sea-risk-cyber-101-july2017.pdf

[14] Logsign, "7 steps of cyber kill chain," *Logsign*, 16 October 2020. Accessed on: May 20, 2021. [Online]. Available: https://www.logsign.com/blog/7-steps-of-cyber-kill-chain/

[15] A. T. Tunggal, "What Is the cyber kill hain and how to use it effectively," *UpGuard, Inc.*, 2 August 2020. Accessed May 20, 2021. [Online]. Available: https://www.upguard.com/blog/cyber-kill-chain

[16] MITRE, "MITRE ATT&CK," *The MITRE Corporation*. Accessed on: May 20, 2021. [Online]. Available: https://attack.mitre.org

[17] Microsoft, "The STRIDE threat model," *Microsoft*, 11 December 2009. Accessed May 20, 2021. [Online]. Available: https://docs.microsoft.com/en-us/ previous-versions/commerce-server/ee823878(v=cs.20)?redirectedfrom=MSDN

[18] FutureLearn, "STRIDE – definition of the STRIDE model," *FutureLearn*, Accessed May 20, 2021. [Online]. Available: https://www.futurelearn.com/ info/courses/cyber-security/0/steps/19631

[19] C. Tannery, "Cyber attribution: essential component of incident response or optional extra," *Exabeam*, 20 July 2018. Accessed May 20, 2021. [Online]. Available: https://www.exabeam.com/incident-response/cyber-attribution-essential-component-of-incident-response-or-optional-extra/

[20] A. Jankovic, "Why the business impact analysis is challenging for an organization with constant changes," *Stratogrid*, 31 May 2020. Accessed May 20, 2021. [Online]. Available: https://www.stratogrid.com/why-the-business-impact-analysis-is-challenging-for-an-organization-with-constant-changes/

[21] L. F. Sikos, "Packet analysis for network forensics: a comprehensive survey," *Forensic Science International: Digital Investigation*, vol. 32, no. C, 2020. DOI: 10.1016/j.fsidi.2019.200892.

[22] MSG, "How to prepare the project risk assessment matrix?," *MSG*, Accessed May 21, 2021. [Online]. Available: https://www.managementstudyguide.com/project-risk-assessment-matrix.htm

[23] F. Wilson, "How to use the risk assessment matrix in project management?," *Ntask*, 11 February 2021. Accessed May 21, 2021. [Online]. Available: https://www.ntaskmanager.com/blog/risk-assessment-matrix/

[24] OAC, "Risk matrix setup," *OAC*, Accessed May 21, 2021. [Online]. Available: https://oac.chris21.com/OAC_ichrisp/Help/ichrisUG/607699.htm

[25] J. Peacock, "Risk register examples for cybersecurity leaders," *CyberSaint Security*, Accessed May 21, 2021. [Online]. Available: https://www.cybersaint.io/blog/risk-register-examples-for-cybersecurity

[26] Logsign, "What is CSIRT? What are CSIRT roles and responsibilities?," *Logsign*, 13 September 2019. Accessed May 21, 2021. [Online]. Available: https://www.logsign.com/blog/what-is-csirt-what-are-csirt-roles-and-responsibilities/

[27] ACSC, "Hacking," *ACSC*, 21 May 2020. Accessed May 21, 2021. [Online]. Available: https://www.cyber.gov.au/acsc/view-all-content/threats/hacking

[28] Greycampus, "Ethical hacking – phases of hacking," *Greycampus*, Accessed on: May 21, 2021. [Online]. Available: https://www.greycampus.com/opencampus/ethical-hacking/phases-of-hacking

[29] I. Upadhyay, "Reconnaissance in hacking: a comprehensive guide in 5 steps," *Jigsawacademy*, 21 October 2020. Accessed May 21, 2021. [Online]. Available: https://www.jigsawacademy.com/blogs/cyber-security/reconnaissance-in-hacking/

[30] Cyber.gov, "Detecting cyber security incidents," *ACSC*, Accessed May 21, 2021. [Online]. Available: https://www.cyber.gov.au/acsc/view-all-content/advice/guidelines-cyber-security-incidents

[31] A. Mujumdar, G. Masiwal, and B. B. Meshram, "Analysis of signature-based and behavior-based anti-malware approaches," *International Journal of Advanced Research in Computer Engineering and Technology (IJARCET)*, vol. 2, no. 6, pp. 2037–2039, 2013.

[32] Bricata, "Layers of cybersecurity: signature detection vs. network behavioral analysis," *Bricata*, Accessed May 25, 2021. [Online]. Available: https://bricata.com/blog/signature-detection-vs-network-behavior/

[33] Y. Fukushima, A. Sakai, Y. Hori and K. Sakurai, "A behavior based malware detection scheme for avoiding false positive," in *6th IEEE workshop on secure network protocols*. pp. 79–84, 2010.

[34] Cisecurity, "Cybersecurity spotlight – signature-based vs anomaly-based detection," *Center for Internet Security*, Accessed May 25, 2021. [Online]. Available: https://www.cisecurity.org/spotlight/cybersecurity-spotlight-signature-based-vs-anomaly-based-detection/

[35] Avinetworks, "Anomaly detection," *Avinetworks*, Accessed on:May 25, 2021. [Online]. Available: https://avinetworks.com/glossary/anomaly-detection/

[36] E. C. Thompson, "The incident response strategy," in *Cybersecurity Incident Response*, Berkeley, CA., 2018.

[37] RSISecurity, "Best practices for testing your cyber incident response plan," *RSI Security*, 8 February 2019. Accessed on: May 21, 2021. [Online]. Available: https://blog.rsisecurity.com/best-practices-for-testing-your-cyber-incident-response-plan/

[38] B. Scott, "Creating an incident response plan. technical library," 24 April 2020. Accessed on: May 21, 2021. [Online]. Available: https://scholarworks.gvsu.edu/cgi/viewcontent.cgi?article=1349&context=cistechlib

[39] J. Creasey, "Cyber security incident response guide," 11 2014. Accessed on: May 21, 2021. [Online]. Available: https://www.crest-approved.org/wp-content/uploads/2014/11/CSIR-Procurement-Guide.pdf

[40] Cipher, "The core phases of incident response & remediation," *Cipher*, Accessed on:May 21, 2021. [Online]. Available: https://cipher.com/blog/the-core-phases-of-incident-response-remediation/

[41] D. Ellis, "6 phases in the incident response plan," *Securitymetrics*, Accessed on: May 21, 2021. [Online]. Available: https://www.securitymetrics.com/blog/6-phases-incident-response-plan

[42] Hartmanadvisors, "The 6 phases of an incident response plan," *Hartmanadvisors*, 18 June 2020. Accessed on: May 21, 2021. [Online]. Available: https://hartmanadvisors.com/the-6-phases-of-an-incident-response-plan/

[43] Cynet, "Incident response SANS: the 6 steps in depth," *Cynet*, 22 November 2020. Accessed on: May 21, 2021. [Online]. Available: https://www.cynet.com/incident-response/incident-response-sans-the-6-steps-in-depth/

[44] Pagerduty, "Incident priority matrix," *Pagerduty*, Accessed on: May 21, 2021. [Online]. Available: https://www.pagerduty.com/resources/learn/incident-priority-matrix/

[45] IBM, "What is a disaster recovery (DR) plan?," *IBM*, Accessed on: May 21, 2021. Available: https://www.ibm.com/services/business-continuity/disaster-recovery-plan

[46] Urbanteach, "Disaster recovery plan," Accessed on: May 21, 2021. [Online]. Available: http://urbanteach.org/uploads/3/4/2/3/34238252/disaster_recovery_plan.pdf

[47] E. Dosal, "How to create an effective disaster recovery plan," *Compuquip Cybersecurity*, 1 April 2020. Accessed on: May 21, 2021. [Online]. Available: https://www.compuquip.com/blog/disaster-recovery-plan

[48] Cybersecuritycoalition, "Cyber security incident management guide," Accessed on: May 21, 2021. [Online]. Available: https://www.cybersecuritycoalition.be/content/uploads/cybersecurity-incident-management-guide-EN.pdf

[49] L. Voigt, "Incident response steps: 6 steps for responding to security incidents," *Exabeam*, 29 September 2018. Accessed on: May 21, 2021. [Online]. Available: https://www.exabeam.com/incident-response/steps/

[50] Atlassian, "Incident management – MTBF, MTTR, MTTA, and MTTF," *Atlassian*, Accessed on: May 21, 2021. [Online]. Available: https://www.atlassian.com/incident-management/kpis/common-metrics

Chapter 5

Cyber-Enabled Crime as an Enabler in Market Manipulation Schemes

Roberto Musotto[1] and Brian H. Nussbaum[2]

[1]Cyber Security Cooperative Research Centre, School of Business and Law, Edith Cowan University, Perth, Australia

[2]College of Emergency Preparedness, Homeland Security and Cybersecurity, University at Albany, Albany, NY

CONTENTS

5.1 INTRODUCTION

Malware, ransomware, and computer intrusion attacks are commonly linked with the idea of cybercrime. As such, cybercrime has not really been considered in market manipulation schemes and it will be suggested here that it has an essential role in these types of crimes. Many types of market manipulation are grounded on information asymmetries or theft. The way information is carried, interpreted, and executed into financial transactions is closely linked to the technology that is employed to spread and filter it. It is this close link that enables misinformation or disinformation to be an important driver of cyber harm. While misinformation and disinformation are both false information, disinformation is done with the intent of causing deception. Without this element of deception, market manipulation through information would not be so challenging or problematic; while misinformation may shape markets, disinformation can be used for profit or political gains. The analysis provided here offers evidence that cyber-enabled

DOI: 10.1201/9781003121541-5

crime enables and facilitates these schemes, which are different from classic forms of market manipulations and other computer crimes.

Market manipulations and disinformation are often treated as recent phenomena resulting from new information platforms, but this is not the case. In February 1814, a hoax letter claiming the death of Napoleon Bonaparte, by the hand of allied Cossacks, caused the London Stock Exchange to ramp up and then crash once truth was revealed [1]. This scheme is not much different in its essential elements from how it would operate today. Almost 100 years later, a hoax letter, carried by email, releasing sensitive and incorrect information caused extensive financial damage to the Australian mining company Whitehaven Coal Limited and anyone related to it. The difference between these two cases is its scale, which has been cyber enabled. Cybercrime is any misuse of information technology to commit crimes [2,3]. Therefore, the cyber element in the crime of market manipulation is a method by which such scheme is carried out.

In this chapter it is suggested that these schemes scale and spread out using the Internet, making them importantly different from traditional market manipulations. Because of this component, market manipulations facilitated through cybercrimes fit into the sub-category of cyber-enabled crimes. These are those cybercrimes that are escalated through the use of information technology in order to unfairly or illicitly take advantage of the vulnerabilities of targeted operators.

The harms that are produced by manipulative attacks on markets are of two types: they can be used to pursue personal profit, but they can also be used for political means [4]. Information can create or destroy wealth, because it is at the basis of any economic choice. Therefore, its malicious use carries the potential for nefarious consequences over the target and stakeholders involved – whether such impacts are financial losses, reputational damage, or other negative impacts.

The dangers posed by market manipulations, as it will be shown through the cases, are immediate effects in terms of stock price impact, and longer-term effects such as the loss of reputation and negative impacts on the brand for a company resulting from cyber-enabled market manipulation.

Three cases are studied here. The first retraces the legal case of Jonathan Moylan, and his attack on the mining company Whitehaven.[1] The second looks at FIN7's targeting of the EDGAR register; a case where the ultimate impacts are somewhat unclear. The third looks at the hijacking of a media companies Twitter account by the Syrian Electronic Army and the subsequent temporary crash of US equities markets.

While many other cases could have been chosen, the cases considered here are emblematic because of the scope of harm caused, actors involved, and techniques employed. It is important to understand what can be done or changed, not just to mitigate these corporate risks, but to distinguish this type of cybercrime from those that follow a different method, so that they can be prevented, where possible, and pursued better.

While complex and sophisticated cyber-attacks occur often, this analysis shows that market manipulation can be accomplished with less technical attacks. Yet, this is one of the most serious cyber risks facing most companies because of the victimization trail and cascading effects produced. It also impacts markets more broadly, beyond merely impacting victim companies. It is also unlikely to be prevented by spending on traditional IT security goods and services, as prevention from cyber-enabled crimes requires non-technological solutions, such as awareness, education [5], and capability spending.

There is therefore a need for the literature to consider whether there is an increased effect[2] when companies are the victims of a cyber-enabled attack as opposed to be the victim of a cybercrime *strictu sensu*. In the case of cyber-enabled crime, there are organizational level and, potentially, larger sector or market-level impacts which are translated in terms of reputation, losses, damages, and market competition.

The chapter is structured as follows: Section 5.2 discusses the literature, Section 5.3 presents the cases, then analyzes and compares them with other international ones, and Section 5.4 concludes.

5.2 LITERATURE REVIEW

Amongst the different methods of manipulating markets, spreading of false information is one of the most common ones. This can be intentional in terms of disinformation or unintentional in terms of misinformation. Once the information is out, the damage is often already done as the information and the damage can be hard to contain and, eventually, stop. [6]. One result is that reported disinformation sensitive to markets becomes conflated by the media or it is underreported by companies, because of its nature and reputational consequences. In the context of market manipulation, these crimes are usually categorized as white-collar crimes [7]. This is so because of the nature of the offender[3] and the stigma attached to the breach of trust committed by the employer or corporation.

One additional reason why these cases have been chosen is because of the extensive documentation available, which made these cases feasible to study. Unfortunately, there is not a broad set of well-documented cases of cyber-enabled market manipulation. While literature has already considered Moylan's case under the right to protest [8–10], right of free speech [11] or from an economic and environmental perspective ([12–15] and 2017; [16–18]), there are still relevant issues on the cyber-enabled criminal action and its victims. The other two cases have not been well analyzed in literature, but they have been widely reported by the media.

Concerning the relation between technology and harm, market manipulation via information technology is a practical application of Wood's [19] *stratigraphy of harm*. In distinguishing technology that is used or not for its intended purpose that is either a means to harm or induces harm, it provides a reading guide for how humans and actors relate to technology. A hoax email, for example, is an object that is neutral to its purpose, yet because of its purpose it creates a set of functions and needs once it comes into existence that exceed its intended use or value [20]. Applying Wood's stratigraphy to Moylan's case, harm is created by *instrumental technicity*: employing an email "for harmful ends not envisioned by the technology's designers" ([19], p.14). In such a design, the focus is on how harm is created, but it does not answer how harm expands on victims. This type of market manipulation can also be read under the light of affordance theories [21,22] where the criminal action is driven by *needs*, made only possible by technological features. While this theory is useful in explaining the deviant action, it stops at explaining repercussions on victims, as well as containing damages.

5.3 THREE MARKET MANIPULATION CASES

Three market manipulation cases have been selected to show how many different variants could exist of the same type of crime and each of them has cybercrime as an essential element to it. These cases describe the different market manipulations operated by Jonathan Moylan, FIN7, and the Syrian Electronic Army.

5.3.1 Jonathan Moylan: Market Manipulation as a Protest

This case concerns the voluntary spreading of false information with a deceitful online public relations campaign. Jonathan Moylan was an environmental campaigner [14] who wished to stop the Australian coal mining company Whitehaven from developing a new mine in Maules Creek, New South Wales. He conducted this campaign by purchasing an internet domain name similar to ANZ (Australia and New Zealand Banking Group) – i.e., typosquatting – and impersonating real employees of the bank in fake documents – i.e., spoofing. On the 7th of January 2013, he disseminated a fake media release announcing that the bank had withdrawn a loan that was meant to be used for the new mine project. He did this through an email sent to 306 recipients at 104 organizations including 295 receivers in 98 media organizations. Minutes after the message had been distributed, media republished the information.

In the 23 minutes that it took for Whitehaven to learn about the false media release and apply to prevent trading orders from being executed, 2,881,334 shares had been sold already which translated into an immediate loss of 8.7% of the total market capitalization of the company. In the first hours the market loss caused by this false statement wiped $314 million of Australian dollars, but in the end of the trading day it had been contained to

$450,360 (Australian dollars), which is still a significant loss which would have not happened had the false statement not been released [23].

Whitehaven tried to mitigate this damage by releasing a media statement confirming, jointly with ANZ bank, that the first media release made by Moylan was a hoax [24]. It was not shared by other media entities until the day after. The company stock kept losing value for the entire following week[4], likely because of the news coverage which had a negative indirect impact on the trade.

This short time lapse also created four types of shareholder victims:

1. Those who sold shares and re-bought them before the trading halt
2. Those who sold shares but were not able to buy them back because of the halt
3. Those who sold shares because of automatic selling contract clauses and they were not able to buy them back after the share
4. Those who bought shares at a higher price but did not make it in time to sell before the halt and saw their investments and profits reduce greatly.

The first category was the least affected as they were hit only by trading fees for selling and re-buying shares. The fourth category suffered more damages in terms of an immediate market loss, but then could face opportunities to recover in the longer term. The second and third categories were the ones that suffered most damages. They were not able to re-buy quickly, thus needing more time to recover. This also does not account for the possibility that this case, or another like it, would create opportunities for gaming markets by selling or selling short, based on prior knowledge of the "announcement." In any case, all these categories should have been able to get compensation, restoring the position investors had before the hoax.

The Moylan case is perhaps the most famous Australian and international market manipulation case that has been enabled by cybercrime. There are, however, others that had a similar end goal and have been carried through the exploitation of Information Technologies – the hacks from Fin7 and SEA.

5.3.2 Fin7: Organized Crime and Market Manipulation

The Fin7 case shows how market manipulation might be exploited by cyber-criminal organizations. FIN7 stole around a billion dollars worldwide and in the United States more than 15 million credit card numbers from over 3600 business locations [25].

In 2017, Fin7 launched a phishing campaign that targeted personnel involved with United States Securities and Exchange Commission (SEC) filings at various organizations (Miller, 2017). Fin7 began targeting numerous organizations, seeking out those in the organizations who were responsible for filing exactly the sort of information that had been previously stolen from the SEC's EDGAR database [26]. In fact, Fin7 even spoofed the email addresses they used to send the phishing emails to appear to be from "EDGAR <filings@sec.gov>" [27,28]. However, the intention of the groups appears to be to steal market-sensitive information that could be monetized, though the details of that usage remain unclear.

Neyret [29] describes several cases in which Fin7 attempted to spoof market regulators to phish companies. There is no complete agreement on why this targeting is occurring, but it is possible that this could have been an attempt to collect intelligence on the market [25] for use in trading on non-public information, or otherwise exploiting information asymmetries for profit.

Stealing information that shapes markets and the value of securities is a cyber-criminal problem and is a very important element that tells how deception is achieved. This is so, because there is:

1. The intention of exploiting IT in order to gain information
   a. Stored or
   b. Transferred through these means

2. The intention of obtaining a gain that can be:
   a. Financial or
   b. Strategic

There are two instances in this example of a growing challenge:

1. There is a growing relationship between hackers and financial criminals, based on the monetization of data [30]
2. The diversification of cyber exploits for offenders. If one operation is not successful, data can be exploited for other types of schemes.

The ability of cyber criminals to team up with financial criminals gives them a means to leverage non-public data and represents a new avenue for cybercriminals to monetize network access. It also allows cybercriminals diversify their risk and income, which seems to be the case the case with the Fin7 EDGAR phishing campaign. Their *modus operandi* used aggressive social engineering "prowess" in calling victims prior to lodging digital complaints laden with malicious documents [31,32], and then calling again after the phishing documents had been sent, in order to check if they were received – a blunt but effective technique.

These potential attempts at accessing material information from SEC filings are the work of a sophisticated cyber-criminal organization and the techniques used were very different to the Moylan case. While the end-result is similar (influencing maliciously the stock market, or the prices of specific securities in the market), the purpose is quite different (personal gain for Fin7 and protest against a particular firm for Moylan).

5.3.3 The Syrian Electronic Army (SEA)

The Assad regime-supported (or at least allied) Syrian Electronic Army (SEA) has been widely involved in website defacements and social media hijackings in an effort to spread information in support of Assad's regime [33]. This latter technique demonstrated an important way in which cyber-enabled criminal activity, even of the simplest variety, can have major implications for markets.

On April 23, 2013 the SEA used a phishing email to hijack credentials enabling them to access the Associated Press's Twitter feed. A 1:07pm, they tweeted "Breaking: Two Explosions in the White House and Barack Obama is injured" [34]. One minute later, the market reacted – at 1:08pm, the Dow Jones Industrial Average began a two-minute decline where it "dropped about 150 points, from 14,697.15 to 14,548.58" [34]. Three minutes later, the news of the erroneous story had spread, and the Dow recovered [34]. This temporary ~1% drop in the market reflected the equivalent of a 136 billion dollars (US) evaporation of market value [33]. SEA actions demonstrate the combined impact of minor and unsophisticated cybercrime and algorithmic trading in securities that create serious market vulnerability.

The SEA had intended to sow panic with the tweets, but the 136 billion dollar impact of the market reaction was a much greater response than could reasonably have been hoped for from the tweet. It is possible this was part of a broader attempt to manipulate the information space, that just happened to have major market impacts; but regardless, it serves as a case study for other threat actors interested in manipulating markets and algorithmic trading. As with the Moylan case, online disinformation involving illicit means caused large unintended effects on the financial market, but purpose and execution were different.

5.3.4 Discussion: The Structure of a Market Manipulation Enabled by Cybercrime

In market manipulations the criminal conduct and its consequences could be broken down in multiple parts:

1. Creation of deception: release of the false statement or action based upon restricted information
2. Loss of control over it
3. Spreading of the information
4. Adjustment effect to the market
5. Spreading of externalities
6. Difficulty in re-addressing the wrong done

The cybercrime element in market manipulations can take different forms. Looking at Moylan's case the cybercrime element relates to the first three parts, because of the misuse of information technologies. The cybercrime element in FIN7 case rests in the way deception is created, which is the assumption that everyone trades in the stock market with a similar amount of information available. The SEA's case is cyber-enabled in respect of the externalities caused by the fake statement.

The release of a false statement using information technologies allow the offender to have a bigger reach, scope, and offers a first patina of inherent credibility to the statement. This is so because, at a first glance, the statement comes from a reputable source (even if it was impersonated or spoofed) and recipients are to believe its authenticity because of all the details (the email, the official wording) that make it look credible [6]. The fact that there is a very low, or almost zero, marginal cost of making copies of digital artefacts, and the ability to automate such an already low-cost activity, enables a single individual to wage enormous spam or phishing campaigns in a way that physical artefacts would never allow.

The collection of email addresses and sending of the same message over to all the recipients maximizes the reach and the offense compared to the effort required to write the fictious email. This level of deception would have not been possible if Moylan would have written a physical letter for each recipient or if FIN7 had to get a physical document out for each company it was tracking. Letters might have taken different times to arrive to each recipient, news of the hoax could have spread before the physical letter would have reached contacts. Different levels of security in each company would have raised an alarm of stolen documents. So, information technologies helped the offenders with the ease of exploitation of deceit coupled with a lower lack of sophistication required.

The release of the false statement over the internet facilitates the second part of the criminal action: the loss of control over it. Once the news starts circulating around, the creator can do little to contain it, limit its interpretation or refute its content or part of it. What is more, when it has passed the minimum standard for being considered credible[5], stakeholders may rely on this information to make their decisions, which will have an impact on the company.

Because in the Moylan case he was impersonating one of the company's real employees, the information was believed to be credible. Because the SEA composed tweets came from the Associated Press account, they were viewed as reputable. Once released, it is not possible to control the final target (i.e., the corporations or government) and it had an impact on investors or other companies [35] too. The use of the internet facilitated the loss of control. In a traditional offline white-collar crime scenario, writing a letter or a media submission might have retained control over it.

The real-time spreading of information is also facilitated by the internet and in the cases analyzed above, its dissemination can be examined under an epidemic model [36]. Once the news is released it reaches some recipients. These are the people that are susceptible to spread the false news around. Not all of them circulate it, but those who do, manage to reach other people that might re-circulate it or not and so on. In the Moylan case, from the moment the false statement had been released (11:55 am) until trades were halted because of it (12:41 pm), 141 shareholders received the news and acted. This is a clear difference from an analog white-collar crime that would have not been enabled using the internet, which would have required a longer time than the 46 minutes in this case.

This is also a sign of the porosity of the trail of information in market manipulations, which required only a few minutes to inform each stakeholder decision. Had more time elapsed, it might well not have been possible to determine which trades and sales were tied to this information; in that sense, this case is an important micro-experiment in the impacts of company-level market manipulation.

In conclusion, in these cases of market manipulation there is an increased effect created using information technologies. This effect relates closely to the way the information has been released and the kinetic effect of deception caused by the loss of control over the hoax itself. Damages touch immediately the company, and its shareholders as well, with higher long-term market and pure economic losses for them than the company itself.

5.4 CONCLUSION

By looking and comparing at actor, motive, target, tactics employed in the cases above as pictured in Table 5.1, there are at least three important points to raise: (1) cyber-enabled market manipulations are often less technical than traditional cyber intrusions and malware infections; (2) there is a need to plan for cyber-enabled incidents because consequences on victims can differ from data breaches and network intrusions; and (3) market regulators need to be aware of the way such attacks unfold, and the inability of both the Internet and an algorithmically powered market to contain consequences to a single firm, country, or other target.

Traditional cybersecurity spending – hardware, software, and tools such as Computer Incident Response Teams (CIRTs) or Security Operations Centers (SOCs) – are helpful for many cybersecurity problems, but do not offer the same resolution of some problems which leverage less technical means or resources outside a company's network (from domain typo squatting, to social media hijacking, to networks of social media bots, and more). Particularly in cases in which a firm's information assets are not directly attacked or penetrated, or those assets are not actually the focus of the attack (like Moylan's attack on Whitehaven Coal) but where the scale of the Internet is leveraged to cause reputational damage, responses will more likely resemble a public relations crisis than a traditional cyber incident response.

Table 5.1 Actor, Motive, Target, Tactic, and Market Impact for the Cyber-enabled Market Manipulation Cases

	Actor	Motive	Target	Tactic	Impact
Moylan Case	Political Activist	Political (Ecological)	Whitehaven Coal Limited	False Press Release, Email Spoofing, Typosquatting	314 millions$ (AUD) in the short term, about ½ million subsequently
Fin7 Case	Cyber-Criminal Organ-ization	Criminal (Financial Gain)	Numerous Companies	Theft of Information that has potential to move markets	Stolen information leveraged from public data[6]
SEA Case	Nation-State Supported Hacktivist Network	Political (Nationalist)	Twitter Account of Media Firm	Social Media Account Hijack, Issuing of False News Story	Temporary 1% decline in US equities markets

Second, firms need to plan for typical and technical cyber incidents (i.e., ransomware, DDoS, SQL injections), but they also need a different and tailored approach for cyber-enabled incidents of other types, such as in the cyber-enabled market manipulations targeting them or their sector. Corporate cyber incident response planning is a quickly growing realm of cyber consulting and information security spending [37]; with a disproportionate amount of that effort focused on what has been the archetypical corporate cyber-attack – the data breach. Even those that do not focus mostly on data breaches tend to focus on events that occur within the networks of a company alone [38]. There is a need to create a targeted response for these kinds of cyber-enabled crimes too.

This is not only true at the organizational level, but at the market and market regulator level. This is the third point. Market regulators too need to be able to understand and respond to events that do not only affect single organizations, like in the case of the SEA Associated Press social media hijacking. These attacks leverage the way information can be released and its effects, and the ability to rapidly spread fear or drive market decisions at an epidemic rate to cause damage to the target, but also in ways that impact multiple stakeholders and the market itself.

This article argues that there is a need for deeper and more systematic study of the cyber element in traditional forms of market manipulation and related financial crimes, their impacts on the corporate risk environment, the information environment, and impacts on markets. Illustrated here, and important for further study, are the differing characteristics and response needs of such cyber-enabled crimes, when compared to traditional network intrusion attacks. Network intrusions and malware related attacks – which often result in data theft or data denial – are a serious problem and must be treated accordingly. However cyber-enabled financial and corporate attacks are only still just beginning to be understood.

ACKNOWLEDGMENTS

The work has been supported by the Cyber Security Research Centre Limited whose activities are partially funded by the Australian Government's Cooperative Research Centres Programme. The authors thank Lyria Bennett-Moses and Rebecca Marples for comments and suggestions.

NOTES

1 *R v Moylan* (2014). NSWSC 944.
2 Compared, for example, with other types of cybercrime attacks and traditional white-collar crime.

3 That comes from a higher socio-economic background and committed during an occupation.
4 On January 7, 2013 the title opened in the market at a price of 3.57 AUD per share. At opening on the 16th of January, the title was worth 3.36 AUD per share (au.finance.yahoo.com, 2020).
5 Which is lower in electronic communications (Greer, 2003).
6 Unknown up to which point it has been done.

REFERENCES

[1] R. Dale, *Napoleon is Dead: Lord Cochrane and the Great Stock Exchange Scandal*. Cheltenham: The History Press, 2007.
[2] J. S. Albanese, *Organized Crime: From the Mob to Transnational Organized Crime*. New York: Routledge, 2015.
[3] Au.finance.yahoo.com, "Whitehaven Coal Limited (WHC.AX) historical data". 2020. Accessed on: March 02, 2020. Available: https://au.finance.yahoo.com/quote/WHC.AX/history?period1=135\\7084800\&period2=1359590400\&interval=1d\&filter=history\&freq\\uency=1d
[4] M. Lewis, *Flash Boys: A Wall Street Revolt*. New York: WW Norton & Company, 2014.
[5] C. Cross and R. Gillett, "Exploiting trust for financial gain: an overview of business email compromise (BEC) fraud", *Journal of Financial Crime*, vol. 27, no. 3, 2020.
[6] M. Haigh, T. Haigh, and N. I. Kozak, "Stopping fake news: the work practices of peer-to-peer counter propaganda", *Journalism Studies*, vol. 19, no. 14, pp. 2062–2087, 2018.
[7] E. H. Sutherland, *White collar crime: The uncut version*. New Haven, CT: Yale University Press, 1985.
[8] M. Mullins, "Coal mining, civil disobedience and the public good", *Eureka Street*, vol. 23, no. 1, pp. 46–47, 2013.
[9] T. Ormerod, "The truth about jonathan moylan", *Eureka Street*, vol. 24, no. 14, pp. 20, 2014.
[10] R. V. Moylan, "NSWSC 944", 2014.
[11] E. Spence, "Whitehaven Hoax was an unethical act that was harmful to all". *The Conversaiton*, 2013 January 11. Available: https://theconversation.com/whitehaven-hoax-was-an-unethical-act-that-was-harmful-to-all-11571
[12] S. Davidson, "Environmental protest: an economics of regulation approach". *Australian Environment Review*, vol. 29, no. 10, pp. 283–286, 2014a.
[13] S. Davidson, "Environmentalists have a right to protest – but not at all costs", *The Conversation*, 2014b July 24. Available: https://theconversation.com/environmentalists-have-a-right-to-protest-but-not-at-all-costs-28322
[14] M. Rimmer, "Coal in court: Whitehaven, climate change and civil disobedience". *The Conversation*, 2013.
[15] S. L. Schwarcz, "Compensating market value losses: rethinking the theory of damages in a market economy". *Fla. L. Rev.*, vol. 63, pp. 1053, 2011.
[16] M. Adams, "Public Nuisance – or Fraud? Whitehaven Hoax Puts Market Creditability at Risk". *The Conversation*, 2013, January 10. Accessed:

3-02-2021. Available https://theconversation.com/public-nuisance-or-fraud-whitehaven-hoax-puts-market-creditability-at-risk-11544.

[17] C. Hamilton, "ASIC and the great coal hoax". *The Conversation*, 2013 January 18.

[18] G. Lewis, "Australia's regulatory panopticon", *AQ – Australian Quarterly*, vol. 84, no. 4, pp. 26–31, 2013.

[19] M. A. Wood, "Rethinking how technologies harm", *The British Journal of Criminology*, 2020.

[20] L. Floridi, "Infraethics–on the conditions of possibility of morality", *Philosophy & Technology*, vol. 30, pp. 391–394, 2017.

[21] S. Deterding, "Situated motivational affordances of game elements: a conceptual model". In *Gamification: Using game design elements in non-gaming contexts, a workshop at CHI*, vol. 10, no. 1979742.1979575, 2011.

[22] A. Goldsmith and D. S. Wall, "The seductions of cybercrime: adolescence and the thrills of digital transgression", *European Journal of Criminology*, 1477370819887305, 2019.

[23] P. Manning, "Don't believe the type over the cost of Whitehaven Hoax", *The Sydney Morning Herald*. 2016. Accessed on: March 02, 2020. Available: https://www.smh.com.au/business/dont-believe-the-hype-over-the-cost-of-whitehaven-hoax-20130115-2crh1.html.

[24] Whitehaven Coal Limited, "Whitehaven comment re hoax media release", *ASX*, 2013. Accessed on: March 02, 2020. Available: https://www.asx.com.au/asxpdf/20130107/pdf/42c9qnsztss8qm.pdf.

[25] B. Barrett, "The Wild Inner Workings of a Billion-Dollar Hacking Group", *Wired*, 2018. Accessed on: March 02, 2020. Available: https://www.wired.com/story/fin7-wild-inner-workings-billion-dollar-hacking-group/.

[26] P. Haskell-Dowland, R. Musotto, B. O'Shea, "Holding the world to ransom: the top 5 most dangerous criminal organisations online right now", *The Conversation*, 2021 July 7.

[27] S. Miller, J. Nuce, B. Vengerik, "FIN7 spear phishing campaign targets personnel involved in SEC filings", *FireEye Threat Research*, 2017. Accessed: 03-02-2020. Available: https://www.fireeye.com/blog/threat-research/2017/03/fin7_spear_phishing.html.

[28] S. Mohurle and M. Patil, "A brief study of wannacry threat: ransomware attack 2017". *International Journal of Advanced Research in Computer Science*, vol. 8, no. 5, 2017.

[29] A. Neyret, "Stockmarket cybercrime", *Autorite de Marches Financiers*. 2020. Available: https://www.amf-france.org/sites/default/files/2020-02/study-stock-market-cybercrime-_-definition-cases-and-perspectives.pdf.

[30] K. Westin, "Black Hats \& White Collars: SEC EDGAR Database Hackers Revealed". *Splunk*, 2019. Accessed on: March 02, 2020. Available: https://www.splunk.com/en_us/blog/security/black-hats-white-collars-sec-edgar-database-hackers-revealed.html.

[31] N. Carr, K. Goody, S. Miller, B. Vengerik, "On the hunt for FIN7: Pursuing an enigmatic and evasive global criminal operation", *FireEye Threat Research*. 2018. Accessed: 03-02-2020. Available: https://www.fireeye.com/

blog/threat-research/2018/08/fin7-pursuing-an-enigmatic-and-evasive-global-criminal-operation.html.

[32] A. Coyne, "AFP, ASIC uncover alleged hacker's plot to boost stock prices", *ITNews*, 2015 August 5. Available: https://www.itnews.com.au/news/afp-asic-uncover-alleged-hackers-plot-to-boost-stock-prices-407481.

[33] J. P. Carlin and G. M. Graff, *Dawn of the Code War: America's Battle Against Russia, China, and the Rising Global Cyber Threat*. Hachette UK: Hachette, 2018.

[34] M. Fischer, "Syrian hackers claim AP hack that tipped stock market by \$136 billion", *Is it terrorism? The Washington Post*, 2013 April 24. Accessed on: March 02, 2020. Available: https://www.washingtonpost.com/news/worldviews/wp/2013/04/23/\syrian-hackers-claim-ap-hack-that-tipped-stock-market-by-136-billion-is-it-terrorism/.

[35] S. Lannin, "Investors told to verify info after fake press release hits Whitehaven". 2013. Accessed on: March 02, 2020. Available: http://www.abc.net.au/am/content/2013/s3665639.htm.

[36] S. Abdullah and X. Wu, "An epidemic model for news spreading on twitter". In *2011 IEEE 23rd International Conference on Tools With Artificial Intelligence*, IEEE, 2011, November, pp. 163–169.

[37] N. K. McCarthy, M. Todd, and J. Klaben, *The Computer Incident Response Planning Handbook: Executable Plans for Protecting Information at Risk*. New York: McGraw-Hill Education Group, 2012.

[38] Kroll, "It's not if but when: how to build your cyber incident response plan". 2016. Available: https://www.sans.org/cyber-security-summit/archives/file/summit-archive-1506371074.pdf.

Chapter 6

Data Lakes: A Panacea for Big Data Problems, Cyber Safety Issues, and Enterprise Security

A. N. M. Bazlur Rashid[1], Mohiuddin Ahmed[1], and Abu Barkat Ullah[2]

[1]School of Science, Edith Cowan University, Australia
[2]School of Information Technology & Systems, University of Canberra, Australia

CONTENTS

DOI: 10.1201/9781003121541-6

6.1 INTRODUCTION

The fabric of our society is built through machines and the Internet. A growing number of users, devices, and applications work together to generate massive data through advanced tools and technologies, such as the *Internet of Things (IoT)* and sensors. The massive amount of data is termed as *Big Data* in the literature and has been characterized by several Vs. However, the most common 3Vs are *volume, variety*, and *velocity*. Volume indicates the amount of data generation; variety represents the different types of data, such as structured, unstructured, and semi-structured; velocity stands for data generation speed [1–4]. Data is important in every aspect of our day-to-day life. The enterprise data is widely used for better decision-making and efficient operation management. The enterprise data needs to analyze frequently for identifying useful information of business needs. The majority of the enterprise data generated is unstructured, such as wearable sensor-based data generation [5]. Figure 6.2 displays the volume of data/information captured, created, copied, and consumed worldwide from 2010 to 2024, in zettabytes (Z.B.)[1] computed by Statista.[2] It can be observed that the data volume has been increased by 2850% from over the years between 2010 and 2020, which is predicted to further increase by 152.54% by 2024 (Figure 6.1).

According to Aparavi's[3] statistics, the worldwide data is expected to hit 175 ZB in 2025. Aparavi also predicts that, in 2025, data from IoT devices alone will be 90 Z.B.[4] According to the projection of I.D.C.,[5] in 2025, 80% of data will be unstructured.[6] With the increasing volume of Big Data from different domains on *information security (I.S.)* events, users, threats, and

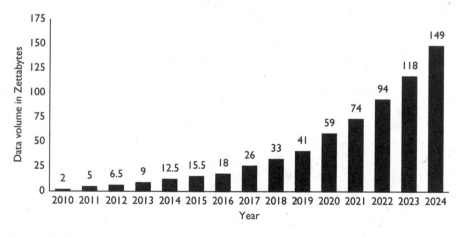

Figure 6.1 Volume of data increased year by year from 2010 to 2024.

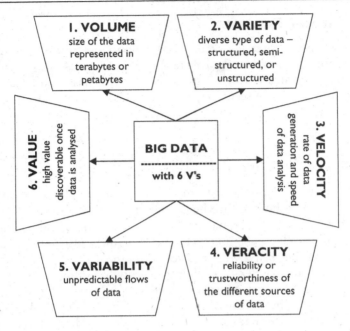

Figure 6.2 Big data with 6Vs.

related information, heterogeneity of the data need to store in its "raw" format for analyzing and monitoring systematic information. However, the challenge of safely capturing and storing data is becoming more complicated with time [6].

Service providers typically use the traditional approaches, such as a data warehouse to store data that is a single repository used to analyze data, consolidate information, and create reports. However, data transferring into a warehouse requires preprocessing. With zettabytes of data in cyberspace, this is not an easy task. Preprocessing requires a substantial amount of computing by high-end supercomputers, which costs time and money. *Data lakes* were proposed to solve this issue. Unlike data warehouses, data lakes store any type of raw data. Both data warehouses and data lakes can be considered as methods of storing and processing Big Data. However, data lakes are often considered a panacea for Big Data problems. The main challenges of Big Data that can be solved by data lake are storing and processing, analyzing heterogeneous data sources; either structured, semi-structured, and unstructured. Also, data privacy can be considered with data lake models to ensure the data security and privacy part. Therefore, data lakes are often considered as a panacea for Big Data problems. Accordingly, many organizations embrace data lakes for attempting to drive innovation and new services for users. To address all these issues, Big Data, data warehouse, data lakes, related cyber safety issues, and enterprise security are discussed in this chapter.

6.1.1 Chapter Roadmap

The rest of the chapter is organized as follows. Section 6.2 presents Big Data. Section 6.3 discusses data warehouses. Section 6.4 covers data lakes. Section 6.5 indicates the cyber safety issues with data lakes. Section 6.6 describes the enterprise security concerns related to data lakes. Section 6.7 concludes the chapter.

6.2 BIG DATA

Big Data refers to datasets that are so large and complex that traditional data processing techniques are inadequate to capture, store, manage, and process them within a reasonable time [7]. The devices and technological settings that produce the Big Data include the sensor networks, IoT, healthcare, cybersecurity, web services, social media, and many other domains. Big Data can refer to explain the growth and availability of data, both structured and unstructured. In 2001, Doug Laney, an industry analyst (currently with Gartner), introduced 3Vs: *Volume*, *Variety*, and *Velocity*, to define the characteristics of Big Data [8]. The 3Vs have emerged as a common framework to describe Big Data [9,10]. For example, Gartner defines Big Data as follows:

> "Big data is high-volume, high-velocity, and/or high-variety information assets that demand cost-effective, innovative forms of information processing that enable enhanced insight, decision making, and process automation" [11].

Similarly, the TechAmerica[7] Foundation defines Big Data as follows:

> "Big data is a term that describes large volumes of high velocity, complex and variable data that require advanced techniques and technologies to enable the capture, storage, distribution, management, and analysis of the information" [12].

Following the above Big Data definitions, the 3Vs can be described as follows [9]:

Volume refers to the size of the data that can be represented in terms of multiple terabytes or petabytes. The volume of Big Data is relative and varies by factors, for instance, time or the type of data. With the increase in storage size allowing bigger datasets to capture, the volume of Big Data will increase in the future. According to recent data generation estimation by IBM, the volume of new data has nearly doubled every two years. IBM also reported that 90% of the world's data was created in the previous two years, with more than 2.5 quintillion bytes of data produced daily [13].

Variety refers to the diverse type of data – structured, semi-structured, or unstructured. Structured data constitutes of about 5% of all existing data, and refers to the tabular data in relational databases or spreadsheets. In contrast, unstructured data usually lacks the structure organization required for analysis purposes. Audio, video, text, and images are examples of unstructured data. Semi-structured data lies in between the structured and unstructured data, and does not follow any strict standards. A typical example of semi-structured data is the *Extensible Markup Language* (XML), which is a textual language for exchanging data on the Web containing machine-readable user-defined data tags. According to IBM, 80% of data is unstructured [13].

Velocity refers to the rate of data generation and the speed of data analysis. The advancements in digital devices, for example, smartphones and sensors, are creating data at an unprecedented rate, which increasingly requires real-time analytics and evidence-based planning. According to IBM, 204,000,000 emails are sent, 216,000 Instagram posts are made, and 72 hours of footage is uploaded on YouTube every 60 seconds, which clearly indicates the speed of data generation and requires advanced data analytics [13].

In addition to the above 3 Vs, there are more Vs introduced in the literature to characterize Big Data. These additional Vs, introduced by IBM [13], SAS [14], and Oracle [15], are Veracity, Variability, and Value, respectively. IBM introduced the fourth V, veracity, which indicates the reliability or trustworthiness of the different sources of data. For example, customer behaviors in social media that are uncertain in nature contain valuable information. According to IBM, one in every three business leaders does not trust the information they use to make a decision [13]. SAS introduced another V, called variability, indicating that the data flows are unpredictable, change often, and vary greatly [14]. Oracle introduced the sixth V, called value, which means that data has a low value relative to its volume when it was collected in the original form. However, a high value can be discovered by analyzing the large volume of data [15].

In summary, the six Vs mentioned above of Big Data are displayed in Figure 6.2. Although Big Data analytics provides opportunities to the research communities to discover new insights, there are several cybersecurity challenges with Big Data, such as handling data packages, false data injection, and data poisoning problems. Furthermore, Big Data storing and processing challenges increase with the increasing heterogeneity and large-scale data size, which also increases privacy and security challenges. Hence, these challenges must be addressed for Big Data storing and processing to ensure data privacy and cyber safety issues.

6.3 DATA WAREHOUSE

Data warehouses are business intelligence tools and technologies and are designed to analyze large datasets. Data warehouses have been successfully used in various application domains, such as healthcare, retail, and marketing. In general, two types of operations are involved with data processing: (1) transactional and (2) analytical. Daily operations, for example, online transactional processing (OLTP), is managed through create, replicate, update, and delete operations on data on a daily basis. These data types are usually structured and stored in a SQL database, for instance, Oracle Database[8]. In the context of Big Data, structured data are processed and stored, and other types of data, including unstructured and semi-structured data, are processed and stored in NoSQL databases, such as MongoDB[9]. Big Data is also selected, cleaned, integrated, summarized, and transformed based on the structure of the data warehouse schema definition for the analytical purpose. Data warehouses are the currently dominant approach of providing analytical data, and they store only transformed data [16].

According to the multidimensional model, data warehouses are designed that defines the analytical axes or dimensions and subjects or facts. Hence, there are two types of tables that form the basis of a data warehouse – dimension tables and fact tables. The fact tables answer the W questions – who, what, when, and where. On the other hand, the dimension tables are supplemented from the databases based on the fields. In a data warehouse, data are extracted (E), transformed (T), and loaded (L), i.e., it follows ETL operations. Enterprise data from various operational databases are collected into a single data warehouse storage to execute ad-hoc queries, which can help retrieve business intelligence conveniently. Transactional data remain in operational databases to provide online transaction processing (OLTP), such as daily business transactions. On the other hand, online analytical processing (OLAP) operations, such as data analysis, reviewing historical data, and analytical systems, perform data correlations. All the complex ad-hoc queries run in the data warehouse, which is built for analytical purposes. Data can be loaded in batch to the data warehouse. Data analytics can be performed on the stored data in the warehouse for better decision-making of the enterprise and for obtaining valuable insights [16].

An alternative to the data warehouse is DataMart that is smaller in size compared to the data warehouse. While data warehouses are large in size and take more time to create, DataMarts take less time to create. Data warehouses store data of an entire enterprise, whereas DataMarts store a part of the organization's data. DataMarts can be built individually, or part of the data warehouse can be extracted to create a DataMart that belongs to a specific department of an organization. Data warehouses can be subject-oriented, integrated, time-variant, and non-volatile. A subject-oriented data warehouse represents real-time objects. An integrated data warehouse consolidates data from different databases for displaying a unified view. In a time-variant data warehouse, data are loaded based on the time interval and stored with appropriate timestamps for later analysis and comparison. In a non-volatile data warehouse, data are collected and loaded into the data warehouse at a point of time for analysis rather than collecting current transition data. Data warehouses provide better performance results with bitmap indexing and materialized views. Data warehouse operations, such as aggregate and join operations, require intensive query load that is computationally expensive. Data warehouses are primarily built to answer complex ad-hoc queries, including historical data, which transactional processing databases cannot handle. Accordingly, to serve the purpose of these complex ad-hoc queries for better business decisions, data warehouses are built as s single consolidated architecture that includes highly summarized data via ETL from transactional databases.

Figure 6.3 shows a subject-oriented, integrated, and non-volatile conventional data warehouse architecture that supports time-variant data for decision-makers. In general, a primary data warehouse contains DataMarts, which are small data warehouses containing a subset of data collected from a central data warehouse. The DataMarts' contents are the information related to a specific domain. A number of data warehouse servers manage and store data. Various front-end tools, such as data mining and query reporting, are used to present multidimensional views of data [17]. Traditional data warehouses have some limitations – they support only structured data and do not support unstructured or semi-structured data.

Similarly, they are not scalable in terms of data volumes. For example, the data warehouse can handle only terabytes of data, while petabyte size is now standard for many applications. Furthermore, performing analytical queries affects the whole query performance, data access, and processing. The decision-making process can also be affected because of the not availability of correct data at a time [18]. Hence, considering the Big Data scenario and for better business decision-making, the data lake concept emerges.

6.4 DATA LAKES

In 2010, James Dixon introduced the data lake concept as a solution to overcome the shortcomings of DataMart, which are the data warehouse's business-specific subdivisions to answer the only subset of questions. In literature, data lake has also been named as data hubs or data reservoirs. The data lake introduced by Dixon is an extensive storage system to store raw and heterogenous data fetched from multiple data sources. It also allows users to discover, extract, and analyze the data [19]. James Dixon, a US data technician who reputedly coined the term, describes data lakes thus:

> If you think of a DataMart as a store of bottled water – cleansed and packaged and structured for easy consumption – the data lake is a large body of water in a more natural state. The contents of the data lake stream from a source to fill the lake, and various lake users can come to examine, dive in, or take samples.

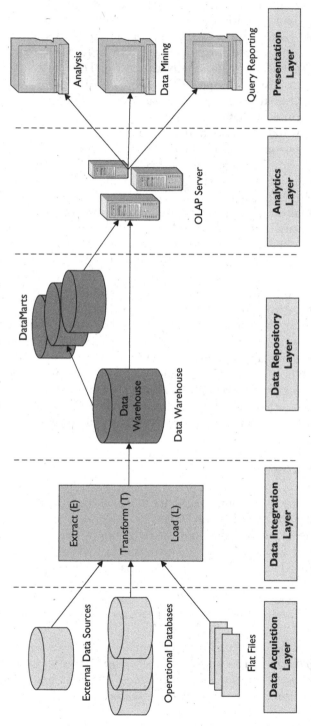

Figure 6.3 A conventional data warehouse architecture [17].

Data lakes can be viewed as central repositories where all data formats are stored with no schema binding. Hence, data lakes have two characteristics: 1) data variety and 2) schema-on-read approach. Data variety stands for different data types, and schema-on-read indicates the schema and data requirements need to be fixed only when data querying – a concept opposite to the data warehouse's schema-on-write approach [20]. Data lakes can combine *structured query language (SQL), not only SQL (NoSQL), online transaction processing (OLTP), and online analytical processing (OLAP)* capabilities. In 2016, Madera and Laurent introduced another definition of a data lake as a logical view of all data sources and datasets in their raw format, accessible by the statistician or data scientist community for knowledge discovery [21]. Madera and Laurent's definition of data lake restricts the use of the data lake to a data scientist or statistician only. Next, they only considered the data lake as the logical view over data sources, while a few data sources can be external to the organization and the data lake. Furthermore, they did not consider the scalability issues of the data lake, which is primarily intended for Big Data storage and processing. To overcome these issues, in 2020, Sawadogo and Darmont defined data lake as follow [20]:

> *A data lake is a scalable storage and analysis system for data of any type, retained in their native format and used mainly by data specialists (statisticians, data scientists or analysts) for knowledge extraction.*

The data lakes are typically built for handling large and rapid arrival unstructured data volumes, which is unlikely to a data warehouse containing mainly structured data. Hence, the dynamic analytical applications can be used in data lakes for finding insights in contrast to the data warehouse using prebuild static applications. Similarly, data in the lake are accessible soon after it is created, unlike the slowly changing data storage in the data warehouse [22]. Data lakes provide highly valuable business insights, real-time analytics, and optimized business intelligence. A comparison between data warehouse and data lake is illustrated in Table 6.1 [16,23,24].

6.4.1 The Concept of a Data Lake

In 2015, Walker and Alrehamy explicitly defined the data lake architecture as [25]:

> *A data lake uses a flat architecture to store data in its raw format. Each data entity in the lake is associated with a uniquely identified and set of extended metadata. Consumers can use purpose-built schemas to query relevant data, which will result in a smaller set of data that can be analyzed to help answer a consumer's question.*

Table 6.1 A Comparison between Data Warehouse and Data Lake

Characteristics	Data Warehouse	Data Lake
Data	Relational, i.e., structured, processed data from operational databases and business applications	Non-relational and relational, i.e., structured, unstructured, semi-structured, raw, unprocessed data from IoT devices, corporate applications, websites, social media, and mobile apps
Storage	Expensive, reliable storage	Low-cost storage
Performance	Faster query results	Query results getting faster
Schema	Schema-on-write (predefined schemas)	Schema-on-read (no predefined schemas)
Data Quality	Highly curated data	Curated or raw data
Data Processing	Time-consuming to new data content	Fast new data ingestion
Agility	Less agile, fixed-configuration	High agility, flexible configuration
Replacement of E.D.W.	Complementary to E.D.W. (no replacement)	Can be source for E.D.W.
Security	Allows better control of the data	Offers lesser control
Data Granularity	Summarized or aggregated level detail	Low-level granularity or detail
Users	Business professionals and analysts	Data scientists, data developers, and business analysts
Analytics	Batch reporting, business intelligence, and visualizations	Machine learning, predictive analysis, data discovery, and profiling
Tools	Mostly commercial tools	Open-source tools, such as Hadoop/MapReduce

Several data lake implementations are primarily based on *Apache Highly Available Object-Oriented Data Platform (Hadoop)*. Different types of data from heterogeneous data sources are collected and stored in the Hadoop Cluster. All data generated by an enterprise are usually dumped into the data lake Hadoop cluster [16]. Hadoop is a widely used and popular Big Data processing tool and supports batch processing. Hadoop consists of two components – *Hadoop Distribution File System (HDFS)* and *MapReduce* engine. HDFS is basically a Java-based distributed file system. It offers faster access to Big Data storage and computing processes, which are fault-tolerant, scalable, and reliable. The input data is divided into HDFS blocks. HDFS blocks can be processed in parallel with no data blocks interaction. There are two main functions of MapReduce: *map* and *reduce*. The map and reduce features are merged in a divide-and-conquer strategy. Here, the map function performs on the data blocks in parallel. On the other hand, the reduce function collects and joins the intermediate result into a final output. (key, value) pairs drive the data flow of the MapReduce model. Indeed, the initial input is split by a master node into several blocks that are identified as (key, value) pairs. The map function distributes the (key, value) pairs into several slave nodes for working in parallel. The same tasks are executed individually on a distinct input block. The map function produces an intermediate list of (key, value) pairs that are shuffled by a shuffling mechanism. The MapReduce library operates on the same key to group the pairs and transfer them to the reduce function. Finally, the pairs are aggregated by the reduce function and generate new (key, value) pairs as output [26,27].

Nowadays, stream processing frameworks, such as Apache Spark or Apache Flink, are used for real-time data load. The data required for analytics systems are transformed on the fly during query time. Data lake may also include semantic databases, a conceptual model, and a layer of context for defining the relationship of data with other data. Data lake eventually can consist of all data types from SQL and NoSQL databases and combine OLTP with OLAP. Here, SQL databases store structured data, and NoSQL databases store semi-structured and unstructured data [6,16]. The merits and demerits of the associated tools and technologies (HDFS, MapReduce, Apache Spark, Apache Flink, SQL, NoSQL, OLTP, and OLAP) are listed in Table 6.2 [28–30].

6.4.2 The Architecture of Data Lakes

Initially, data lake architecture was proposed as a flat architecture with a mono-zone for storing all raw data in their native format. Every data element in a Data Lake is given a unique identifier and tagged with a set of metadata information. This architecture was similar to the Hadoop environment and allowed loading large volumes and heterogeneous data. However, data lake users were not able to process data and record users operations [31]. The next level data lake architecture is comprised of five data ponds – raw, analog, application, textual, and archival. The raw data pond stores the current ingested data and data not fitting in other ponds. The next three data ponds store classified data from raw data ponds according to their characteristics. Archival data ponds store data, which are no longer used. This data lake architecture supports classifying different data and storing useless data in archival ponds that can make faster data find and easier data analytics. However, storing data in various ponds, especially the archival pond, fails to make raw data available, contradicting the fundamental idea of data lake

Table 6.2 Merits and Demerits of HDFS, MapReduce, Apache Spark, Apache Flink, SQL, NoSQL, OLTP, and OLAP

Tools/ Technologies	Merits	Demerits
Hadoop	Extra storage and computing power through additional nodes to Hadoop cluster; Supports semi-structured and unstructured data; Offers distributed computing; Fault-tolerant and supports data replication; Scalable and reliable; Prevents network overloading.	Not suitable for real-time and small data applications; The complex joining of multiple data set operations; Does not support encryption at network or storage level; Cluster management is too hard; Scalability issue with operating by a single master; Restrictive programming model.
HDFS	Stores large data files on multiple machines; Offers very high aggregate bandwidth across the cluster; Streaming access to data; Portable across different hardware platforms; Compatible with various operating systems; It prevents filesystem corruption and loss of data.	Problems with storing a large number of small files; Data processing overhead because of no in-memory calculations; Single point of failure, scalability issues, and the bottleneck in massive metadata requests; Restricted programming model.
MapReduce	Fault-tolerant and provides redundancy; Supports parallel execution in distributed platforms; Both unstructured and structured data can be processed.	The computation cost vs Communication cost optimization required for a proper design of MapReduce; Restricted programming model; High latency; Batch processing not iterative.
Apache Spark	Faster than Hadoop; Easy-to-use APIs to operate on large datasets; Provides advanced analytics; Spark is dynamic in nature; Supports multilingual for coding; Spark is very powerful; Offers increased access to Big Data.	The optimization process is not automatic; It uses a file management system; Provides fewer algorithms; It has a problem with small files; Multi-user environment is not supported; It has limitations with window criteria.
Apache Flink	Unifies streaming and batch processing via low latency streaming engine; No out-of-memory exception throwing; Efficient at disk spilling and transfers over networks; Runtime tuning is not required; Reliable and provides stable performance; Built-in programmer optimizer.	Less community and forums support; Less open-source projects availability; Not matured yet; API support is complex for many domain languages; Challenging to write a program because of internal data representation as raw bytes.

(Continued)

TABLE 6.2 (*Continued*)

Tools/ Technologies	Merits	Demerits
OLTP	Integrates all analytics in a single platform; Database consistency using fully normalized schema; Protects sensitive data from unauthorized users and objects; Supports on-time transaction modifications; Supports large databases; Ensures database atomicity; Easy data manipulation;	Higher dependency on skilled I.T. professionals; High-level data security required to protect sensitive data; Not the fault-tolerant, causing risk of data loss; Concurrent data modifications by multiple users may lead to many issues; Supports limited queries and updates.
OLAP	Offers high-speed data processing; Data are aggregated and supports data detailing; Multidimensional representation of data; Easy-to-use by the non-technical users; Provides what-if data representation without data loss;	High cost of data storage and processing; Data structure need to define before data storage; Lack of computational facilities for business computing; Cannot provide sufficient information for business decision-making.
SQL	No formal coding is required; Well-defined standards used comparable to ISO and ANSI standards; SQL queries are portable; Supports database connection and answering queries via domain language; Offers different views of data and structure.	Complex user interface; Does not offer full control to the programmers; Operating costs of SQL versions cause difficulty to access by programmers; Many SQL features are vendor lock-in.
NoSQL	Non-relational or table-less; Low-cost or open-source dataset; Easily scalable; Outperforms SQL databases.	Relatively more minor support to the community; Lack of standardization, unlike to SQL standards; Issues with interfaces and interoperability;

storing all raw data and processing them upon request [31]. Figure 6.4 shows the data flow of the pond data lake architecture.

To overcome limitations of flat or ponds architecture, data lake architecture with multi-zones proposed in the literature. The Amazon Web Services (A.W.S.) data lake architecture consists of four zones – ingestion, storage, processing, and govern and secure. The ingestion zone loads the raw data, and the raw data are stored in the storage zone. The processing zone is used for data processing when required. The data security, data quality, metadata management, and data life cycle are controlled by the govern and secure zone [32]. Figure 6.5 displays the zone data lake architecture.

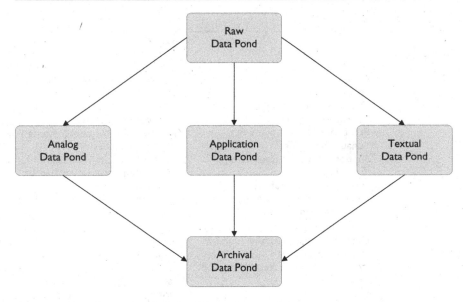

Figure 6.4 Data flow in a pond data lake architecture.

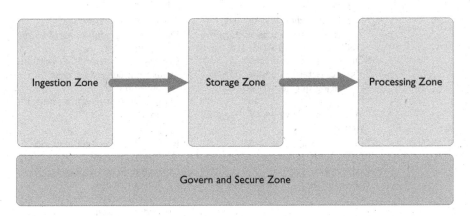

Figure 6.5 Data flow in a zone data lake architecture.

Another data lake architecture divided the data processing into real-time processing zone and batch-processing zone. This architecture also proposed a processed data zone for storing all cleansed data [33]s. Likewise, the above data lake architectures, several other data lake architectures are proposed in the literature and still an emerging area of research for a standard data lake architecture. A conceptual data lake architecture can be viewed as illustrated in Figure 6.6.

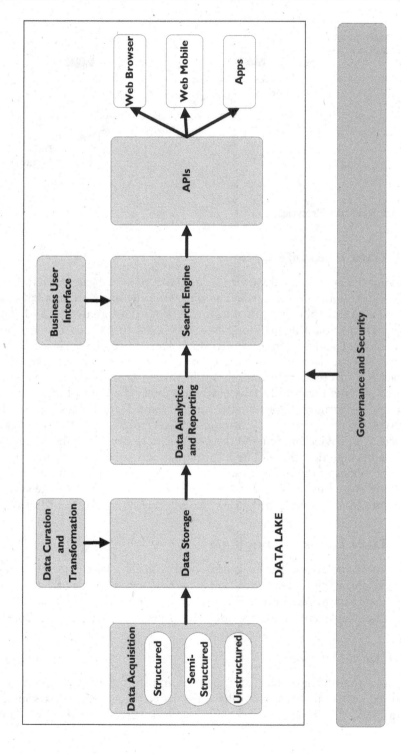

Figure 6.6 A conceptual data lake architecture.

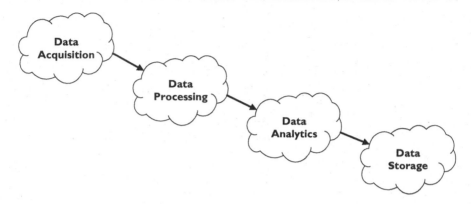

Figure 6.7 Data lake life cycle.

6.4.3 Data Lake Life Cycle

Following the architectural view of a data lake, the life cycle of a data lake can be illustrated in Figure 6.7. The data lake life cycle starts with data acquisition, then follows with data processing, data analytics, and data storage. During data acquisition, data may exist in various formats and require diverse acquisition methods. Raw data is usually retrieved to become part of the data lake. In the data processing phase, the retrieved data is processed to create information applicable to businesses, for example, business insights and product recommendations. The data processing can use machine learning algorithms to process data. Data processing can be converted to any intermediate format. However, the raw data is always retained. To provide on-demand data access, data can be further analyzed in the data analytics phase. The information access mode typically drives the requirement of data analytics. In the data storage phase, data analytics results are stored in suitable data storage systems. The data storage system in the data lake is based on the specific data service requirement [34].

6.4.4 Data Lakes Technologies

Several tools and technologies are associated with data lake implementation, such as data ingestion, data extraction, data cleaning, data storage, data processing, data access, data integration, dataset discovery, dataset versioning, and metadata management. These are discussed in the following sections: [20,35]

6.4.4.1 Data Ingestion

Data ingestion technologies are used to transfer data (structured, unstructured, or semi-structured) physically from the various data sources, such as IoT, databases, emails, FTP, and web servers, to the data lake.

Multiple ingestions can be performed, for example, real-time, batch, or one-time load. The fundamental task of data ingestion is the bookkeeping of files for versioning and indexing purposes. Because of the frequent inter-faces' requirement with external data sources at the limited bandwidth, data ingestion tasks need to complete with low latency and a high degree of parallelism. This eventually indicates that the data ingestion usually does not perform deep analysis on the data downloaded from external sources. However, the shallow data sketches can be applied to the downloaded data and its metadata for maintaining a basic organization of the data down-loaded by data ingestion. Checksums, for instance, can be applied for du-plicate detection multi-versioning of datasets. For immediate data analysis purposes, data ingestion requires supporting real-time ingestion for high-velocity data with more sophisticated indexing.

One type of data ingestion tool is software, which gathered data via predesigned and industrialized jobs iteratively. Apache Foundation pro-posed a number of data ingestion tools that can also aggregate, convert, and clean data before ingestion. Examples of such tools are Apache Flink, Flume (Hadoop log transfer service), Samza (distributed stream processing frameworks), Kafka (real-time data pipelines and stream processing), and Sqoop (data ingestion from SQL and NoSQL databases into Hadoop). Other types of data ingestion tools are based on typical data transfer tools and protocols, such as HTTP, FTP, wget, rsync. Data lake managers use these tools with the data ingestion scripts. Furthermore, application pro-gramming interfaces (APIs), such as CKAN and Socrata, are used to access the catalog of open data and associated metadata and serve the data re-trieval and transfer jobs from the Web into the data lake.

6.4.4.2 Data Extraction

The raw datasets created by the data ingestion are in specific data formats, such as binary encodings or textual. Data extraction transforms the raw data into a predefined data model for different purposes, for example, data dis-covery, cleaning, and integration. Data cleaning can be performed by CLAMS that unify heterogeneous data from the data lake into RDF. Similarly, for data discovery, table extraction can be used. The abstraction of data into attributes for indexing allowing efficient data discovery can be performed table extraction. Data extraction tools, such as DeepDive, extract the relational data from the data lakes consisting of tables, texts, and images bases on user-defined schemas and rules. Google Web Table project is an example of an automatic data extraction tool that combines statistically trained classifiers and hand-written heuristics. Google Web Table is used for detecting relational tables from HTML tables and assigning synthetic headers when required. For extracting relational data from semi-structured log files, DATAMARAN can be used. The declarative data description language, such as PADS, also parses and extracts data files and a compiler and tools.

6.4.4.3 Data Cleaning

Logical and relational data cleaning usually needs correct schema information that may also include integrity constraints. With the data lake characteristics, it is quite common that data are stored with schema-less heterogeneous formats and schemas are required only at the application level. Data with schema information is usually performed during metadata management. However, keeping data cleaning for the later stages can also result in errors, such as during data discovery or data integration operations. CLAMS can enforce the data quality constraints just after the data ingestion and data extraction. This can be done by loading heterogeneous raw data sources into CLAMS using a unified data model enforcing data quality constraints.

6.4.4.4 Data Storage

Data storage in the data lake can be performed in two different ways: classic databases and HDFS storage. In the case of the former approach, various types of databases are used to store different types of data – structured, semi-structured, and unstructured. Relational databases, such as Oracle, MySQL, and PostgreSQL, are used to store structured data. NoSQL databases are used to store unstructured and semi-structured data. In the latter case of data storage, the most common data lake storage is using HDFS (see section 4.1). HDFS is well suited for unstructured data for schema-free bulk data storage. HDFS needs to combine with SQL or NoSQL databases for handling all types of data formats.

6.4.4.5 Data Processing

For data processing in a data lake, MapReduce is usually used, which is a ready-to-use parallel data processing framework given by Apache Hadoop. Because of working on disk-level, MapReduce is suitable for Big Data. However, it is less effective with fast data. Apache Spark is the alternative solution for fast data with the cost of using full memory to store intermediate results instead of using a file system. Apache Spark is, therefore, most appropriate for real-time data processing. Apache Flink and Apache Storm can also perform real-time data processing similar to Apache Spark. The combination of MapReduce and the real-time processing framework can be more suited for Big Data with stream processing.

6.4.4.6 Data Access

Classical data query languages, such as SQL for relational databases, XQuery for XML databases, JSONiq for MongoDB, or SPARSQL for RDF, can be used for data access in a data lake. However, because of storing heterogeneous data in a data lake, a simultaneous query cannot be performed in the heterogeneous databases using the above query languages. Query techniques, such as Spark SQL and SQL++ from multistore, can be used for querying relational databases and semi-structured data in JSON format. Scalable query rewriting engine (SQRE), CloudMdsQL, Apache Phoenix, and Apache Drill are other query languages that can be used for data access in the heterogeneous data lake. For business users, interactive and user-friendly tools, such as Microsoft Power B.I. and Tableau, are also used for data reporting and visualization tasks over data lakes.

6.4.4.7 Data Integration

Data integration is a challenging task of integrating raw data from a data lake during query time. On-demand data integration requires finding datasets containing relevant data and integrating them in a meaningful way. Relevant data can a modeled data that augments known entities with new properties or attributes. Relevant data can also be a schema described by keyword queries expressed over attribute names or other metadata. The information exchange between datasets with different schemas can be performed by schema mapping. In a sample-driven schema mapping, users can describe the schema using a set of records. Similarly, in multi-resolution schema mapping, users can describe schemas using incomplete records, data types, and value ranges. Apart from these, schema mapping, query-driven discovery can find tables to join or union with a query table.

6.4.4.8 Dataset Discovery

Because of the incompleteness of comprehensive schemas or data catalogs, data discovery in a data lake is important. In line with query-driven data discovery, the generation and enrichment of data catalogs are used for dataset discovery purposes. In a query-driven data discovery, first, a user initiates a search with a query, for example, searching for datasets or keywords. The objective is to find similar datasets as the query or datasets, which can be joined or unioned (i.e., integrated) with the query. Efficient indexing and defined measures that are specialized for the data lake characteristics can achieve query objectives. Exploration or navigation can also be used instead of search in a data lake for data discovery. A user can be navigated through the linkage graph, or a hierarchical structured can be created to explore the data lake for dataset discovery.

6.4.4.9 Dataset Versioning

The data lake has been originated to provide dynamic characteristics. New datasets and new versions of an existing dataset can be entered into the data lake at the data ingestion stage. Besides, over time, extractors can be evolved and generating new versions of raw data is typical. Therefore, the versioning of a data lake is very important in all stages of a data lake. Accordingly, vanilla-distributed file systems are not sufficient for data lake versioning operations. This is because of a higher cost of storing all versions of Big Dataset. In addition, without using any version manager, tracking versions can be error-prone using only file names. Dataset versioning is also important because of a large number of data lake users. Hence, with the increase of dataset versions, an efficient and cost-effective data lake system to provide storage and versions is very crucial. A git-like approach, called DataHub, is providing data lake operations, including version creation, viewing, branching, and merging between datasets.

6.4.4.10 Metadata Management

Data lakes usually do not accompany descriptive and complete data catalogs, common to data warehouse or database management systems. A data lake becomes only a data swamp without any metadata information. On-demand data discovery, data integration, and raw data cleaning in a data lake require data catalogs. Metadata management systems provide efficient metadata storage and querying over metadata to extract metadata from data sources and enrich data with meaningful metadata. Google Dataset Search (GOODS) is an example of a metadata management system to extract and collect metadata for datasets generated and used by Google. Metadata consists of dataset-specific information, such as schema, time-stamps, and owners, for identifying the relationship (e.g., similarity or provenance) between multiple datasets. GOODS uses metadata to make datasets accessible and searchable. Metadata in a data lake can be categorized into two types – functional metadata and structural metadata.

- **Functional Metadata:** Functional metadata are the metadata that is used for different operational activities and can be classified into three types:
  - *Business metadata* – a set of descriptions to make the data more understandable with defined business rules. For example, data fields consisting of names and integrity constraints defined by business users during the data ingestion stage.
  - *Operational metadata* – information that are automatically generated at the time of data processing. For example, descriptions of source and target data, including data location, number of records, file size, and process information.
  - *Technical metadata* – information about data representation, including data format. For example, data structure consisting of names, lengths, and types obtained from a database.
- **Structural Metadata:** Structure metadata is associated with the objects, where an object can be a relational table or an XML document. Structure metadata can be classified into three types:

- *Intra-object metadata* – a set of characteristics related to a single object in the data lake. Intra-object metadata further divided into four types.
  - *Properties* – general description of an object retrieved from the filesystem as (key, value) pairs, such as file name and size and location.
  - *Previsualization and summary metadata* – contents overview or an object's structure, such as schema extraction for structured or semi-structured data or wordclouds for textual data.
  - *Version and representation metadata* – obtained via data updates, and metadata representation comes from data refining operations. For example, by generating a data object from an existing one, the new data object can be considered as metadata for the existing one.
  - *Semantic metadata* – annotations describing the data meaning in an object generated using semantic resources (e.g., ontologies) or added by business users manually. For example, title, description, descriptive tags, and categorization of objects that allow data linking.
- *Inter-object metadata* – links between objects. Inter-object metadata further divided into three types:
  - *Object groupings* – the grouping of objects into a collection where an object may belong to more than one collection and deduce from intra-object metadata, such as data format, tags, owner, and language.
  - *Similarity links* – the strength of an object's likeness and obtained using custom or standard similarity measures, such as affinity and joinability.
  - *Parenthood links* – save data linkage and generated automatically when data joins, such as recording process information when creating a new object from a combined group of other objects.
- *Global metadata* – provides a context layer for easier data processing and analysis. Global metadata is related to the entire data lake rather than associating with any specific object. Global metadata further divided into three types:
  - *Semantic resources* – knowledge bases that help enhance analysis and build manually or obtained from the Internet, such as ontologies, thesauri, and taxonomies.
  - *Indexes* – an indexing system automatically builds and enrich indexes for faster pattern-based or term-based data retrieval.
  - *Logs* – information that tracks user's activities in a data lake, such as connection history and query execution.

6.5 CHALLENGES OF DATA LAKES AND BIG DATA

Data lake architecture can be divided into three modules: 1) data integration, 2) data storage, and 3) data analytics. Data integration describes data arriving into the lake from a wide range of data sources. The data integration can occur without a reasonable security policy in place. If the incoming data is not verified against security threats, cybercriminals get a golden opportunity to inject false data. The second module is data storage. It is the place of dumping all the raw data. Again, this can occur without any consideration of cyber safety issues. The most critical module of data lakes is data analytics. It merges the expertise of scientists, analysts, and data officers. Data analytics aims to design and develop modeling algorithms. For producing meaningful insights, this module uses raw data. For example, data analytics is how Netflix[10] learns about its subscriber's viewing habits. A data lake provides a simplified format for storing an organization's Big Data and creates scopes for data crunchers. However, their digital doors remain exposed.

Hence, cyber safety issues require attention and remain an afterthought. Our ability to analyze and discover intelligence from data lakes are compromised in the areas of cyberspace. This is evident via many recent data breaches and cyber-attacks worldwide. For example, any deviation in data may lead to wrong diagnosis or even casualties because of compromised data lakes healthcare. We are becoming even more prone to cyber-attacks together with technological advances. Dealing with malicious cyber activities, therefore, should be a priority concern in the modern digital environment. In recent years, research has flourished in this area. A strong relation between effective cybersecurity and data lakes is yet to be implemented [36–38].

6.5.1 Challenges Ahead for Data Experts

A smallest change or data manipulation in data lakes can massively mislead data crunchers and have a widespread impact. For example, any deviation in data can lead to a wrong diagnosis or even casualties with the compromised data lakes for healthcare. Furthermore, government organizations using compromised data lakes can cause mayhem in international trade and affairs situations. The government, finance, defense, and educational sectors are at risk of data lake attacks. The results of cyber-attacks are far away from trivial with the volume of data stored in data lakes. Because of generating of large amounts data in today's digital world is inevitable, data lake architects must try harder to ensure these at-risk data depots are correctly looked after [36].

6.5.2 Challenges with Big Data Storing and Processing

Considering the Big Data scenario, the data lakes need to address a number of challenges, including heterogeneity, scalability, fidelity, security, and privacy. These are briefly discussed in the following sections:

6.5.2.1 Heterogeneity

Big Data are required to collect, store, integrate, and analyze from various data sources, heterogeneous in nature. Therefore, data lakes need to face the challenges with heterogeneity, such as 1) how to identify and curate the various data sources? 2) how to organize the process of collecting, storing, integrating, analyzing, and handling the data coming from those identified data sources? 3) how to address structural and semantic changes in data and the availability of data sources with time? [39]

6.5.2.2 Scalability

The number of Big Data sources is increasing continuously. Hence, new data are generated, and older data become obsolete, which in turn results in data lake scalability issues in terms of storage capacity. Furthermore, the performance of data lakes is not guaranteed [39].

6.5.2.3 Fidelity

In a data lake, it is trivial to make a difference between raw data and clean data. Raw data is not always ready to be used in decision-making. However, a data lake should be able to ingest arrival data in its full-fidelity as much as possible [40].

6.5.2.4 Security and Privacy

Data in the data lake can be replaced without the oversight of the contents and data governance. Thus, the security and privacy of data in the data lake become an issue [16].

6.6 ENTERPRISE SECURITY

The enterprise data indicates the data shared by employees and partners in a company, master data, transaction data, and analytic data. Enterprise data quality has some characteristics, such as accuracy, consistency, completeness, timeliness, metadata management, and data lineage. Residence of enterprise data includes intranet, cloud, social media, data stores, traditional data warehouse, and file stores. Enterprise data lakes provide a centralized data repository, meaningful business insights, and superior business operations with the help of *artificial intelligence (A.I.).* Enterprise data lakes are used for data governance, A.I. application for business intelligence, predictive analysis, information hygiene (i.e., traceability and consistency), historical analysis, and future growth analysis.

Because of the advances in malicious software, especially in malware obfuscation, hackers can easily hide a risky virus within a harmless-looking file. A typical example of attacks nowadays is the false data injection attacks, which have increased throughout the past decade. The attack occurs when a cybercriminal uses freely accessible tools to compromise a system that is connected to the Internet. The foreign data injected gains unauthorized access to the data lake. It then manipulates the stored data for misleading its users. There are many prospective motivators behind such an attack. Another example of attacks in the data lake is mining sensitive information. Because enterprises dump their all raw data into the data lake, it becomes a rich source of sensitive data. Without appropriate security control and governance, cybercriminals can easily corrupt an organization's business by mining unprotected data. These sensitive data can be sold later in the underground market or rival organizations for financial benefits. Because of the massive amount of raw data are stored in the data lake, the consequences of cyber-attacks are far from trivial. Hence, designing and implementing data lakes to store an organization's valuable data must also protect and secure external cyber-attacks [37,41].

Enterprise security tasks include the following major things to consider:

- How to mitigate or eliminate the risks of private data leaks?
- How to keep data safe in the data lake from intruders?
- How to prevent a data lake from becoming a data swamp?
- How to find out that some data in the data lake are corrupted?
- How to ensure the sensitive data are not compromised?
- How to protect the privacy data in the data lake?

6.7 CONCLUSION

In this chapter, we tried to explore the existing research on data lakes. Traditional data warehouses can store summarized and aggregate data for better business analytics. However, it lacks storing all sorts of data in its native format. With the advancement of modern technologies, several tools and technologies create massive data, called Big Data. One of the characteristics of Big Data is the value, and it indicates that every data element can have a business value. Hence, storing all raw data from originating heterogeneous data sources is very effective for later data analytics and business insights. Data lakes provide that panacea for storing Big Data and for later analytics. Accordingly, in this chapter, Big Data, traditional data warehouse, data lake with its architecture, data life cycle, and associated technologies are discussed. Storing raw data in the data lake also opens the door to cybercriminals to explore sensitive information from the data lake and compromise the overall business. Cybercriminals can also inject false data into the lake, resulting in severe consequences, as observed in healthcare wrong diagnosis. Therefore, enterprises need to measure and mitigate a number of issues to protect their data and keep it secured.

NOTES

1 https://www.statista.com/statistics/871513/worldwide-data-created/
2 https://www.statista.com/
3 https://www.aparavi.com/
4 https://www.aparavi.com/data-growth-statistics-blow-your-mind/
5 https://www.idc.com/
6 https://solutionsreview.com/data-management/80-percent-of-your-data-will-be-unstructured-in-five-years/
7 https://www.techamerica.org/
8 https://www.oracle.com/au/database/
9 https://www.mongodb.com/
10 https://www.netflix.com/

REFERENCES

[1] A. N. M. B. Rashid, M. Ahmed, L. F. Sikos, and P. Haskell-Dowland, "A novel penalty-based wrapper objective function for feature selection in big data using cooperative co-evolution," *IEEE Access*, vol. 8, pp. 150113–150129, 2020.

[2] A. N. M. B. Rashid, M. Ahmed, L. F. Sikos, and P. Haskell-Dowland, "Cooperative co-evolution for feature selection in Big Data with random feature grouping," *Journal of Big Data*, vol. 7, no. 1, Dec 4, 2020.

[3] A. N. M. B. Rashid, and T. Choudhury, "Cooperative co-evolution and mapreduce: a review and new insights for large-scale optimization," *International Journal of Information Technology Project Management*, vol. 12, no. 1, pp. 29–62, Jan-Mar, 2021.

[4] A. N. M. B. Rashid, and T. Choudhury, "Knowledge management overview of feature selection problem in high-dimensional financial data: cooperative co-evolution and MapReduce perspectives," *Problems and Perspectives in Management*, vol. 17, no. 4, pp. 340–359, 2019.

[5] F. Ali, S. El-Sappagh, S. M. R. Islam, A. Ali, M. Attique, M. Imran, and K. S. Kwak, "An intelligent healthcare monitoring framework using wearable sensors and social networking data," *Future Generation Computer Systems-the International Journal of Escience*, vol. 114, pp. 23–43, Jan, 2021.

[6] N. Miloslavskaya, and A. Tolstoy, "Application of big data, fast data and data lake concepts to information security issues." *2016 IEEE 4th International Conference on Future Internet of Things and Cloud Workshops (Ficloudw)*, pp. 148–153, 2016.

[7] A. N. M. B. Rashid, "Access methods for big data: current status and future directions," *Eai Endorsed Transactions on Scalable Information Systems*, vol. 4, no. 15, pp. 4–9, 2017.

[8] D. Laney. "3D data management: controlling data volume, velocity and variety," 6, No. 70. Available: http://blogs.gartner.com/doug-laney/files/2012/01/ad949-3D-Data-Management-Controlling-Data-Volume-Velocity-and-Variety.pdf. (accessed date: 26-Apr-2021).

[9] A. Gandomi, and M. Haider, "Beyond the hype: big data concepts, methods, and analytics," *International Journal of Information Management*, vol. 35, no. 2, pp. 137–144, Apr, 2015.

[10] O. Kwon, N. Lee, and B. Shin, "Data quality management, data usage experience and acquisition intention of big data analytics," *International Journal of Information Management*, vol. 34, no. 3, pp. 387–394, Jun, 2014.

[11] I. Gartner. "Gartner information technology glossary." Available: https://www.gartner.com/en/information-technology/glossary/big-data. (accessed date: 26-Apr-2021).

[12] S. L. S. Mills, L. Irakliotis, M. Rappa, T. Carlson, B. Perlowitz. "Demystifying big data: a practical guide to transforming the business of government." Available: https://bigdatawg.nist.gov/_uploadfiles/M0068_v1_3903747095.pdf. (accessed date: 26-Apr-2021).

[13] I.B.M. "Big data solutions: changing the way you work." Available: https://www.ibm.com/au-en/it-infrastructure/solutions/big-data. (accessed date: 26-Apr-2021).

[14] S.A.S. "Big data: what it is and why it matters." Available: https://www.sas.com/en_au/insights/big-data/what-is-big-data.html. (accessed date: 26-Apr-2021).

[15] Oracle. "What is big data." Available: https://www.oracle.com/au/bigdata/what-is-big-data.html. (accessed date: 26-Apr-2021).

[16] P. P. Khine, and Z. S. Wang, "Data lake: a new ideology in big data era," *4th Annual International Conference on Wireless Communication and Sensor Network (Wcsn 2017)*, vol. 17, 2018.

[17] E. Saddad, A. El-Bastawissy, H. M. O. Mokhtar, and M. Hazman, "Lake data warehouse architecture for big data solutions," *International Journal of Advanced Computer Science and Applications*, vol. 11, no. 8, pp. 417–424, Aug, 2020.

[18] A. Sebaa, F. Chikh, A. Nouicer, and A. Tari, "Research in big data warehousing using Hadoop," *Journal of Information Systems Engineering & Management*, vol. 2, no. 2, pp. 10, 2017.

[19] J. Dixon. "Pentaho, hadoop, and data lakes." Available: https://jamesdixon.wordpress.com/2010/10/14/pentaho-hadoop-and-data-lakes/. (accessed date: 26-Apr-2021).

[20] P. Sawadogo, and J. Darmont, "On data lake architectures and metadata management," *Journal of Intelligent Information Systems*, vol. 56, no. 1, pp. 97–120, Feb, 2021.

[21] C. Madera, and A. Laurent, "The next information architecture evolution: the data lake wave." *Proceedings of the 8th International Conference on Management of Digital Ecosystems (Medes 2016)*, pp. 174–180, 2016.

[22] N. Miloslavskaya, and A. Tolstoy, "Big data, fast data and data lake concepts." *7th Annual International Conference on Biologically Inspired Cognitive Architectures, (Bica 2016)*, vol. 88, pp. 300–305, 2016.

[23] A. A.W.S. "What is a data lake?." Available: https://aws.amazon.com/big-data/datalakes-and-analytics/what-is-a-data-lake/. (accessed date: 26-Apr-2021).

[24] Guru99. "What is data lake? It's architecture." Available: https://www.guru99.com/data-lake-architecture.html. (accessed date: 26-Apr-2021).

[25] C. Walker, and H. Alrehamy, "Personal data lake with data gravity pull, *Evolutionary Computation*, vol. 26, no. 4, pp. 160–167, 2018.

[26] F. Ferrucci, P. Salza, and F. Sarro, "Using hadoop mapreduce for parallel genetic algorithms: a comparison of the global, grid and island models," *Evolutionary Computation*, vol. 26, no. 4, pp. 535–567, 2018. doi: 10.1162/ evco_a_00213 Epub 2017 Jun 29. PMID: 28661707.

[27] A. Sinha, and P. K. Jana, "A hybrid MapReduce-based k-means clustering using genetic algorithm for distributed datasets," *Journal of Supercomputing*, vol. 74, no. 4, pp. 1562–1579, Apr, 2018.

[28] M. Sharma, and V. Devi, "APS: Dynamic platform selector for big data analysis," 2016 IEEE International Conference on Recent Trends in Electronics, Information & Communication Technology (RTEICT), pp. 2072–2076, 2016, doi: 10.1109/RTEICT.2016.7808204.

[29] D. Guo, and E. Onstein, "State-of-the-art geospatial information processing in NoSQL Databases," *ISPRS International Journal of Geo-Information*, vol. 9, no. 5, pp. 331, 2020.

[30] A. Mohamed, M. K. Najafabadi, Y. B. Wah, E. A. K. Zaman, and R. Maskat, "The state of the art and taxonomy of big data analytics: view from new big data framework," *Artificial Intelligence Review*, vol. 53, no. 2, pp. 989–1037, 2020/02/01, 2020.

[31] F. Ravat, and Y. Zhao, "Data lakes: trends and perspectives," *Database and Expert Systems Applications, Pt I*, vol. 11706, pp. 304–313, 2019.

[32] R. Nadipalli. "Effective business intelligence with QuickSight." Available: https://www.packtpub.com/product/effective-business-intelligence-with-quicksight/9781786466365. (accessed date: 26-Apr-2021).

[33] P. Menon. "Demystifying data lake architecture." Available: https:// rpradeepmenon.medium.com/demystifying-data-lake-architecture-30cf4ac8aa07. (accessed date: 26-Apr-2021).

[34] Jingxuan. "Data lake: concepts, characteristics, architecture, and case studies." Available: https://www.alibabacloud.com/blog/data-lake-concepts-characteristics-architecture-and-case-studies_596910. (accessed date: 26-Apr-2021).

[35] F. Nargesian, E. K. Zhu, R. J. Miller, K. Q. Pu, and P. C. Arocena, "Data lake management: challenges and opportunities." *Proceedings of the Vldb Endowment*, vol. 12, no. 12, pp. 1986–1989, Aug, 2019.

[36] M. Ahmed. "Data lakes: where big businesses dump their excess data, and hackers have a field day." Available: https://theconversation.com/data-lakes-where-big-businesses-dump-their-excess-data-and-hackers-have-a-field-day-123865. (accessed date: 26-Apr-2021).

[37] C. H. News. "Identifying security challenges against data lakes." Available: https://cyware.com/news/identifying-security-challenges-against-data-lakes-c4e19226. (accessed date: 26-Apr-2021).

[38] M. Ahmed, A. Naser Mahmood, and J. Hu, "A survey of network anomaly detection techniques." *Journal of Network and Computer Applications*, vol. 60, pp. 19–31, 2016.

[39] H. Mehmood, E. Gilman, M. Cortes, P. Kostakos, A. Byrne, K. Valta, S. Tekes, and J. Riekki, "Implementing big data lake for heterogeneous data sources." *2019 IEEE 35th International Conference on Data Engineering Workshops (ICDEW 2019)*, pp. 37–44, 2019.

[40] A. Farrugia, R. Claxton, and S. Thompson, "Towards social network analytics for understanding and managing enterprise data lakes." *Proceedings of the 2016 Ieee/Acm International Conference on Advances in Social Networks Analysis and Mining Asonam 2016*, pp. 1213–1220, 2016.

[41] A. N. M. B. Rashid, M. Ahmed, and A.-S. K. Pathan, "Infrequent pattern detection for reliable network traffic analysis using robust evolutionary computation," *Sensors*, vol. 21, no. 9, pp. 3005, 2021.

Chapter 7

The Battle for Cloud Supremacy and the Remaking of Enterprise Security

Matthew Ryan[1] and Frank den Hartog[2]

[1]Macquarie Group Limited

[2]School of Engineering and Information Technology, UNSW Canberra

CONTENTS

7.1   INTRODUCTION

Since the turn of the century, globalization has ushered in a new wave of disruptive technologies that have generated new and exciting business opportunities for enterprises. Simultaneously, the rapid adoption of these technologies has exposed enterprises to an array of unintended human errors and malicious cyber threats. From ransomware, misconfigurations, to intellectual property theft, there are a myriad of cyber threats that enterprises require protection against. As part of a never-ending process to counter these threats, enterprises

DOI: 10.1201/9781003121541-7

Table 7.1 Example CSP Responsibility Model

RESPONSIBILITY	SAAS	PAAS	IAAS	ON-PREM	
INFORMATION AND DATA	E	E	E	E	RESPONSIBILITY ALWAYS RETAINED BY CUSTOMER
DEVICES (PC AND MOBILE)	E	E	E	E	
ACCOUNTS AND IDENTITIES	E	E	E	E	
IDENTITY AND DIRECTORY INFRASTRUCTURE	S	S	E	E	RESPONSIBILITY VARIES BY SERVICE TYPE
APPLICATIONS	CSP	S	E	E	
NETWORK CONTROLS	CSP	S	E	E	
OPERATING SYSTEMS	CSP	CSP	E	E	
PHYSICAL HOSTS	CSP	CSP	CSP	E	RESPONSIBILITY TRANSFERS TO CLOUD PROVIDER
PHYSICAL NETWORK	CSP	CSP	CSP	E	
PHYSICAL DATA CENTER	CSP	CSP	CSP	E	

E = ENTERPRISE, S = SHARED RESPONSIBILITY, CSP = CLOUD SERVICE PROVIDER.

have invested trillions of dollars into security tools and capabilities, increased the size and skillsets of their cyber workforces, provided cyber awareness training to their staff, and many executive leadership teams now exhibit a relatively high degree of cybersecurity acumen. Yet in spite of all these actions, the volume and impacts from cyberattacks against enterprises continues to grow exponentially.

This research explores how the search to develop a panacea for cyber-attacks is redefining the existing Cloud Service Providers (CSPs) security operating model, as detailed in Table 7.1 [1–3], whilst simultaneously creating an opportunity for CSPs to profit and monopolize the enterprise cybersecurity market. This chapter begins by examining the genesis of cloud, before exploring how cloud computing is revolutionizing how enterprises operate and secure their business information systems and data. It discusses the advances in security control systems, the potential for CSPs to engineer new solutions, and why the cloud revolution continues to be challenged by repeated security failings. This forward-looking research hypothesizes that the aggregate sum of a series of technology advancements and prevailing market conditions will create a technology race for CSPs to provide a new Technology-as-a-Service (TaaS) model for their enterprise customers.

7.2 RESEARCH LIMITATIONS

This research is broadly focused on large modern enterprises. At a macro level it appears easy to define high-level parameters of what constitutes a large modern enterprise such as revenue or employee numbers to determine the correct categorization. However, when we examine these enterprises at a more granular level, such as the state of their technology environment or cybersecurity maturity, they start to become ambiguous. To demonstrate this, consider the Fortune 50 companies Exxon Mobile, United Health Group, and Starbucks. Today they represent three of the largest companies in the world, operating across three different market sectors, each using a different business operating model. As a result, they will have significant differences in their approach to risk management, technology adoption, and their ability to respond to cyber threats. These differences expand further when compared to other comparative sized companies, such as Amazon, Google, Microsoft, and Apple. This example demonstrates that despite large enterprises sharing generic business similarities in parameters such as revenue, profits, and their employee numbers; in practice they operate very different technology and cybersecurity operating models.

This simple example highlights that whilst this research is primarily focused on large modern enterprises (i.e., with over ~5,000 employees such as financial institutions, logistics, hospitals, and technology companies), the outcomes of the research will not apply equally to all large modern enterprises. The research outcomes should also not be broadly applied to enterprises that operate small networks, or networks with large volumes of Industrial Control Systems (ICS) and Internet of Thing (IoT) devices. This is due to the type of cyber security tools and systems deployed in these types of organizations potentially being vastly different from what is deployed in a typical large enterprise's network.

7.3 PROLOGUE TO THE CLOUD

From reaching new markets to providing scalability and competitive advantage, throughout the 21st century enterprises have continuously looked to emerging technologies to innovate, solve business problems, and to create new market opportunities. In their endless pursuit of profits, enterprises have adopted and deployed emerging technologies at increasing rates; whilst simultaneously trying to protect their business information systems through a reactive process of continuously adding layer upon layer of the latest and greatest security tool to their technology environment. For venture capitalists, cybersecurity vendors, and service providers, this continuous cycle of uplift has created an endless profit loop. However, after decades of promises and innovation, and the investment of trillions of dollars into cybersecurity, cyberattacks against enterprises continue to occur. In fact, for far too many enterprise networks have become so complex and convoluted, and filled with layers of obsolete technologies, that they now require an ever-growing volume of scarce cybersecurity expertise on hand just to keep their business information systems operating.

Whilst enterprises were frantically deploying emerging technologies, criminals and nation states were also busy adapting their business models to the prevailing conditions of a new interconnected and internet-enabled world. These activities led to a flood of cyberattacks against enterprises that included Distributed-Denial-of-Service (DDoS) attacks, data theft, phishing, fraud, to crypto-jacking. The term crypto-jacking refers to the process of using malware to steal Central Processing Unit (CPU) revolutions from victims' devices to illegally mine cryptocurrencies. For decades these cyberattacks have continued to pose serious threats to enterprises and their business operations. Despite the endless barrage of cyberattacks, Ryan (2020) argues that it was the rise of ransomware that really made enterprises stop, and re-evaluate their cyber preparedness.

> "The emergence of new anonymising technologies enabled ransomware to evolve into a prodigious cyber threat. Ransomware attacks are a phenomenon that have repeatedly displayed the capacity to rapidly monetise both crown jewels and innocuous data with limited or no monetary value" [4].

In the wake of a series of global ransomware attacks, enterprises, providers, and governments sought increased collaboration to prevent and respond to cyberattacks. This has led to increased information sharing efforts and new communication channels such as the Financial Services Information Sharing and Analysis Center (FS-ISAC) being established [5]. Cultivating a greater understanding about what cyberattacks have transpired, and how they happened is fundamental to developing cloud-based technologies that promise to deliver the panacea enterprises have long been promised for cyberattacks.

It was not that long ago when every enterprise used to operate their entire technology stack from the murky shallows of their basement and communications rooms within their commercial buildings. Since those days, many of these enterprises have already (or are in the process) of uplifting their infrastructure from data centers to cloud infrastructure [6,7]. The move to the cloud is being driven by the business, with business cases commonly citing performance, resilience, scalability, operational costs, or simply to enable the business to bring new products and services to the market faster as the reasoning for the switch.

Another driving force behind this shift is the broader industry move towards Software-as-a-Service (SaaS) business applications. Whilst many enterprises still install and configure operating systems and core business applications onto their own hardware, this practice is rapidly declining. Instead, many enterprises are opting for SaaS solutions to service their changing business demands, and to reduce their hardware capital expenditure and operating costs. This shift can be observed through the growing adoption of SaaS products such as Microsoft Office 365, Teams and Outlook, which in FY19/20 saw grow revenue by 24% and subscribers soar to 42.7 million [8].

Based on the continued growing demand for SaaS solutions, it is also foreseeable that SaaS will not only be the default option, but it may imminently become the only option for enterprise-related software products.

During the early stages of cloud adoption, CSPs, business leaders, and users will continuously highlight the clouds' ability to rapidly access new products, storage capacity, reliability, and performance of SaaS products to justify their choice. However, deeper analysis reveals the potential security advantages behind adopting cloud architectures and native security controls. One major advantage of SaaS is that the vendor of the application does not need to cater to a myriad of configurations and different operating systems. This simplification of the design and integration process enables increased standardization, whilst in-turn reduces complexity and enables the baseline security of the product to be improved. Another benefit is that software vendors no longer need to send out security patches, instead they can be applied by the vendor in almost real time. This does not remove the change management process, however due to the resiliency of cloud architectures, this will significantly speed up the ability of enterprises to implement changes. As a result, there should be a decline in horror cyber stories such as Boeing, who was breached because they failed to implement a critical patch that the vendor released a year prior [9]. Changing how vulnerability management occurs may have an enormous impact on the cybersecurity posture of enterprises, and the volume, and severity of the cyberattacks they incur in the future.

7.4 THE GENESIS OF CLOUD

In its simplest form, cloud computing is defined as the delivery of on-demand computing services such as storage, servers, databases, networking, software, or analytics over the internet. The origins of cloud computing can be traced back to the 1960's, however it wasn't until 2006 when Google CEO Eric Schmidt introduced the term to an industry conference that cloud computing as we commonly understand it today began to appear [10]. Since then, there has been no shortage of CSP' that have promised users and enterprises alike that the cloud is:

> "A game-changing experience that is unparalleled with on-prem security efforts. Because native cloud platform services are all integrated seamlessly, it offers an opportunity to leverage consistent monitoring, detection, logging, and auditing, all combined with powerful analytics and discovery tools enabled by machine learning to provide insights and control. Beyond monitoring and logging, centralized management of security controls provides unified single-pane-of-glass visibility into how security for data is applied across your organization. There is simply no way on-prem security programs can achieve the same level" [11].

Table 7.2 Worldwide Public Cloud Service Revenue Forecast (Millions of USD) [14]

	2019	2020	2021	2022
Cloud Business Process Services (BPaaS)	45,212	43,438	46,287	49,509
Cloud Application Infrastructure Services (PaaS)	37,512	43,498	57,337	72,022
Cloud Application Services (SaaS)	102,064	104,672	120,990	140,629
Cloud Management and Security Services	12,836	14,663	16,089	18,387
Cloud System Infrastructure Services (IaaS)	44,457	50,393	64,294	80,980
Desktop as a Service (DaaS)	616	1,203	1,951	2,535
Total Market Value	**242,697**	**257,867**	**306,948**	**364,062**

The perceived opportunity for enterprises to capitalize from new technology advances has led to strong growth for cloud computing solutions. Industry analysis undertaken by Deloitte indicated that "for the past three years, cloud was consistently the top emerging technology in which respondents from large financial institutions said they wanted to invest" [12]. The global demand for enterprise cloud computing services continues to increase year-on-year. In 2019 Microsoft reported a "27% increase in revenue from its Intelligent Cloud business, and that overall revenue associated with the cloud were up by 39%. During the same period Amazon Web Services (AWS) also reported a 33% growth in sales to smash through the $10 billion (USD) barrier" [13]. These strong growth numbers are further supported by Gartner, whose research as depicted in Table 7.2 demonstrates the year-on-year growth of cloud computing services since 2019.

Global events such as the COVID-19 pandemic and SolarWinds attacks will only further accelerate enterprises uplift their technology and cybersecurity modernization programs [15]. After years of resistance, the pandemic has abruptly forced thousands of enterprises to allow and adopt remote working for their survival. This has also forced enterprises to scour for and swiftly deploy cloud-based technology solutions to enable their staff to work remotely. It is estimated that 75 million people in the United States alone were required to work from home during the pandemic [16]. This shift to remote-based was not without challenges, with many enterprises questioning the security of their remote access points, data security, and their ability to protect edge-based devices. It should also be acknowledged that the ability for enterprises to uplift core business operations, and for large volumes of their staff to work remotely would not have been possible at the beginning at the 21st century.

A year on from the start of the COVID-19 pandemic, many enterprises continue to operate significant portions of their business operations remotely. It can be argued that the success of enterprises throughout this period is in part due to the availability and ability of the major CSPs to rapidly deliver an array of scalable cloud-hosted solutions. Ultimately government agencies and enterprises were able to rapidly adopt and deploy products such as COVID safety-related applications, cloud computing, virtualization, and SaaS applications to keep their core businesses services operating during a global pandemic [17].

7.4.1 Cloud Shortfalls

For business and security leaders, it is easy to foresee the potential business benefits of cloud computing when it comes to the ease and speed of deployment, scalability, and reliability. But if we look deeper into this popular narrative, and consider the current state of play holistically—the cloud has not fully lived up to all the hype, and more broadly it has not provided a cyber sanctuary for enterprises against cyberattacks. When examining the challenges that are preventing clouds' advancement, security practitioners are faced with some difficult verities. Whilst there have certainly been technical flaws and vulnerabilities in the solutions developed by major CSPs such as AWS and Apple [18], this research is not the first (and unlikely to be the last) to highlight that human error is increasingly at the heart of a plethora of major cybersecurity incidents [19].

The Ponemon Institute has gone further, declaring that "human error is the enemy of cyber resiliency [20], and this is where things may become a little uncomfortable for some security practitioners. It is important to distinguish that human error is not always the fictitious character Karen or Warren in the accounts department clicking on a precarious link saying that they have won a free trip to Hawaii. This standard analogy of a non-security savvy user clicking on a link is a failure of the security industry, as it is far from the single point of failure in this scenario. Leaders and practitioners alike need to understand it is impossible to prevent enterprise users from clicking on links, as embedded links often come trusted sources that may be compromised. Therefore, it is important to recognize that security failures are increasingly the result of having no end-point protection, a misconfigured bucket, firewall, or phishing tool, lack of network segregation, or poor vulnerability management practices.

In recent years, major CSPs have been talking more and more about errors that security professionals are making in the design, deployment, and maintenance of enterprise security controls systems. Far too often the root cause of the security failure is the way in which the solution has been configured and deployed, not a weakness in the solution being provided. For example, the problem has become so common that the U.S. Securities and Exchange Commission (SEC) released a risk alert stating that "firms did not adequately configure the security settings on their network storage solution to protect against unauthorized access... Often, misconfigured settings resulted from a lack of effective oversight when the storage solution was initially implemented" [21].

This statement is not designed to be a thinly veiled swipe at the thousands of cyber security practitioners that everyday are trying to do so much with so little to protect the enterprises and the customers they serve. Instead, it is a reflection about the realities of the current security environment. It reflects on years of observations about how cybersecurity is actually being conceived, designed, and performed inside enterprises every day. These observations are supported by Maurer and Hinck (2020) whose research into cloud security discovered that the "main finding is that many cloud incidents are not caused by malicious adversaries but rather by human error" [22]. This reinforces the notion that security teams are ultimately constrained by their available resources, their collective knowledge, and the tools available for them to defend their given environments. Even finding more expertize is problematic because there is a global talent shortfall in cybersecurity. Despite the best efforts of governments, enterprises and academia, the demand for top cyber talent continues to significantly outstrip supply. Rudimentary analysis of company filings indicates that cybersecurity is both: a) an expensive endeavor to perform, and b) a problem too big and complex for most enterprises to solve on their own.

Our research argues that another underlying problem of the current cloud computing model is the use of the "shared responsibility model" [1–3]. This is because the "shared responsibility model" does not adequately leverage the internal expertise of the CSP, or protect the provider from the fallout of major cybersecurity attacks or disruptions against their clients. In effect, it means that CSPs such as Amazon, Google, and Microsoft are not responsible for remediating incidents beyond their control, nor are they liable for their client's applications and/or data from being compromised. However, that does not mean they do not suffer any ramifications in the wake of an incident. For instance, "the Capital One incident illustrated the reputational cost for CSPs and their clients that accompany any shortcomings in this area" [22]. Ultimately, when a CSP's client suffers a major security incident or disruption, there will be an erosion of trust and reputational damage for both the enterprise and the CSP. This erosion of trust can manifest through the enterprise's customers and the broader public towards. Internally, the enterprise's executive leadership team may have sold the cloud solution to their Board as a remedy for their security and technology problems; therefore, any subsequent failure will naturally diminish the level of confidence about the solution within the organization.

Businesses and security professionals alike are all too familiar with news stories about enterprises making grand announcements about how they are now going all in on the cloud "This is going to be a technological revolution for the business and its customers." Only to read in popular media a year later that the same enterprise has suffered a data breach due to its data repository's security being misconfigured, resulting in personal information of millions of customers being compromised [23]. Due to these repeated failings, this research argues that major cloud vendors will increasingly be required to provide services that extend beyond the existing "shared responsibility model." Instead, the CSPs will need to develop, implement, and support new models where they accept more and more responsibility for the entire security of an enterprise's business information systems environment.

At first this will present itself as small incremental shifts in responsibilities for applications and providing niche security services and support for top tier clients. But over time, more and more CSPs will see an opportunity to generate extraordinary revenue by adopting increased responsibility models at scale. This realization will trigger a technology race that has the potential to remake the cybersecurity industry. As CSPs ramp up their quest for market supremacy, they will rapidly develop, acquire, implement, and monopolize cybersecurity technologies and resources. This has the potential to create market conditions where smaller security innovators will face extreme pressures to join forces, or risks going head-to-head with major CSPs, and the Slack platform may be an early example of this occurring [24]. The transition towards a complete all-in-one CSP model is not a radical proposition, and in many ways a transition towards this model is already in flight [25]. A look into the rear-view mirror indicates that CSPs are not averse to engaging in fierce competition or taking more responsibility, and this notion is supported by the ongoing in-house development of their own chipsets, hardware for data centers and end users, and the battle for internet search engines and applications supremacy.

7.5 INSIDE THE ENTERPRISE

Despite many of these enterprises investing billions of dollars to secure their environments and after years of effort trying to build world-class teams of cyber defenders, the stark reality is that today many enterprises still do not have the required resources to defend themselves from common cyber-attacks. Sadly, they are unable to accurately assess their cyber risk, have limited visibility of their environments or operational effectiveness of their critical security controls, and they have become increasingly reliant on third parties to perform and protect their business operations. A recent research study into the efficacy of cybersecurity by Hubback (2020), which interviewed over 100 business and cybersecurity leaders, discovered that "nine in ten leaders agreed that products fail in the most basic way imaginable—stopping cyberattacks... Customers being robbed is becoming normal... Everybody suffers ransomware now... It is all so normal now that the risk has been accepted" [26].

7.5.1 Profit versus Overhead

The unfortunate reality of the current global market is that cybersecurity is a burden for most enterprises. It is not a market differentiator, and it does not provide a comparative business advantage for businesses not directly involved in industries such as defense, cybersecurity, or associated data and asset management type services. On the other hand, cloud computing can easily be sold as a market differentiator, and as an opportunity to gain a competitive advantage for many enterprises. This is because "cloud services provide tools for businesses to leverage, so that companies can direct their focus on innovative and value adding uses of the technology rather than replicating the existing technologies" [27]. When business leaders talk about moving their enterprises to the cloud, the driving forces behind their strategies are business and cost reduction opportunities, not improving the enterprises' cybersecurity capability. Whilst cybersecurity will undoubtedly be a component of the business cases rationale for uplifting, it is unlikely to be the primary reason for an enterprise undertaking a large migration to the cloud [28].

Whilst this summation does not accurately portray all enterprises, it reflects a significant portion of the global market. This gives rise to the notion, that should an alternative cybersecurity model be offered by the major CSPs, a large number of enterprises may be interested. In practice, CSPs do not have to offer technology or security services that are cheaper than the current cost; they just have to be relatively comparative. Due to the benefits of scale, many enterprises may already be unable to compete with product price points of the major CSPs. When enterprise leadership teams make outsourcing decisions, they generally consider the total cost of ownership, but they also consider the management effort, efficiency and resilience gains, and any potential transfer of risk opportunities. Provided there are adequate governance practices in place, outsourcing may potentially provide a layer against regulatory action in the event of an incident or major disruption. As the third party may not be regulated, this can be problematic in some jurisdictions. The aggregate of these considerations enables the CSPs to propose a fee that may be significantly higher than the current operating cost; however, this may still be an attractive offer for the enterprise's leadership.

Globally there is a continued push by enterprises to further outsource their business information systems and technology-related services. Whilst being slow to respond, this shift has not gone unnoticed, with many financial regulators now expressing "the possibility of systemic risk arising from concentration in the provision of some outsourced and third-party services to financial institutions" [29]. This shift was detailed by Australian Prudential Regulatory Authority (APRA) Chairman Wayne Byres who stated that "outsourcing and partnering are far from new concepts, but increasingly it is occurring for business-critical functions, not just at the periphery of activities" [30]. The shift highlights businesses increasing desire to focus more on their core business objectives, not their technology and cyber security operations.

7.5.2 Governance and Regulation

The rapid adoption of cloud services is changing the internal governance models and practices for enterprises, and how their regulators oversee their changing technology environments. The accessibility and ease of use of these services is beginning to render many traditional security and governance models all but obsolete. For instance, internal policies that have always been documented as reports and guidelines are now being implemented as rulesets that are programmed into the enterprises cloud environment. This shift in governance practises is not just limited to business enterprises but also extends to governments agencies. For instance, the United States Department of Defense (DoD) cloud strategy outlines that "cloud infrastructure will allow for provisioning and deprovisioning of resources automatically" [31]. The DoD's cloud strategy goes further, detailing the potential security benefits of increased cloud adoption:

> "CSPs will be integral to combating cyber challenges and securing the cloud. The CSPs will automatically scan infrastructure resources and generated logs, which will be used to identify vulnerabilities early and to make intrusion detection and mitigation in near-real time a reality across much of the enterprise" [31].

Simultaneously on the enterprise regulatory front, Levite and Kalwani (2020) forecast that "there is also likely to be increasingly charged policy discussions and regulatory actions on the need for standards and adequate levels of transparency in CSP security and risk management practices, including both systemic controls and operational defensive measures" [32]. As major CSPs continue to battle for increased market share, it is likely that they will increasingly be considered critical infrastructure by governments, and this will lead to heighted expectations and regulations for CSPs.

7.5.3 Resourcing Challenges

In a world where there is a chronic shortage of top cybersecurity talent, the battle to attract and retain talent will be pivotal for all enterprises. Blumberg (2020) argues that "if providing cloud-based infrastructure is not your core business, it will be impossible for you to match the CSPs on the talent needed to build and run these platforms in a scalable, efficient, and secure way" [33] The resourcing challenge presents another potential area of delineation between enterprises and CSPs, because the ability to entice, tolerate, and effectively manage unique and challenging staff may be very problematic for many enterprises. Curry (2019) argue the future design, development, and implementation of technologies that underpin advances in cybersecurity are most likely going to be produced by a limited number of individuals who have unique technical skills but may also be neurodiverse, apply unconventional approaches to problem solving, or exhibit abnormal social skills [34]. The term neurodiverse refers to individuals with differences in brain function and behavioral traits as part of normal variation in the human population.

Whilst modern enterprises continue to build and refine their cultural diversity models, the level of flexibility and tolerance required to manage the diverse teams of people required to build advanced technological solutions may be beyond the appetite of many modern enterprises' human resources and management teams. When former Google executives Eric Schmidt and Jonathan Rosenberg (2019) were discussing their book "How Google Works" they explained "in our experience, most smart creatives have strong opinions and are itching to spout off... You need these aberrant geniuses because they're the ones that drive, in most cases, the product excellence... They are better than other technical people" [35]. These perspectives may be very difficult for many leaders to accept; thus, I would postulate that it would be difficult for these enterprises to entice, manage, and retain what Schmidt and Rosenberg describe as aberrant geniuses.

7.6 CLOUD SECURITY

In isolation, native security controls in the cloud are indifferent to existing security controls that are deployed on-prem or in hybrid cloud environments. The sole fact that a control was simply built natively in the cloud does not improve the strength of that control. However, when deployed in a complex environment with numerous other controls, there are differences in the effectiveness of each control to function in unison as a system. Business leaders and cybersecurity practitioners alike love to talk about how their enterprises security was designed using defense-in-depth. Unfortunately, in practice, that is generally not the case, and their design would be more accurately defined as a defense-in-breadth. Wolf (2018) examined this notion of defense-in-depth, "whereby the defenders layer their controls (defenses) along the dimension of time – as soon as an attacker defeats one control, he or she comes up against another. This assumes a fairly linear and static progression, in which the defenders are always certain they know exactly how a perpetrator will progress through the target system" [36].

The crux of this problem is that, despite the designers' best intentions, in legacy (non-cloud native) controls there is generally a lack of interlock functionality in the security system. An interlock is defined as a mechanism that makes the state of two mechanisms or functions mutually dependent. This lack could be reflective of the design of the control itself, and/or that the control is being deployed with numerous other controls that were potentially designed by different vendors, and implemented at different stages of the product lifecycle. This does not mean that controls designed by different vendors cannot be used together, but the practitioner must acknowledge that as the number of controls and layers increases, the level of complexity increases across the enterprise's security environment. As the level of complexity increases, it is unlikely that each control will continue operating at its optimum level whilst working in unison as a system. As Schneier (1999) postulates "as systems get more complex, security will get worse" [37]. Therefore, as enterprises develop and implement more controls and bespoke configurations, their ability to operate in unison becomes more challenging, and the risk of a control being misconfigured increases sharply.

Problems associated with control effectiveness are not limited to integration issues, with several cybersecurity leaders arguing that some cyber controls are not being developed for their defensive effectiveness, but instead for their marketability. An investigation in 2020 by Forbes into the cybersecurity industry revealed "the problem starts with a fragmented industry this is configured to invent products they think VCs will invest in, that larger companies might want to integrate, that customers can be convinced to buy" [38]. Whilst most security vendors continue to build tools to secure their clients, many continue to profit from a model of endless cyber insecurity, whereby enterprises are in a constant state of uplift and transformation.

7.6.1 Strategic Compatibility

Another common misconception is enterprises applying the same security strategies, tools, and controls in their cloud environments. This notion is supported by Google's Lance and Chuvakin (2021) who argue, "simply applying a data security strategy designed for on-prem workloads isn't adequate. It lacks the ability to address cloud-specific requirements and doesn't take advantage of the great amount of security services and capabilities the cloud has to offer" [39]. In reality, once an enterprise has migrated to cloud, many of the controls from their on-prem environments are not required anymore or can be replaced by cloud native controls. Despite moving some or all of their workloads to the cloud, many enterprises have failed to acknowledge that in the cloud we are talking about an entirely new set of technologies being operated.

When designed and implemented correctly, the cloud may offer an unparalleled level of security for enterprises. Gartner forecasts that "in 2020 public cloud Infrastructure-as-a-Service (IaaS) workloads will suffer at least 60% fewer security incidents than those in traditional data centers" [40]. Whilst this may sound like marketing spin, there is some logic in this forecast. Proponents of the cloud security argue the cloud offers:

"Native cloud platform services are all integrated seamlessly, it offers an opportunity to leverage consistent monitoring, detection, logging, and auditing, all combined with powerful analytics and discovery tools enabled by machine learning to provide insights and control. Beyond monitoring and logging, centralized management of security controls provides unified single-pane-of-glass visibility into how security for data is applied across your organization. There is simply no way on-prem security programs can achieve the same level" [39].

To further detail some of the differences between legacy and native cloud security, Figure 7.1 illustrates a high-level generic ransomware attack sequence following an enterprises user credential becoming compromised. This event could occur because of a myriad of cyberattacks such as a phishing attack, weak password security, password recycling, or the connection of corrupted device (i.e., phone and USB device) to the enterprises network. As detailed below within Figure 7.1, the cautionary symbol illustrates common areas of control interdiction, whereby enterprise security controls should have detected and/or prevented the ransomware attack from progressing further. Despite the popular dramatization of ransomware attacks, when we talk about attacks against enterprises it is generally not a simple scenario of one user clicking on a nefarious link, and seconds later all the enterprises data is encrypted, and the entire network is offline. From the victim's perspective, it may appear that everything is happening so fast, and that reflects the design of the attack being executed. Non-human driven ransomware attacks (self-propagating) may also spread faster than human driven, as they require limited preparatory work [41]. Instead, Figure 7.1 highlights the level of complex steps that an attacker must successfully overcome to execute a ransomware attack against an enterprise utilizing common cybersecurity controls from the SANS top 20 [42].

By comparison we could explore all the various points of potential interdiction using cloud native security controls. For simplicity, we demonstrate this point by analyzing the step of the process of the attacker attempting to delete the enterprises backup data. This process is arguably one of the critical processes required for the attacker to successfully complete the ransomware attack. This is because it is highly unlikely that an enterprise would pay any ransom demand, should they have ready access to a snapshot or backup data repository which would enable them the ability to restore their systems. Whilst an enterprise may pay to prevent their data from being leaked, commonly referred to as a 'double tap' type of ransomware attack, there are no guarantees to ensure this will not occur after payment, so paying any form of ransom may be a moot point.

Within the cloud the use of automation, analytics, and generic cloud controls may drastically increase the security of an enterprise technology environment. The example detailed below in Figure 7.2 highlights that increasing an environment's overall security is not the result of strengthening individual controls, instead it is the result of strong controls working in unison to increase visibility and to create interlocks. In turn this also creates

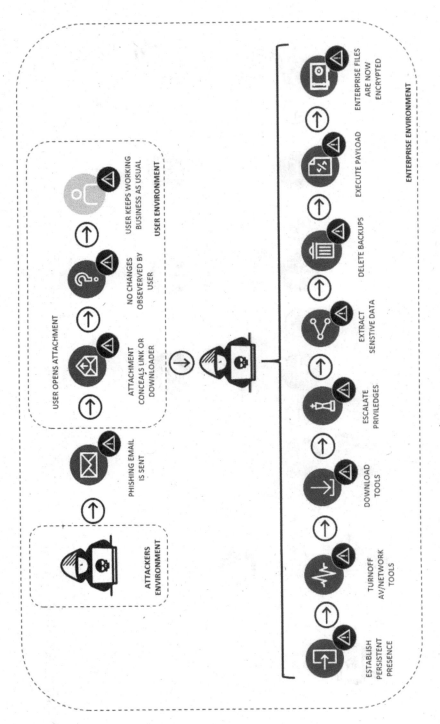

Figure 7.1 Compromised user credential ransomware attack sequence.

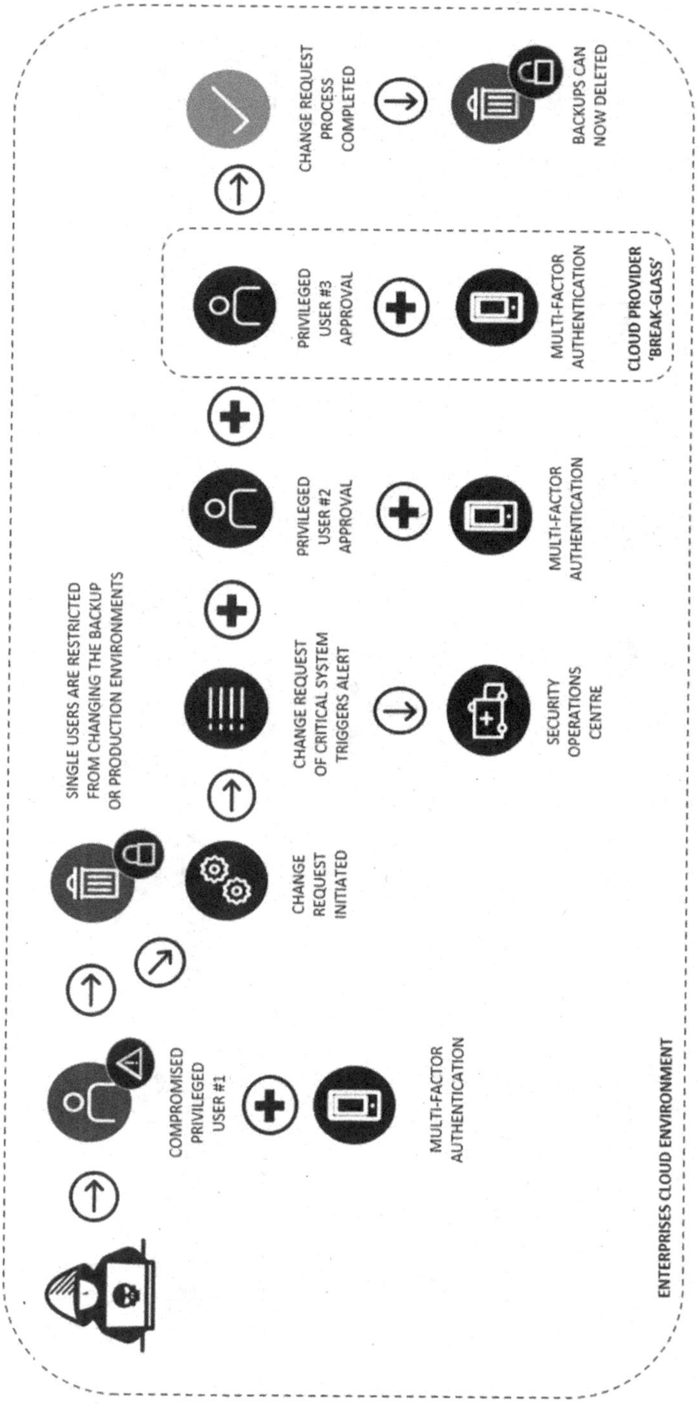

Figure 7.2 Cloud backup data security.

complexity for the attacker, which has the potential to lower an attackers' Return-on-Investment (ROI), and this should be considered a fundamental component of winning the cybersecurity battle with organized crime. This concept is supported by former National Security Agency (NSA) cyber-warfare officer and Dragos CEO Robert Lee (2020) who argues the notion that:

> "Defence is far behind... The adversaries only need to get one thing right, and we have to get everything right... This premise that the adversaries somehow have the upper hand is utterly ridiculous... They have to get everything right and stay stealthy...We just have to get one thing right and pivot to investigate and we win" [43].

Above Figure 7.2 details a potential compromised user credential-based ransomware attack against a high-level generic cloud environment. The users' credential may have become compromised through a phishing attack or by an alternative method. In spite of this, straight away we can see how the deployment of Multi-Factor Authentication (MFA) on the first users' (and subsequent users) accounts increases the level of complexity required to execute a successful ransomware attack. Moving forward, the attacker will at some point need to delete the data backups; however, this is prevented in this scenario because this process is governed (secured) by a formal change management process within the enterprises cloud management system. This attempted change can also be configured to automatically trigger an alert to notify the Security Operation Center (SOC) about the event, and to even notify other privileged users through automated email or SMS mechanisms.

In a worst-case scenario, the enterprises environment in Figure 7.2 may become heavily compromised (including the enterprises MFA mechanism), however the deployment of a break-glass mechanism will provide an additional layer of protection against cyberattacks such as ransomware. To further elaborate on this, the implementation of a break-glass function may require the CSP to approve or provide part of the security key required to execute specific configuration changes within the enterprise's cloud environment (i.e., delete backups or turn off security controls). The activation of a break-glass function is a highly unusual activity to be undertaken ad-hoc, and its activation will naturally trigger robust security protocols on the CSPs-end before any keys are exchanged or processes are to be approved. In heavily automated and mature cloud environments, the deployment of 'break-glass' functions is becoming standard practice to protect an enterprises' configuration settings for critical applications such as pricing engines, critical system configurations, and to provide a safety mechanism for high-risk change management activities such as rotating master encryption keys. Expanding on an insurance company's policy pricing tool example, the pricing tool may be configured to run autonomously, using multiple streams of data, algorithms, and pre-defined parameters to automatically generate prices for insurance policies. In this scenario, any unauthorized change to the pricing tools parameters may result in major financial and security incident for the insurer.

The process detailed in Figure 7.2 is not unique to cloud native environments, and similar environments may be designed and implemented using legacy technologies. However, the underlying problem in legacy environments is that this level of security, visibility, automation, and operability is not the default. The security controls detailed in Figure 7.2 are not only the standard controls that all enterprises can readily access and deploy in the cloud, but numerous controls were omitted for simplicity purposes. These removals include security controls such as: continual threat monitoring, suspicious login and activity monitoring, continuous validation, and data redundancy (e.g., snapshots). Other crucial elements not depicted in the cloud management system are application whitelisting, network logging of every user action (visibility), and the deployment of user behaviors analytics tools (AI/ML).

7.6.2 Visibility and Clarity

Today, many enterprises rely on a patchwork of reports from different sources to manage their cyber risks. Too often internal security teams lack access to the required threat intelligence, and real-time information related to the operational status and effectiveness of their key controls. Boehm (2019) argues that "analytics are the backbone of the information security management system; having a strong, smart analytical system in place enables users to integrate data from different sources across a network and aggregate risks as needed" [44]. Real-time visibility of the complete environment remains a significant deficiency in legacy environments, with many enterprises unable to see who is on their network, what they are doing, and what data they are accessing.

One of the foundation principles of establishing and maintaining an effective cybersecurity environment is implementing effective access control. Despite this, Identity and Access Management (IAM) and Privileged Access Management (PAM), has remained one of the MitreCorporations top security weaknesses for the past decade [45]. Typically, this problem is magnified through the use of legacy on-prem solutions because they are often weak in providing proper visibility over the provisioning and validation of the access logs. For example, many legacy (non-cloud) and hybrid-cloud enterprise environments may utilize a specialized IAM platform, maybe a PAM platform, and a Security Information and Event Management (SIEM) system. The SIEM system may also be outsourced to a third-party Managed Security Services Provider. Additionally, internal audit functions are generally geographically separated from their business and information security departments. For some enterprises, this function may even be outsourced to an external auditor due to a lack of internal technology expertise. As a result, this often makes it very difficult to accurately and efficiently validate the access permissions and activities for potentially up to a few hundred thousand staff that are spread across global offices. To address some of these challenges, many enterprises have implemented a formal attestation process, where business owners are required to periodically validate user access to their systems. The problem is that some systems may have thousands of users, of which the system owners only know very few.

Control visibility weaknesses associated with IAM are not limited to legacy (non-cloud) environments. An analysis by Google into IAM's usage on its own Google Cloud Platform (GCP) found that "most permissions granted to cloud users aren't actually used within 90 days" [39]. This discovery is at odds with the principle of least privilege, and provides practical insight into some of the challenges faced by enterprises to uplift IAM. However, Google's analysis does highlight some of the advantages that cloud can provide enterprises in the IAM space through the increased visibility, and by enabling enterprises to easily and rapidly implement advanced analytics and automation capabilities without the need to develop bespoke solutions.

Using the scenario above where a user has not accessed an application for over 90 days, the Google Cloud Command Center will automatically recommend that the user's access to the application be suspended or removed[1]. However, in the cloud this can easily be automatically (or manually) designed to be restored by the user by self-requesting access to the application through a user interface, with the outcome and provisioning to be automatically determined by the user's role. Microsoft has also automated this process for some applications with Azure [46]. Automated processes such as this IAM example can be implemented for legacy (non-cloud) systems too, but the primary reasoning why it has not been implemented in most enterprises is simply that the IAM solution is not capable of performing this process, and the resources required to replace the IAM solution are too high.

7.7 ENGINEERING SOLUTIONS

Arguably some of the greatest foreseeable advantages of CSPs taking increased responsibly for enterprises technology environments are: a) the reduction in misconfigurations through automated provisioning using robust templates and guardrails, b) access to readily deploy advanced analytics and scanning tools to automatically mitigate threats, and c) enterprises having access to specialized teams of global cybersecurity experts that understand their environment, and can help them safeguard their business assets and data at all times. Whist there are no technological barriers that are preventing this shift, holistically there remain a series of minor business and technology challenges (i.e., the efficiency, security, co-ordination, and level of automation) that require further improvements before an enhanced responsibility model can be deployed at the scale. The following section outlines some of these challenges, and potential approaches that may speed up the transformation process.

7.7.1 Mutable to Immutable Infrastructure

Prior to the adoption of cloud computing, building server infrastructure and software was an expensive process that required dealing directly with each physical server. Replacing or updating these physical servers was a costly and time-consuming process, and as a result a practice called mutable infrastructure was born. Mutable approaches allow infrastructure updates and configuration changes to be undertaken in-place. However, this highly open and adaptive practice inevitably led to a series of critical problems including unreliability, increased complexity, and inconsistency in change management outcomes. Through advances in virtualization and cloud technologies, the industry was able to begin addressing some of these problems. In order to increase the predictability and efficiency of the replacement process, immutable infrastructure was implemented into major cloud and enterprise providers' environments. This concept is based on "the core idea of immutable infrastructure, in which no modification to a running server is allowed unless the server is completely replaced with a new instance that contains all the necessary changes" [47].

Looking to the future, the broader adoption of immutable infrastructure and software could offer significant gains through simplified deployments, faster rollback, and increased security to the enterprise's environment. For example, removing a user's ability to alter the underlying operating system's code could prevent the user from introducing misconfigurations and errors into the environment. This design change could limit or remove an adversary's ability to maliciously alter the underlying code, which may prevent the adversary from launching other types of attack. These types of design change have the potential to drastically reduce potential attack vectors, with limited to no impact on user functionality for the majority of enterprise users.

7.7.2 Reduced User Functionality

At the turn of 21st century, software developers were marketing to businesses and home users that their products could help them do almost anything. To help deliver on those promises their operating systems and applications were designed with a high degree of compatibility, connectivity, and interoperability. However, this high level of flexibility and functionality generally was not without consequence, and it generally came at the price of security. Through the ongoing collection of data related to user behaviors, software providers now have a much deeper understanding of what applications are being used, what users are doing, when, and for how long. Within modern enterprises, the vast majority of user activities being performed are basic user tasks such as emails, writing reports, data entry, and video conferencing. Therefore, the removal of non-essential user functionality from operating systems and applications for general users represents an area of development that may provide significant security advancements for enterprise environments. This removal of non-essential user functionality is supported by Lee (2020) who argues:

> "Microsoft own the physics of their operating system... Everything you can and cannot do, Microsoft own that... I guarantee you that within five years Microsoft just take away the functionality related to a user being able to mass encrypt all the files on a system... They just do away with it" [43].

In cloud native environments, general users have limited reasons to encrypt data, especially at bulk-data. By default, databases and share drives are encrypted at rest in most CSPs environments. Of course, there are legitimate needs for general users to encrypt data, for example to transfer sensitive or legal documents to an external third party. However, a suite of different secure-exchange products by vendors and CSPs that perform this function securely already exist. When we consider the aggregate volume of change in the cloud, and the potential for reduced operating system user functionality, then one of the first place we may see this change is through a Desktop-as-a-Service (DaaS) product. This is supported by Vaughan-Nichols (2020) who states that "the folks at Microsoft have been pushing Windows to a DaaS model for years now. Recently, and with the release of Microsoft 365 and Windows Virtual Desktop (WVD), there's no question Microsoft wants you to move your office work to the cloud" [48].

7.7.3 Throttling

Throttling is not a new process in cybersecurity or engineering, and it can be observed across multiple disciplines in engineering. Within cybersecurity throttling is generally defined as process that is used to limit the number of user actions, bandwidth, or concurrent calls (by script or code) to prevent overuse of resources. As detailed in Figure 7.3, this process is useful in cybersecurity, as it can be used to detect (and prevent) inadvertent or malicious actions by single users. The throttling limit can be used as a monitoring (detection) tool which can be used to trigger an alert, or even automated to prevent (by stopping) the activity.

The implementation of throttling is a useful tool for detecting threats such as browser compromise (illegal crypto mining), DDoS attacks, scripted attacks, and other forms of brute force attacks. Another common throttling example used is restricting the number of logins that a user can attempt in a given time period at a customer access portal, or even the speed of keystrokes being entered at the portal. Throttling can also be used to detect (and prevent) a user trying to encrypt large volumes of data due to the processing power (resources required) will surge at the point of mass file encryption. There are also alternative types of throttling such as Melton's (2018) power analysis technique, which was used to classify the steps of encryption and correlate them to identify when encryption is occurring on a computer may also be useful. Melton discovered that:

> "Due to the nature of the malware, encryption processes are detected. When such processes are observed, it is possible to stop the computer processes until verified by the user. As a result, ransomware activity can be halted before continuing to encrypt data and possibly preventing further encryption early in the ransomware's process limits the amount of data being no longer accessible by the user while saving most of the files on a computer" [49].

Whilst this type of throttling to action process is not standard practice, the technology to implement these types of processes and controls already exists within cloud security systems. Moving forward, as the level of automation in cybersecurity systems increases, it is likely that events that trigger alerts today will be followed by automated responses by the security system. To meet the security needs of enterprises, cybersecurity systems will need to increase their level of autonomy in mitigating security threats. To further aid this process, enterprises will be required to drastically consolidate the volume of assets and

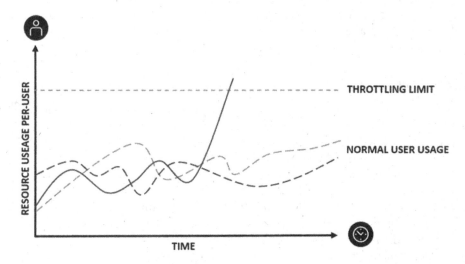

Figure 7.3 Throttling diagram.

applications operating in their environment, and the cloud provides an opportunity for both of these endeavors to occur in the near future.

7.8 AGGREGATE OF CHANGE

This research has highlighted the increasing appetite from enterprises for cloud computing services, and the rapid adoption of IaaS/SaaS solutions. It has also highlighted enterprises growing reliance on third parties for cybersecurity, and the prevalence of security incidents from security misconfigurations in the cloud. These events not only produce friction, but they also cause financial and reputational damage to the enterprises and as well as the CSPs involved. Whilst these incidents and more incremental changes have been transpiring over the last decade, in the background CSPs have been collecting an enormous amount of data to determine their future options. In principle the path forward is relatively simple, the CSPs need to; a) provide a secure environment that is easy for enterprises to on-board too, b) provide business services that enterprises demand, and c) implement an operating model that is comparable to alternative options but is profitable for themselves. The latter is where the shared security model comes in.

From the outset of enterprise cloud adoption, CSPs have exhibited a genuine desire to build secure and resilient systems that protect their clients from cyberattacks such as ransomware, data theft, and DDoS attacks. They also acutely understood the risk, which is why they were quick to draw a line in the sand about defining shared responsibilities. Broadly they were happy to accept responsibility for the underlying network and infrastructure, but were also clear that they wanted nothing to do with the user level applications or data. It is our expectation that in the coming years this approach will increasingly be challenged for a variety of reasons. The primary reason is that enterprises are adopting SaaS at unprecedented rates, and this has drawn Microsoft and Google into the security of elements beyond the shared responsibility model. The adoption of SaaS is driven by the needs of the business, as AWS does not provide a suite of business products, it has not been drawn into the security of SaaS at the same rate as the other two CSPs. Additionally, in the wake of continued technological advances in virtualization, analytics, and automation, CSPs are becoming increasingly confident about their ability to defend their clients native cloud environments. This can also be evidenced by Microsoft's submission to Parliamentary Joint Committee Intelligence and Security Review of the Security Legislation Amendment (Critical Infrastructure) "the danger of having a government direct a private sector entity's response without complete knowledge of the situation and the technology cannot be understated" [50].

This growing confidence is further evidenced by Google Cloud's CISO Phil Venables (2021) announcement that "we are pushing the boundaries of the security capabilities customers should expect a cloud platform to deliver. Shared fate goes beyond the existing cloud security model" [25]. The shift in language to a 'shared fate' model is indicative that CSPs are already moving closer towards taking an increased level of responsibility and control. Based on this notion, we argue that a shift towards a TaaS model will continue to evolve incrementally until the CSPs effectively become an all-in-one service provider. However, there will be some limitations, such as entities will still need to provide personal staff data and detail access rights to enable IAM and PAM provisioning.

As this shift towards what is best defined as a TaaS model continues to evolve, there are numerous challenges that will need to be resolved or uplifted. Ultimately, for the TaaS model to be successful, the CSPs will require all applications within their environment to be built to a robust application development specification. Chiodi (2021) explains that "in the next 18 months, we will start to see examples of ML deployed within some very specific use cases. It will start to show up in areas like data classification, malware detection, and automated reasoning. For example, ML that can evaluate security configurations from multiple different angles, as an attacker would" [51]. These advancements are essential for the CSPs to perform functions such as the provision access controls, monitoring network events, vulnerability management, and to respond to security threats. The proposition of an TaaS model naturally raises concerns about provider concentration risk. However, in many ways the risk of concentration is already present in industry. For example, if an enterprise uses a SaaS business suite in a multi-cloud environment (a common practice to try an achieve resilience), if the SaaS provider becomes the victim of a major global disruption (e.g., a cyberattack), ultimately the product they support may be down irrespective of which CSP or Data Center the provider or the enterprise are using. This scenario also raises a growing underlying problem, many enterprises are insufficiently aware of their own, and their third-party providers critical interdependencies (fourth-party providers).

There may also be concerns in relation to the reduction of security through the removal of obscurity. This is a double-edged sword, because obscurity often conceals an enterprises applications and security defenses, and attackers are frequently detected and thwarted by controls they were unaware existed. By standardizing architectures and security controls, this potentially increases the value of exploits against those systems, which encourages criminals and intelligence agencies to further develop them. The other side of the sword argues that obscurity increases complexity, which requires bespoke integrations and reduces the effectiveness of some controls; thus, increasing the potential for security gaps in the environment to be created and go untreated.

This series of discussions raise the issue of cybersecurity resourcing and expertize. In the existing model, developers and security practitioners of varying ability are responsible for task such as developing an enterprises' security strategy, applications, configuring security controls and systems, and the ongoing security of the business' information systems and data. A fundamental difference in the advancement of the TaaS model will be the continued standardization of architectures and controls. Security architectures and controls such as IAM are already standardized in Microsoft Azure and GCP for native SaaS applications. This standardization process would also drive the consolidation of cybersecurity resources within the major CSPs. Global teams of cybersecurity experts, the same experts who built the architecture and controls, will now be working in unison with advanced analytics, tools, and automation to provide continuous protection of their cloud environment. No longer will attackers be able to exploit the absence of basic security controls, misconfigurations, or SIEM alerts being dismissed. The overarching system will become highly autonomous, using colossal amounts and streams of data to manage, detect and respond to suspicious activities. The development and implementation of the TaaS model is unlikely to be an easy or inexpensive process. Although the development and implementation of the required stages may be challenging, we argue that the financial and security benefits are likely to be great enough for the CSPs to rapidly pursue them.

7.9 CONCLUSION

Throughout the last decade, enterprises have increasingly outsourced their information systems to the cloud; however, this transition continues to be challenged by misconfigurations by enterprise staff, which have been the root cause of numerous high-profile disruptions and cybersecurity incidents. For enterprise management teams and CSPs, the financial and reputational ramifications of these incidents are becoming increasingly problematic for their brands. In response, through bulk-data collection activities, CSPs are increasingly becoming aware of potential ways forward that may solve or reduce the threat to enterprises from cyberattacks. The research explored how these developments are increasingly pointing towards CSPs taking more responsibility and control of the overall technology environment. It also highlighted that any shift in operating model that alters the responsibility and control of CSPs inevitably triggers discussions about the sustainability of the existing shared responsibility model.

This research postulates that a shift towards a TaaS model may create significant financial opportunities for CSPs, whilst simultaneously improving the cybersecurity capabilities of their customers. Should Boards and management teams be presented the opportunity to outsource their technology and cybersecurity worries to a leading CSP for a comparative price, this option is likely to be a very attractive proposition for businesses who are not in the technology or cybersecurity business themselves. This is further illustrated by the ongoing challenges large enterprises face in relation to technology and cybersecurity costs, talent deficiencies, product effectiveness, incidents related to misconfigurations, complexity of control integration, regulatory changes, and the dynamic nature of cybersecurity threats. It is therefore easy to conceive a future where enterprises would jump at the opportunity for CSPs take over their entire technology environment. The pathway to implement a successful TaaS model still has many challenges that require resolution, and there may be diverse routes beyond those outlined in this paper. Whilst it may take years for some of these advancements to fully materialize, this research has sought to draw attention to the silent battle for cloud supremacy, and how this battle is shaping the future of enterprise security.

This research explored how advances in technology have led enterprises to rapidly adopt cloud computing services, which has transformed how enterprises select, operate, and secure their business information systems and data. Whilst the research revealed that there are numerous security advantages for enterprises migrating to cloud native security systems, the driving forces behind most enterprises uplifting to cloud are the perceived opportunities to reduce costs, scalability, and the potential to creating competitive advantages. This chapter also identified shortfalls across the cybersecurity industry, highlighting that after investing trillions of dollars and years of effort, many enterprises have made little or no relative improvements in their cybersecurity capabilities. For many enterprises, the adoption of robust cloud native security systems will significantly increase the effort required for adversaries to undertake cyberattacks such as ransomware attacks and IP theft. This will also provide enterprises easy access to advanced security controls and analytics, and the ability to leverage the internal expertise of CSPs. Future cloud adoption may improve the security of enterprise, which inadvertently may begin to challenge the ROI for cyber adversaries.

NOTE

1 This notification is not unique to Google Cloud. It can also be amended for different time periods and automated responses for different applications.

REFERENCES

[1] Amazon Web Services, "Shared Responsibility Model." Accessed on: February 27, 2021. Available: https://aws.amazon.com/compliance/shared-responsibility-model/
[2] Google, "Google Cloud Platform: Shared Responsibility Matrix." Accessed on: February 22, 2021. Available: https://services.google.com/fh/files/misc/gcp_pci_srm__apr_2019.pdf
[3] Microsoft, "Shared responsibility in the cloud." 3 February 2021. Available: https://docs.microsoft.com/en-us/azure/security/fundamentals/shared-responsibility

[4] M. Ryan, "The ransomware revolution: how emerging encryption technologies created a prodigious cyber threat," *Doctorate of Cybersecurity, School of Engineering and Information Technology.* UNSW, 2020. Available: http://unsworks.unsw.edu.au/fapi/datastream/unsworks:72179/SOURCE02?view= true

[5] Financial Services Information Sharing and Analysis Center, "Safeguarding the Global Financial System by Reducing Cyber Risk." Accessed on: March 20, 2021. Available: https://www.fsisac.com/

[6] S. Arons and N. Grant, "Deutsche bank to move 'Heart' of IT systems Into Google's cloud." in *Bloomberg.* 5 Dec 2020. Accessed on: 5 December 2020. Available: https://www.bloomberg.com/news/articles/2020-12-04/deutsche-bank-to-move-heart-of-it-systems-into-google-s-cloud

[7] K. Nash, "J.P. Morgan set to run first apps in public cloud," *The Wall Street Journal*, 30 March 2017. Accessed on: 30 March 2017. Available: https://www.wsj.com/articles/BL-CIOB-11770

[8] Microsoft, "Microsoft annual report FY19/20," Redmond, Washington. 2021, Accessed on: Fenruary 24, 2021. Available: https://www.microsoft.com/investor/reports/ar20/index.html

[9] L. Matthew, "Boeing is the latest wanna cry ransomware victim." *Forbes*, 30 March 2018. Accessed on: June 1, 2018. Available: https://www.forbes.com/sites/leemathews/2018/03/30/boeing-is-the-latest-wannacry-ransomware-victim/#218e8ea96634

[10] E. Schmidt, "Conversation with Eric Schmidt." in *Search Engine Strategies Conference*, 2006: Google.

[11] A. Lance and A. Chuvakin, "Designing and Deploying a Data Security Strategy With Google Cloud." January 2021. Accessed on: February 4, 2021. Available: https://services.google.com/fh/files/misc/designing_and_deploying_data_security_strategy.pdf

[12] J. Bernard, D. Golden, and M. Nicholson, "Reshaping the cybersecurity landscape," *Deloitte Insights*, 24 July 2020. Accessed on: October 18, 2020. Available: https://www2.deloitte.com/content/dam/Deloitte/pt/Documents/risk/Cybersecurity.pdf

[13] B. Borcherding, "Why enterprises are accelerating cloud adoption." *Forbes*, 17 July 2020. Accessed on: March 5, 2021. Available: https://www.forbes.com/sites/forbestechcouncil/2020/07/17/why-enterprises-are-accelerating-cloud-adoption/?sh=37e4a045f498

[14] Gartner, "Gartner forecasts worldwide public cloud revenue to grow 6.3% in 2020," *Gartner*, 23 July 2020. Accessed on: 23 July 2020. Available: https://www.gartner.com/en/newsroom/press-releases/2020-07-23-gartner-forecasts-worldwide-public-cloud-revenue-to-grow-6point3-percent-in-2020

[15] Microsoft Security Response Center, "Microsoft Internal Solorigate Investigation – Final Update." 18 February 2021. Accessed on: March 8, 2021. Available: https://msrc-blog.microsoft.com/2021/02/18/microsoft-internal-solorigate-investigation-final-update/

[16] K. Lister, *U.S. Employers Stand to Save Over $500B a Year with a Combination of In-Office/Remote Work Strategies.* San Diego, CA: Global Workplace Analytics, 2021.

[17] Businesswire, "United States virtualization security market report 2021," *Dublin* 18 February 2021. Accessed on: March 7, 2021. Available: https://www.businesswire.com/news/home/20210218005726/en/United-States-Virtualization-Security-Market-Report-2021---Growth-Trends-COVID-19-Impact-and-Forecasts-to-2026---ResearchAndMarkets.com

[18] M. Honan, "How apple and amazon security flaws led to my epic hacking," *WIRED*, 8 June 2012. Accessed on: March 7, 2021. Available: https://www.wired.com/2012/08/apple-amazon-mat-honan-hacking/

[19] Microsoft, "Human-Operated Ransomware Attacks: A Preventable Disaster," 5 March 2020. Accessed on: March 20, 2020. Available: https://www.microsoft.com/security/blog/2020/03/05/human-operated-ransomware-attacks-a-preventable-disaster/

[20] P. Institute, "The cyber resilient organization: learning to thrive against threats." Ponemon Institute, September 2015. Accessed on: March 12, 2021. Available: https://www.ponemon.org/local/upload/file/The%20Cyber%20Resilient%20Enterprise%20Final%2010.pdf

[21] *Safeguarding Customer Records and Information in Network Storage – Use of Third Party Security Features*. 2019. Available: https://www.sec.gov/files/OCIE%20Risk%20Alert%20-%20Network%20Storage.pdf

[22] T. Maurer and G. Hinck, "Cloud security: a primer for policymakers." in "Cloud Security," Carnegie Endowment for International Peace, 2020. Accessed on: March 16, 2021. Available: https://www.jstor.org/stable/resrep25787.9

[23] C. Smith, "How the cloud has opened new doors for hackers." in *The Washington Post*. 2020. Accessed on: 2 March 2020. Available: https://www.washingtonpost.com/technology/2020/03/02/cloud-hack-problems/.

[24] L. Feiner, "Slack accuses microsoft of anticompetitive practices in EU complaint." 22 July 2020. Accessed on: March 7, 2021. Available: https://www.cnbc.com/2020/07/22/slack-accuses-microsoft-of-anticompetitive-practices-in-eu-complaint.html

[25] P. Venables and S. Potti, "Announcing the risk protection program: moving from shared responsibility to shared fate." *Google Cloud*, 2 March 2021. Accessed on: March 2, 2021. Available: https://cloud.google.com/blog/products/identity-security/google-cloud-risk-protection-program-now-in-preview

[26] J. Hubback, "Cybersecurity technology efficacy: is cybersecurity the new "Market for Lemons"?," *Debate Security* 2020. Accessed on: March 6, 2021. Available: https://www.debatesecurity.com/downloads/Cybersecurity-Technology-Efficacy-Research-Report-V1.0.pdf

[27] Deloitte, "The economic value of cloud services in Australia," July 2019. Accessed on: June 15, 2020. Available: https://www2.deloitte.com/au/en/pages/economics/articles/economic-value-cloud-services-australia.html

[28] Q. Hardy, "How cloud computing is changing management," *Harvard Business Review*, 8 February 2018. Accessed on: March 2, 2021. Available: https://hbr.org/2018/02/how-cloud-computing-is-changing-management

[29] Financial Stability Board, "FSB consults on regulatory and supervisory issues relating to outsourcing and third-party relationships," *Financial Stability Board*, 9 Nov 2020. Accessed on: 9 November 2020. Available: https://www.fsb.org/2020/11/fsb-consults-on-regulatory-and-supervisory-issues-relating-to-outsourcing-and-third-party-relationships/

[30] W. Byres, "Peering into a cloudy future," in *Curious Thinkers Conference*. Sydney: APRA, 2018. URL: https://www.apra.gov.au/news-and-publications/apra-chair-wayne-byres-speech-to-2018-curious-thinkers-conference

[31] (2018). *DoD Cloud Strategy*. Available: https://media.defense.gov/2019/Feb/04/2002085866/-1/-1/1/DOD-CLOUD-STRATEGY.PDF

[32] A. Levite and G. Kalwani, "Cloud governance challanges: a survery of policy and regulatory issues," in *"Cloud Security,"* Carnegie Endowment for International Peace, 2020, Accessed on: March 16, 2021. Available: https://www.jstor.org/stable/resrep27699.5

[33] S. Blumberg, T. Delaet, and K. Swami, "Ten 'antipatterns' that are derailing technology transformations," *McKinsey Digital*, 21 July 2020. Accessed on: March 21, 2021. Available: https://www.mckinsey.com/business-functions/mckinsey-digital/our-insights/ten-antipatterns-that-are-derailing-technology-transformations

[34] S. Curry, "Neurodiversity: a competitive advantage in cybersecurity," in *Forbes*, 13 May 2019. Accessed on: 13 May 2019. Available: https://www.forbes.com/sites/samcurry/2019/05/13/neurodiversity-a-competitive-advantage-in-cybersecurity/?sh=53f9e29e6265

[35] N. Tiku, "Three years of misery inside Google, the Happiest Company in Tech," *WIRED*, 13 August 2019. Accessed on: September 4, 2019. Available: https://www.wired.com/story/inside-google-three-years-misery-happiest-company-tech/

[36] J. Wolff, *You'll See This Message When It Is Too Late: The Legal and Economic Aftermath of Cybersecurity Breaches*. Cambridge, Massachsetts: The MIT Press, 2018.

[37] B. Schneier, "A Plea for Simplicity: You can't secure what you don't understand.," *Information Security*, 19 November 1999.

[38] J. Dunn, "Is The Cybersecurity Industry Selling Lemons? Apparently Lots Of Important CISOs Think it Is," in *Forbes*. New York, 2020. Accessed on: 22 Oct 2020. Available: https://www.forbes.com/sites/johndunn/2020/10/22/is-the-cybersecurity-industry-selling-companies-lemons-apparently-lots-of-important-cisos-think-it-is/?sh=181af01574dc

[39] A. Lance and A. Chuvakin, "Google Cloud Whitepape: Designing and Deploying a Data Security Strategy with Google Cloud," January 2021. Available: https://services.google.com/fh/files/misc/designing_and_deploying_data_security_strategy.pdf

[40] Gartner, "Cloud Strategy Leadership." Accessed on: February 23, 2021. Available: https://www.gartner.com/imagesrv/books/cloud/cloud_strategy_leadership.pdf

[41] M. Ryan, *Ransomware Revolution: The Rise of a Prodigious Cyber Threat* (Advances in Information Security) S. Jajodia, Ed. Fairfax, VA, USA: Springer, 2021.

[42] Center for Internet Security, "The CIS Critical Security Controls for Effective Cyber Defense," 1 April 2019. Accessed on: March 7, 2021. Available: https://www.sans.org/critical-security-controls

[43] R. Lee, "The threat to industrial control systems." in *S4 Events*, Miami, Florida, 2020. S4X.

[44] J. Boehm, J. Kaplan, P. Merrath, T. Poppensieker, and T. Stähleand, "Enhanced Cyberrisk Reporting: Opening Doors to Risk-Based Cybersecurity," 9 November

2019. Accessed on: April 11, 2020. Available: https://www.mckinsey.com/
~/media/McKinsey/Business%20Functions/Risk/Our%20Insights/Enhanced
%20cyberrisk%20reporting%20Opening%20doors%20to%20risk%20based
%20cybersecurity/Enhanced-cyberrisk-reporting-Opening-doors-to-risk-based-cy-
bersecurity.ashx

[45] MITRE Corporation, "Common weakness enumeration: top 25 most dangerous software weaknesses," 26 Oct 2021. Accessed on: 10 December
2020. Available: https://cwe.mitre.org/data/definitions/1350.html

[46] Microsoft, "What is Automated SaaS app user provisioning in Azure AD?,"
8 February 2021. Accessed on:February 17, 2021. Available: https://docs.
microsoft.com/en-us/azure/active-directory/app-provisioning/user-
provisioning

[47] J. Cavallaro, S. Sonnenberg, and S. Knuckley, *Living Under Drones*. Stanford:
Stanford Law School, 2012.

[48] S. Vaughan-Nichols, "Desktop-as-a-Service: will you soon be running your
"Desktop" from the cloud?," *Insider Pro*, 4 September 2020. Accessed on:
March 21, 2021. Available: https://www.idginsiderpro.com/article/3565755/
desktop-as-a-service-will-you-soon-be-running-your-desktop-from-the-
cloud.html

[49] J. Melton, "Detecting ransomware through power analysis," in *Master of
Science Electrical Engineering Naval Postgraduate School*. Monterey, CA,
2018. P. 40.

[50] Microsoft, "Microsoft Submission to the PJCIS Review of the Security
Legislation Amendment (Critical Infrastructure) Bill 2020," in *Parliamentary
Joint Committee on Intelligence and Security*, 2021.

[51] M. Chiodi, "Cloud security 2021: 4 key trends you shouldn't miss," in Paloalto
Blog, no. 17, April 2020, Available: https://blog.paloaltonetworks.com/2020/
04/cloud-security-2021/

Chapter 8

Security, Privacy, and Trust of Emerging Intelligent Transportation: Cognitive Internet of Vehicles

Khondokar Fida Hasan[1], Antony Overall[1], Keyvan Ansari[2],
Gowri Ramachandran[1], and Raja Jurdak[1]

[1]School of Computer Science, Queensland University of Technology (QUT)
[2]School of Science, Technology, and Engineering, University of the Sunshine Coast (USC)

CONTENTS

8.1 INTRODUCTION

The transportation system is an indispensable part of modern civilization and a primary contributory sector in today's economy. In the past two

DOI: 10.1201/9781003121541-8

decades, the vehicular industry has experienced sharp growth, especially in first world countries. According to the Motor Vehicle Census in 2020, there are 19.8 million registered motors for 25 million people in Australia, with an annual average increase of 1.7% [1]. The whole world has more than 1.4 billion vehicles, and this number is projected to be doubled in 2040 [2]. With an increase in cars on roads, there comes a substantial rise in traffic-related incidents, such as vehicle and pedestrian accidents and increased congestion [3]. However, noticeable efforts in developing the transportation system are observed so far. Among them, the recent technological development utilizing cloud-based artificial intelligence and machine learning towards developing cognitive computing technology is considered a revolutionary step in addressing some burning issues such as driving behavior and providing the necessary rapid response on the road.

Meanwhile, the tech world experienced penetration of the novel concept of communication between humans and things and among things themselves over the past few decades. The Internet of Things (IoT), as it is named, is a technological advancement that enabling such interactions mobilizing the Fourth Industrial Revolution. The concept of IoT is to make every single "network enabled" object in the world connected and represents a vision in which the Internet extends into the real world, embracing everyday objects from the Internet of Computers to the Internet of Things. This paradigm already demonstrated its potential and reshaping the future of communication, bringing further improvements and radical transformations to human lives, including homes, transportation systems, the environment, and human well-being [4].

Under the umbrella of the Internet of Things (IoT), transportation evolution is considered a breakthrough in respect of trends and traffic management approaches to enable safety and comfort on the road is also popularly termed as the Internet of Vehicles (IoV). IoV makes sensor platforms that can receive information from other vehicles, the environment, and the driver to ensure a safer road transport system. Although a significant improvement in automation and connectivity is observed, IoV-based model is still inefficient due to the lack of technical sophistication to reduce the road causalities to zero [5]. The IoV framework-based solution cannot address many issues. One of the primary issues, perhaps, is the driving errors and misjudgment by drivers. For autonomous vehicles, this can relate to onboard sensors' errors and misinterpretation of data. According to road research statistics, over 90% of road accidents are caused by humans at present [6]. Such accidents are primarily due to fatigue while driving, overspeeding, blocked line of sight in the road are directly caused by human factors such as cognitive limitations and judgments. Limits of human and existing technology-based solutions encourage the necessity of applying emerging technologies, such as machine-enabled cognition using Machine Learning (ML), Artificial Intelligence (AI), and related technologies with system automation that can control decision-making. These can offer technical support to enable error-free driving, emergency response, and advanced driving assistance resulting in the idea of the Cognitive Internet of Vehicles (C-IoV). C-IoV is an evolved paradigm of IoV that introduces cloud-based AI/ML into the transportation system. Therefore, cognitive technology has allowed for more significant enhancements in IoV and its capabilities. However, cybersecurity issues pose the greatest threat to effective implementation of the future to safe mobility.

8.1.1 Chapter Roadmap

In the following sections, at first, a brief of intelligent transportation systems' evolution is presented in Section 8.2. Later a close look at the evolved framework, the Cognitive Internet of Vehicles (C-IoV), is discussed in Section 8.3. The primary issues of Security, Privacy, and Trust around the developed layer in the cloud are outlined in Section 8.4. Section 8.5 discusses countermeasures employing the cognitive layer. However, additional issues of security and privacy utilizing the cognitive engine are presented in Section 8.6 before the concluding remarks in Section 8.7.

8.2 EVOLUTION OF INTELLIGENT TRANSPORTATION SYSTEM

Transportation systems constitute an indispensable part of modern life that plays a critical role in coordinating all forms of transport and related traffic to offer safety by tackling a range of challenging issues. Since the invention of the wheel, we have witnessed the evolution of transportation in all forms, from automobiles to personal commuters like bicycles, motorcycles, scooters, etc. This evolution was perhaps slow over thousands of centuries, has gained impetus in the last two centuries. However, the greatest breakthrough is observed perhaps in the past two decades with the introduction of Information and Communication Technologies (ICT) to the transportation sector. ICT is the driving force behind some of the remarkable innovations in the transportation industry in modern society. Novel ICT-enabled technologies are irresistibly integrating into automobiles to improve driving experiences and tackle some burning issues, such as traffic congestion, road accident, and other road fatalities that cause death and property lost.

Aiming towards smart transport and traffic management systems, combining different technologies and different modes of applications, in the 19th century, the umbrella term Intelligent Transportation System (ITS) has emerged and is widely used to identify transportation innovation. In the 20th century, however, we had observed remarkable innovation and rapid penetration of disruptive ICT technologies over the past 20 years. This leads to having three successive frameworks after ITS are: Cooperative ITS (C-ITS), Internet of Vehicles (IoV), and Cognitive Internet of Vehicles (C-IoV). A graph showing the evolution of intelligent transportation is presented in

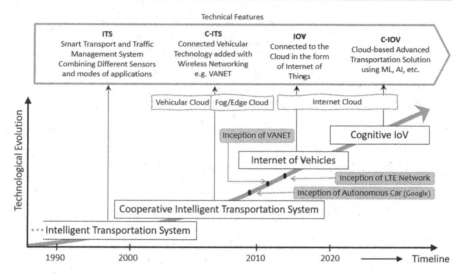

Figure 8.1 Evolution of intelligent transportation system [7].

Figure 8.1, outlining the primary technical features, different stages of the cloud and market inception of the prime technology. Four significant phases from the 1980s can be seen where around 2010, Autonomous cars, VANET, and LTE networks were incepted into the market. With CITS, both vehicular cloud and edge cloud are introduced. At the same time, the Internet cloud is the platform of the frameworks IoV and C-IoV.

While evolution is a continuous process, the transportation system is evolving following different authorities' guidelines to enable full autonomous driving levels (Level-5) defined in the Society of Automotive Engineers (SAE) levels of driving automation [8]. The penetration of technologies is accelerating the required evolution to achieve road safety and efficiency utilizing in different assistive manners.

While defining, ITS is a set of technologies, applications, and services to tackle road safety issues and empower mobility to assist with productivity and comfort. Conceptually, the term ITS broadly refers to a transportation system with various sensors and assisting technologies integrated on vehicles and infrastructures to monitor their local environment to understand their surroundings accurately. Additionally, wireless communication lets vehicles exchange information with each other and with other road elements.

Although both sensor-based autonomous and communication-based assisted technology march in parallel, the technological evolution under each set-up has been treated differently; and different groups of scientists, researchers, and developers are working under two technology directions: Autonomous vehicles (AV) and Connected Vehicles (CV). Thus, technologically, the Intelligent Transportation System generally refers to a range from Autonomous Vehicle (AV) to Connected Vehicles (CV), as shown in Figure 8.2.

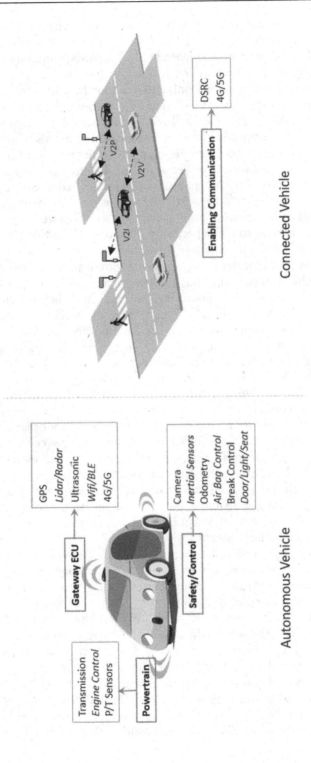

Figure 8.2 The concept of intelligent transportation system. (a) Autonomous vehicle (b) Connected vehicles [9].

More closely, in autonomous vehicles, a broad range of sensors is integrated into the vehicle to collect the data about the surrounding environment enabling them to operate independently. Primarily, autonomous vehicles can be considered as self-controlled robots that operate independently and take a wide range of decisions onboard without human interaction [10]. While traveling on the road, these vehicles can perceive, understand, and interpret traffic scenarios, make intelligent decisions, and act upon them. The ability to operate independently is facilitated mainly by the innovation in robotics and available tools and techniques. Noticeable breakthroughs in robotics have been observed in recent years due to the advancement of Artificial Intelligence (AI). AI enables machines to make independent, intelligent decisions like humans. AI-powered vision and signal processing techniques gather information around the road environment, interpret, and model the information to make necessary decisions. The actions may further change the environment, requiring subsequent decisions. This results in a close-looped system that tightly integrates the physical and digital realms.

A single vehicle presumably has limited perception ability on the road, therefore, limited knowledge about the road and the other vehicles' intent. Thus the Connected Vehicle (CV) emerged to allow the vehicles to communicate with each other and share information about vision, diving intents, and other road information such as weather reports, traffic scenarios, and even entertainment for the passengers.

In Connected Vehicles (CV), drivers have access to wireless connections to other neighboring vehicles, infrastructure, pedestrians, and other devices within their proximity. The principal advantage of having wireless communications is the ability to access information that may otherwise be beyond the driver's immediate awareness. Such wireless communications would help prevent possible collisions by exchanging status information (such as the location, speed, and direction of travel of nearby vehicles, etc.), and event-driven safety messages (such as lane changing and collision warnings etc.). Along with these safety warning messages, such communication would also support sharing traffic information, weather updates and Internet-based infotainments.

At its earlier stage, this technological endeavor evolved with integrating cooperative and assisting communication technology termed as Cooperative Intelligent Transportation System (CITS), which is essentially enabled by Vehicular Ad-hoc Networks (VANET). Vehicular Ad Hoc Network (VANET) is a special kind of Mobile Ad-Hoc Network (MANET) to the domain of vehicles on the road. The basic communication architecture in VANETs consists of two blocks: On-Board Units (OBU) which is essentially the vehicle, and Road Side Units (RSU) Figure 8.3.

The idea of VANET received significant attention in both academia and industry helped to flourish it over the past decade. The core principle of VANET is that a vehicle connects to other vehicles and roadside units to share and propagate information. Meanwhile, with the advancement of the

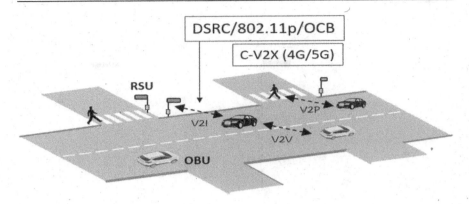

Figure 8.3 Vehicular Adhoc Network (VANET).

Internet of Things (IoT), vehicles are being connected to the internet. It is aiming at providing ubiquitous access to information alike to the drivers and passengers. Within this merge, vehicles are in the process of evolution equipped with a range of sensors, powerful onboard computational units, Internet connectivity over IP, a range of communication technologies with direct or indirect connection capabilities. Those evolved features enabled new characteristics of the data traffic in the vehicular network to the concept of Big Data [11]. With this paradigm shift, one of the critical issues VANET faces is its incapacity to process large amounts of data collected by themselves and other devices around them. This overall leads to the technological evolution named Internet of Vehicle (IoV). The IoV framework includes the Internet as a permanent asset to the vehicular network systems. It allows forming an interconnected set of vehicles to offer Internet-based services such as storage and computation to assist with road safety, road management, and infotainments [12].

In contrast to VANET, IoV fundamentally has two interrelated but separate technological directions: Internet-based networking and intelligence service. Internet-based networking is primarily enabled through a combination of three; VANET (known as vehicles' interconnection), Vehicle Telematics (known as connected vehicles), and Mobile Internet. On the other hand, intelligence is assumed in two stages. One is onboard to the vehicle, which combines driver and vehicle as unity using internal onboard intelligent sensors and technologies. The other is cloud-based intelligence. Overall, IoV is a centralization concept compared to VANET that focuses on the intelligent integration of humans, vehicles, things, and environments around it in a meaningful way to provide the necessary services on the road.

While conceptualizing the cloud services in the vehicular ecosystem, it can be seen that there are three levels of cloud; vehicular cloud, fog/edge cloud, and Internet cloud, as shown in Figure 8.4. In the vehicular cloud concept, the vehicles on the road communicate with each other and share their

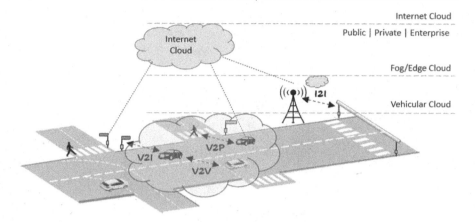

Figure 8.4 Conceptual diagram of Internet of Vehicles.

computing resources, storage resources, and spectrum resources. Every vehicle should have access to the cloud to utilize services. The prime motivation behind this paradigm is that; it use to happen, vehicles spend many times in rest, for example, in a parking garage, driveway, parking lot, or even on the road. Since vehicles have resources, the resources can be potentially used in all those situations, especially the parked vehicles that may have vast unemployed and wasted resources. Considering these features, vehicles are considered to form a vehicular cloud network [13]. In comparison to an individual vehicle, the vehicular cloud offers more resources. [14].

Fog or edge cloud services, on the other hand, are hosted in the vicinity of end-users (edge of the network, roadside units). It also includes computation, storage, and networking. The prime motivation of having fog is to complement the centralized cloud by moving down some computing resources to the edge to offer services with reliable access to some delay-sensitive mobile applications [15].

Compared to the other two cloud formation, the Internet cloud is vast, where internet-based services can offer extensive storage, powerful computation, and scalability. Such an Internet cloud can be public, for example, to access infotainment services. It can also be private, for example, cloud services of any car manufacturing company, or it can be an enterprise cloud such as the back office of the road transportation system [12]. Such Internet and cloud-centered network is the basis of the concept of Internet of Vehicles (IoV)

With the recent rapid advancement of Internet of Things and future autonomous driving expectations, the Internet of Vehicles (IoV) has attracted wide attention. The high penetration of sensors onboard and roadside generates trillions of data propelling to leverage the cloud-based IoV resources for big data processing. However, the emerging issues on how IoV could handle the big data intelligently and how the big data-enabled IoV could better support the ITS applications and improve the driving experiences are not well

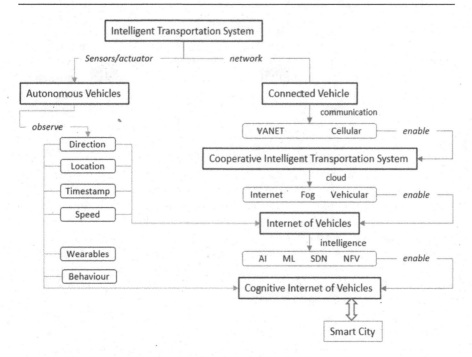

Figure 8.5 High-level ontology to map development relationship.

understood with the proposed IoV structure [5]. Additionally, network automation, stable connectivity, and reasonable connectivity and service cost to optimal uses of the resources cannot be guaranteed by the existing proposed IoV framework utilizing cellular networks and ad-hoc networks [5].

To alleviate those issues, a redefined and well-structured framework named Cognitive IoV is first proposed by a group of researchers [5,16]. This framework utilizes artificial intelligence, cloud/edge computing and 5G network slicing to deal with the top-level issues of IoV, such as the comprehensive modeling of the intelligence access to the network, automation in network control, and network healing.

The overall development and relationship are presented in Figure 8.5, and a close look at the cognitive Internet of Vehicles (C-IoV) architecture is presented in the following section.

8.3 COGNITIVE INTERNET OF VEHICLES (C-IOV): MOTIVATION AND FRAMEWORK

8.3.1 Overview of C-IoV

Road traffic is fundamentally a dynamic network that usually hosts enormous numbers of vehicles and commuters passing through each other and also the road infrastructure at every point in time. Utilizing collected data from different deployed sensors and shared information on the road, it is possible to locate traffic congestions, deadlocks on the road, slow-moving traffic, and other road-related affairs by advanced data analytics modeling. In recent days there have been significant attempts to model and study traffic more effectively than ever, thanks to big data analysis. This development attempts to make meaningful operational policies that could maximize resource utilization and lead to a safe travel experience.

The original idea of the Internet of Vehicles (IoV) is limited to the concept of connecting vehicles and road infrastructures to the Internet to share their observation and receiving existing Internet-based services such as infotainments. However, it is now understood that the idea of only connection over the Internet and its limited service is not enough to meet the demand and expectation. In fact, beyond that, the Internet cloud can be employed to enable the capability to sense, understand, learn, and think independently from both the physical and social worlds by themselves utilizing advanced technologies. Such expectation leads to having a new paradigm named Cognitive Internet of Vehicles (C-IoV), which supports cognitive computing capacity to the network employing ML, AI, SDN, and similar technologies. It fundamentally aims at bridging the transportation system such as a vehicle, road infrastructure, and the social world such as human demand, awareness, and social behavior and so on. It also aims to enable smart network operation and optimization, resource allocation, emergency responses, and intelligent service provisioning [5,7,17,18].

However, the question is, what does Cognitive refer to here? The term "cognition" originally received from the general definition of human (animal) cognition system of intelligent behavior, which refers to the states, experience, and process of knowing by utilizing senses and all conscious and unconscious processes [19]. The process includes perceiving, recognizing, and reasoning for intuitive problem solving and decision-making.

Cognitive in the context of engineering, on the other hand, generally refers to cognitive computing, a branch of computer science that deals with computerized models to simulate the human thought process in complex situations. Using self-awareness and self-learning algorithms and models that use advanced artificial intelligence and techniques such as data mining, pattern recognition, and natural language processing, the computer can mimic the human brain's works. There is indeed much talk about machine learning and artificial intelligence, and recently cognitive computing. The following analogy with a human brain can clarify the differences between these terms.

The term ML generally refers to the computerized techniques that basically take data, data streams, and look for patterns to quickly react based on what the algorithms are learning over time. It is analogous to the lower part of our brain stem, where if somebody touches something sharp, s/he immediately reacts to it because it's going quickly back and forth to the

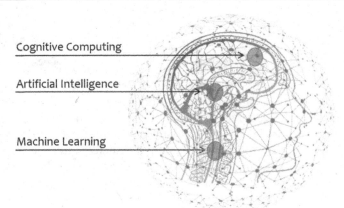

Cognitive Computing

Artificial Intelligence

Machine Learning

Figure 8.6 An analogy of cognitive computing: what is it?

base of the brain. It is recognized as the lowest level of cognitive capability. Above that level, then, is artificial intelligence, which resembles the part of the human brain where humans start to develop a form of intelligence that begins to work together in a more complex way, using a more complex set of algorithms. Those are typical human functions for daily activities and similar functions of other animal creatures.

Cognition, however, is in the upper frontal lobe of the brain, as shown in the Figure 8.6. That is where humans differentiate, and that's where humans start to bring together different concepts and start reasoning. It not just about reading a simple image, speech, transferring a message from place to place; it rather brings together the human factors, contexts and all of the data sources into a more complex set of reasoning. And that's where cognitive is, where the exponential value can be unlocked in IoV.

Scientists and researchers in various disciplines, notably neuroscience, computer science, engineering and mathematics, use the term cognition to build and represent understanding by learning. In line with this, networking exclusively started using this term and applied it in the emerging Internet of Things (IoT) as Cognitive IoT (CIoT).

However, in the vehicular networking concept, Arooj et al. [17] define C-IoV as a network-based framework for intelligent vehicles, where vehicles are primarily considered a context-aware agent. It is a sensory network of road elements such as vehicles and related infrastructure to receive real-time information from the road and surrounding physical world, including humans and the environment with minimal human interaction. It observes real data in live streams and conducts computing operations such as pattern matching using integrated intelligent algorithms in-vehicle applications. Thus evolved framework supports the communication between vehicles (V2V) and things (V2X) in the respective cloud and stores data. This heterogeneous datastore is used for knowledge discovery using advanced machine learning technologies such as deep learning, artificial neural networks, and data mining techniques for better sensing, learning, prediction, and efficient resource management.

C-IoV also applies the SDN and associated control services and systems such as Self-Organized Networking (SON), Network Flow Virtualization (NFV), and network slicing to enable cloud-based service. It supports high manageability, high controllability, high operationalization, and credibility of the network to increase driving assistance and improve road safety. The evolved C-IoV host multiple users, multiple vehicles, multiple things, and multiple networks and initiates intelligence cooperation. It offers an in-depth integration of the human-vehicle-thing-environment with services and resources, increases transportation efficiency, improves the service level of cities, and ensures safe and comfortable travel [5,17,18,20].

Therefore, it can be said that the emerging C-IoV is a paradigm that goes beyond connected vehicles. It supports storing, analyzing, and exchanging context-aware information among road transportation entities more intelligently.

8.3.2 C-IoV Framework

C-IoV is an advanced and well-defined framework evolved from IoV. In contrast to IoV, the C-IoV offers hierarchical cognitive engines, that is, control and cognition, and conducts joint analysis in both physical and network data space. From the network perspective, it can be said that VANET is a sub-network of IoV. And C-IoV is a refined and enhanced paradigm of IoV that offers more sophistication, management, and security. Figure 8.7 shows the conceptual diagram of future transportation in relation to the smart city, outlining the cognitive engine within the framework of C-IoV.

The evolved cognition and control layer is part of the internet cloud that allows initiating cognition process utilizing cloud-based advanced features, such as storing, processing, and computing the data collected from the lower layers of the C-IoV architecture. The lower layers fundamentally consist of the communication layer and sensory, physical layer where a range of short to long-range communication technologies (cellular and non-cellular) and protocols resides. The sensory, physical layer addresses both in-vehicle and roadside heterogeneous sensors, ranging from wearables to camera to external GPS with data acquisition ability during the vehicle's movement [5,12,17,21–23]. The upper layer is the application layer responsible for management and service to coordinate and cooperate among different users and parties. It is also responsible for designing application services from intelligent transportation applications such as intelligent driving, intelligent transport management to customized application services such as driving guidance, emotion monitoring, etc. [5,18,24].

The cognition engine slices between those layers serve as the bridge between the real-world observations and application realization. The fundamental

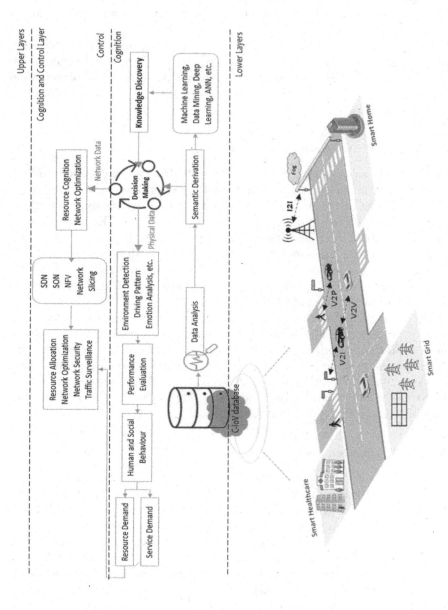

Figure 8.7 Evolved layer of cognition and control in C-IoV framework.

purpose is to create knowledge from received data and treat them accordingly to the service required. In general, the physical data is intended to be processed to detect the environment, driving pattern, or drivers' or passengers' emotion analysis. On the other hand, resource cognition is derived from network data to conduct real-time traffic surveillance network optimization, enforcing security, and resource allocation.

Overall, as shown in Figure 8.6, the key process involves data processing of the received data to understand appropriate use and management through several steps, for example, semantic derivation and knowledge discovery, where both lead to the decision-making process to conduct behavioral analysis and system performance evolution.

8.3.3 Use Case Analysis

Primarily the services enabled by the evolved C-IoV can be divided into two categories, strategic service, and control service, as shown in Figure 8.8.

The purpose of the strategic service is to process and analyze data flow using cloud-based computing and storage technologies. The strategic services are enabled through different operations and analysis tools. Examples of some services include monitorization, behavior analysis, optimization of the network, pattern analysis, and more. The indicated tools primarily are ML, neural networking, deep learning, distributed and federated learning, and other AI-based tools [3,10].

On the other hand, the control services are responsible for determining system performances by utilizing a variety of different facilities such as network optimization, resource allocation, network-wide security, etc. The technologies used to allow these services include software-defined networks, network slicing, and more [3,10]. Let us consider the following two scenarios to understand how road transportation under the evolved framework can enable travel safety.

8.3.3.1 Application Scenario 1

Within the C-IoV framework service, the smart vehicles are assumed to be capable of detecting, disseminating, and intelligently providing the content. Ideally, a myriad of sensors works together in the future look of the vehicular environment. Which includes intra-vehicle and inter-vehicle sensors for sensing and receiving information among road users, such as pedestrians, route environments, and other real-world contexts. To understand the typical application of C-IoV, we can think of a situation where a traveler on a car is traveling home from work. Suddenly, assume that the vehicle senses some irregular seismic waves, raised temperature of the environment, high magnitude, and airflow frequency. These irregularities are detected on board the vehicle using various sensors. At the same time, vehicle continuously sharing the data with the cloud. Suppose other connected smart vehicles also observe

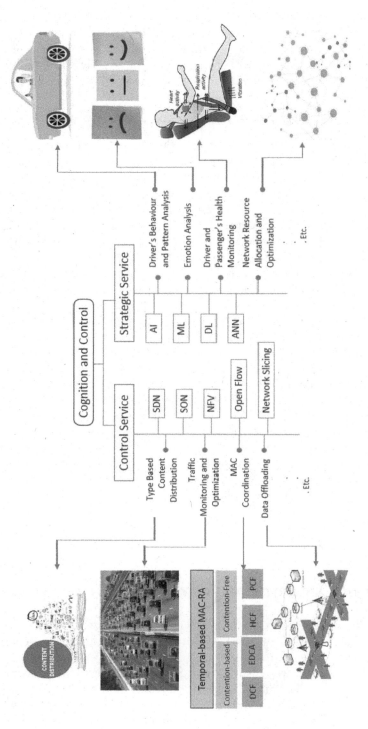

Figure 8.8 Services of C IOV: strategic service and control service.

the same abnormality from the same road and send the data to the cloud engine. At this point, the cognition engine will inherently analyze the data to detect any disaster that may occur proactively. It will initiate necessary measures at this stage, including the generation of early warnings and safe navigational route for the way home or safe place [17] Figure 8.9.

8.3.3.2 Application Scenario 2

Let us consider another scenario where the future driving scenario can help the vehicle's driver or passenger get sick or unwell. Under the proposed C-IoV framework, the deployed intra-vehicle network can carry out people's emotion detection and analysis. It can also perform driving behavior surveillance and physical health surveillance. Such surveillance is usually being conducted using onboard cameras and embedded sensors. For example, the intra-vehicle network camera can extract and analyze the driver and passengers' facial expressions. It can detect the eyelid state of the commuter to understand sleepy or dizzy behavior. Combining other data such as steering wheel movement for drivers, odometer readings can also be recorded to predict the subject's emotion or physical condition. Utilizing this information can deduce to generate necessary warnings to prevent any accident or take any measures needed as required. This level of operation can be achieved within the context of existing autonomous vehicular concepts through onboard computation. However, from the perspective of cognitive facilities, the evolved C-IoV framework offers more resource support, such as the cellular network's communication resources, the remote data center's computing resources, nearby fog or edge devices, such as roadside units or other vehicles. These resources can be used to conduct comprehensive condition analysis extensively for the sick passenger or driver. Simultaneously, the cognitive engine initiates some other necessary actions such as contacting the ambulance, doctor, and family members at home and sharing the onboard analysis result carried out using sensors to the doctor. All those activities would be taken autonomously without human involvement is the sole role of the evolved cognition engine that certainly can increase the survival of the sick on the road [5].

8.4 WHAT SECURITY, PRIVACY AND TRUST MEANS IN ITS?

Generally, in short, security in a cyber system refers to safeguarding data, privacy refers to safeguarding identity, and trust indicates a reliable relationship between parties. However, cybersecurity in practice is a set of technological measures ensuring that a system performs without interruption, achieving the tasks while mitigating unintended, external, unauthorized, and unexpected interference. On the other hand, privacy can be defined as the reliance that the confidentiality of, and access to, sensitive

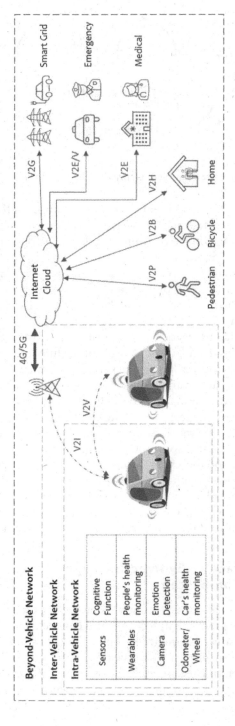

Figure 8.9 Ubiquitous communication of future transportation system: cognitive ITS [5].

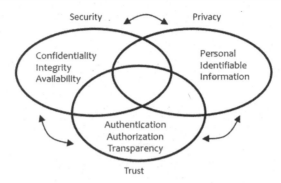

Figure 8.10 Inter dependency between security, privacy, and trust in cyber physical system.

information (such as Personal Identifiable Information (PII)) about the system or entity is protected and concealed. Privacy is often seen as an aspect of security, an affordance of confidentiality because a secure system should protect its users' privacy. Security also plays a central role in preventing service failures and cultivating trust in the network Figure 8.10.

With the rapid advancement of ICT and the necessity of multifaceted connectivity, cybersecurity is becoming a challenging concern nowadays in every enterprise and industrial systems where transportation is no different. Direct attacks by malicious parties and security vulnerabilities expose the data of cyber technology-enabled transportation technologies. It is a threat to privacy and can be the reason for developing untrusted connections, which could jeopardize the entire system. Since transportation is a critical sector directly influencing humans, any technological failure can lead to road fatalities or property losses; in extreme cases, it can have catastrophic consequences, including death. Therefore, successful, safe and secure deployment of the intelligent transportation system is vitally important, which depends on the design of the cyber secure framework. While aiming for that, it is important to understand vulnerability and attack surface that may be associated with the evolved transportation. In the following subsections, at first, the high-level overview of the attack surface concerning the security and privacy of C-IoV is discussed. Later potential trust issues are presented.

8.4.1 Attack Surface in Evolved Intelligent Transporation System

The evolved paradigm of transportation depicted in the above sections means, the entire system, both in automated and connected vehicular means, now carries more sensitive information. This includes vehicular telematics data to individual health data, which must be managed securely and privately. However, cyber threats are eminent as the transportation system is exposed due to the high accessibility and interdependence among systems that create new possibilities for different cyber-attacks and vulnerabilities.

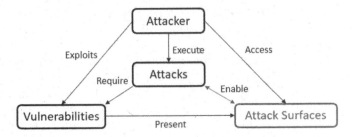

Figure 8.11 Attack surface: a relation between security-related terms in ITS.

In general, security breaches can happen through cyber system vulnerabilities that an attacker can exploit to enter the system. The attacker can also breach the system directly by other means, such as by injecting malware through hardware or communication channels or hardware ports. All are system entries termed as Attack Surface, shown in Figure 8.11 [25].

As shown in Figure 8.11, any system vulnerability leads to an attack surface that the attackers can exploit to access the system. An attacker can also execute a series of small attacks to expose a larger attack surface to get into the system unauthorizedly. However, most often, an attacker requires an understanding of system vulnerabilities to execute an attack.

As the emerging ITS is exclusively a hybrid system over ubiquitous connections, the attack surface extends from hardware to service, software to applications. For instance, all the automated car's hardware systems are attack surface. When vehicles communicate with each other, any infected vehicle can be a potential source to breach the security.

The attack surface can be the onboard system interface or a remote interface. Any physical interface, such as Onboard hardware like the On-Board Diagnostics (OBD) port, allows the vehicle to access the roadside infrastructure, disk reader, USB port, etc. can be the sources for the attack to gain access to the vehicle. Other physical parts of the bodies from different OEMs are also potential interfaces and are considered an attack surface. Compared with that, the remote attack surface is all possible entities that the vehicles are wirelessly connected. Several wireless technologies, such as DSRC, 4G/5G, Bluetooth, Wi-Fi, Remote Keyless Entry, GNSS, etc., can be the remote surface access interface.

Furthermore, the vehicles rely on an external cloud, edge, and fog infrastructure for processing and storing of data. The remote infrastructure that handles the vehicles' data must not be vulnerable, meaning it should not suffer from any hardware or software faults and failures. Faulty software may expose an attacking surface to malicious attackers, who may then intercept the vehicles' private and sensitive data and use it for malicious purposes. In addition to the data leakage, a malicious attacker may also compromise the integrity of the computation processes on the remote node, which would lead to either incorrect or delayed output. Making critical decisions relies on a remote infrastructure is not safe for the vehicles. Hence, the attack surface on the remote infrastructure such as cloud must also be minimized.

Overall, the attack surface resides within the vehicle, among the vehicle's connections and beyond the vehicle interactions. In a top-layer view, the attack surfaces for all potential cyber-attacks and data breaches fundamentally can be viewed again in a three-tier diagram shown in Figure 8.12, where intra vehicle-based ECUs, between vehicles communication and cloud, cloud-connected parties are seen as the potential attack surface.

8.4.2 Trust in the Evolved C-ITS Framework

Trust has many meanings across different disciplines; however, trust in networking implies a reliable multiparty relationship. It narrates the state to which a network node or entity accepts others' dependence [26]. Therefore, any network party has to provide a notion about the condition such as the correctness of the data within the context. In a vehicular network, this notion or signature is complex and depends on accuracy, timeliness, accessibility, and also interoperability. And with the introduction of large volumes of data through C-IoV, trust becomes diversified.

The multifaced and growing connectivity within and beyond the smart city's transportation system, trust becomes more important than ever. The evolved C-IoV in the smart city context is in a process to connect the wide real physical world with digital control by sensing the world, understanding it and programming it. This leads to the possibility of losing information and the loss of control over the device or host. Any breach of information security can endanger commuters' lives on the road and social loss in personal life. To achieve absolute security to the emerging transportation system and exchange reliable and authentic information among network nodes, peers, and the cloud, an attack-free and trusted environment is foremost.

Within the vehicular network context, trust ensures expected result of communicating with peers in every session. However, the concern is that the outcomes can be a positive value or being hacked and or cheated somehow. When processing application data on remote infrastructure, including cloud, edge, and fog nodes, it is important to ensure that the remote nodes are not compromised and they are strictly adhering to the service-usage agreements. However, a compromised node may behave maliciously. Imagine a vehicle is employing an object detection application to count the objects in a long distance. Due to the lack of local processing power and soft real-time requirements, the vehicle offloads the images and the object detection code to a remote node. If a remote node is honest and un-compromised, it would correctly execute the code using the vehicle's provided input image and then return the number of objects found in the image. However, when a remote node is compromised, it may simply return

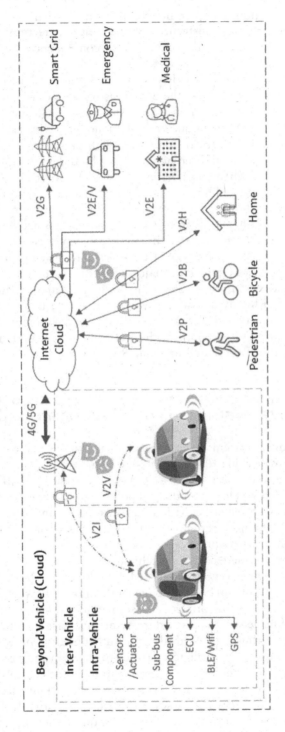

Figure 8.12 Three-tire view of the possible attack surface.

random results without running any computation, which may hamper the performance and the responsiveness of the object detection application. Note that this attack may lead to catastrophic consequences if it is a safety-critical application.

In the evolved framework of C-IoV, there exist multilevel interactions. For example, road-level interaction where vehicles wirelessly communicate with other vehicles, sensors, pedestrians, roadside units, intelligent city entities. Interaction and cooperation among multiple cloud service providers (CSPs) as a single cloud would not provide all devices with satisfactory quality of services due to performance and the high cost of cloud deployment or country policy. Additionally, while coordinating with other smart city services, the transportation cloud would have to interact with the targeted service cloud to enable the services shown in Figure 8.13. Ensuring trust among all these untrusted parties is a highly desirable challenge of such a network.

However, with such multifaceted interaction, C-IoV is exposed to a range of threats to security and privacy. Any dishonest and misbehaving peers and malicious CSP in the system is a major concern, increasing the system's vulnerability and endangering lives. Ensuring trust among all these untrusted parties is a highly desirable challenge of such a network.

Considering security, privacy, and trust with the technological evolution of smart transportation system, a high-level comparative table to different system architecture is presented in Table 8.1

8.5 PROSPECTIVE COUNTERMEASURES ENABLED BY COGNITIVE ENGINE IN LEGACY SECURITY ISSUES

The evolved transportation framework can face significant security issues over the predecessors due to its multifaced connectivity with other sectors towards realizing the smart city, which would introduce additional attack surfaces to the system. However, the technology associated with the evolved cognitive engine in the emerging C-IoV framework can improve the system's overall security. The IoV framework suffers many security issues that primarily stem from the network side of IoV [27]. In relation to that, we have identified four areas where cognitive technology, as it is defined, can be used to improve the existing security issues of IoV [28–30], are following:

Authentication: Authentication, in general, allows network devices to distinguish between outside attacks and source nodes. It is an essential security feature for networks that address identity-based attacks such as spoofing and Sybil attacks [31]. Ideally, the authentication process starts by comparing the physical layer characteristics to the transmitter's characteristics following in determining the authentication of the transmission. This can be done by comparing the characteristics to a particular threshold built on the classification model's accuracy. Over time, a set of ML-based techniques, for example, reinforce learning techniques, such as Q-Learning,

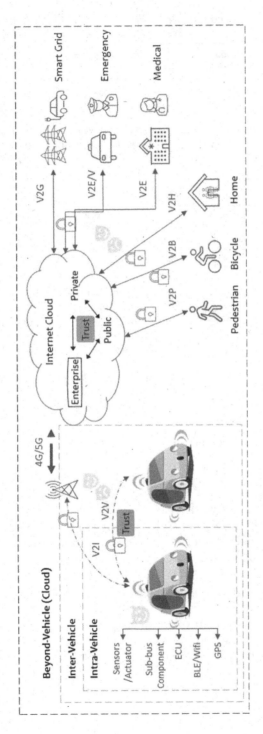

Figure 8.13 Issue of trust in smart transporation.

Table 8.1 Evolution of ITS and Its Corresponding Technologies, Security Concerns, and Threats

System Architecture	Fundamental Technology	Security Concerns	Security Threats
Intelligent Transportation System (ITS)	Sensors, Modes of Applications	Data Validity, Privacy, Open communication link, Behavior privacy, Breaching of identity and liability of vehicles	Incorrect data in network, Eavesdropping, Reply attacks, Location privacy attacks, Msg manipulation, Sybil attack
Cooperative Intelligent Transportation System (C-ITS)	Edge/Fog technology, Wi-Fi, 3g/4g, VANET	Information Modification, Data Leakage, Message manipulation, Authentication, Access Control	Spoofing, Replay attack, Eavesdropping, Denial of Service, Data Manipulation, Repudiation, Identity Spoofing
Internet of Vehicles (IoV)	Internet Cloud	Access, Trust, Dynamic Provision, Availability, Multitenancy, Transborder data flow	Data leakage and loss, Malicious insiders, Identity Theft, Service hijacking, Insecure interfaces
Cognitive Internet of Vehicles (C-IOV)	Machine Learning, Deep Learning, Neural Learning	Evasion attacks, Data poisoning, Model stealing, Influence attacks	Data leakage, automotive car accidents, Unawareness of malware

Dyna-Q, and deep Q-network (DQN), have been proven to select the required threshold to acquire authentication accuracy [32–34]. Besides, Convolution Neural Network (CNN) model shows promise to extract driver behavioral characteristics from the original data in the experimental vehicles achieving higher accuracy driver identification that can be potentially used for authentication [35].

Access control and verification: The use of access control prevents unauthorized users from accessing resources within the network. The emerging transportation network is essentially heterogeneous, and it is challenging to design an effective access control mechanism for such a network. However, some machine learning-based access control mechanisms such as Support Vector Machines (SVMs), K-Nearest Neighbors (K-NNs), and Nearest Neighbors (NNs) have come up with optimal solutions that can be employed to achieve access control support from and within C-IoV [34,36].

Within the evolved paradigm, it is possible to integrate a verifiable computation framework that allows the vehicle or other third parties to verify the correctness of data independently. Emerging cryptographic implementations such as ZKSnarks are offering viable solutions. Besides, a new class of verifiable computation systems based on run-time profiling is being introduced – verifiable Python (vPython) is a new verifiable computation framework that helps the application developers to gather proof from a remote node that it has correctly executed the computation [37].

Secure network offloading: Secure offloading allows for networked devices in the vehicular network to use external, storage, and cloud computation resources for specific tasks that would require heavy computational power. Q-Learning, a ML tool and a feature of the proposed cognitive engine, can be used to identify an optimal threshold for authentication, can also be used to identify the best rate of offloading data to provide security against specific attacks, such as jamming and spoofing attacks.

Malware detection: Cloud-based vehicular network is prone to attack from a wide range of malware such as viruses, worms, and trojans [38]. ML-based malware detection techniques, for example, supervised learning techniques such as naïve Bayes, neural networks, or K-nearest neighbor, can be used to label the traffic going into the IoV network and build classification models to detect network intrusion [34].

Along with the above-mentioned support, the cognitive engine can be used for continuous software updates. Contemporary software frameworks and operating systems are prone to bugs. The software community is continuously describing the potential vulnerabilities and release patches to minimize the damage. Therefore, running outdated software frameworks and operating systems would open up a large attack surface, which can be minimized by employing good software and security practices. Again, when relying on third parties for computation and storage, it is important to verify their actions to ensure correctness and safety. By including verifiable computation and storage solutions within the concept of cognitive framework, the application developers can get assurance from the remote infrastructures. Additionally, the hierarchical cloud model with a robust centralized cognition model can fit the emerging federated learning model to be adopted. In federated learning, each independent vehicle need not share their complete data to a central server for learning purposes. Instead, each vehicle can run a learning algorithm locally within their vehicle and share only the updated model parameters with the remote server. This model helps the vehicle retain their sensitive data while still contributing to the learning process and contribute to security and privacy improvement.

Finally, the cloud-based C-IoV framework essentially gives a centralized infrastructure, which is one of the inherent concerns as relying on a centralized architecture would lead to a central point of failure. A malicious attacker may compromise the infrastructure that serves the vehicles. Since the vehicular network is dispersed and inherently decentralized, decentralized frameworks involving blockchain and distributed ledger technologies help the application developers include stakeholders in the application processes, which prevents the central points of failure and provides more transparency. A cognitive engine can play a vital role in enabling such a hierarchy to apply decentralized solutions under centralization.

8.6 SECURITY AND PRIVACY CONCERNS IN C-IOV

Under the umbrella of C-IoV, a composite network can be observed; thus, system vulnerabilities can be a common reason to execute successful attacks. Besides, any active attacking mechanism such as injecting malware or even sufficient knowledge about the system can help attackers hack into a targeted system. It happens that vulnerabilities in the transportation system may exist; for example, simply it can be due to the weakness of the system design or software bugs that can be exploited to enter the system. Therefore, vulnerabilities are subjected to exist at all tiers, intra, inter, and beyond vehicular networks.

In the case of autonomous intra-vehicular networks, many recent studies highlighted the internal bus's limitation and weakness, which possibly can allow unauthorized access to the system without any restriction [23,39–42]. For inter-vehicular networks, many vulnerabilities around DSRC (IEEE 802.11p) have also been addressed; for example, Ucar et al. [43] conducted a vulnerability test that shows the technology gap using omnidirectional antennas that is a potential cause of jamming attacks. Similarly, Lyamin et al. [44] show jamming DoS attacks in DSRC while exchanged beacons are corrupted. The recent proposal of IEEE 802.11-OCB as a replacement of IEEE 802.11p does not offer cryptographic protection since it operates outside the context of a basic service set. This also indicates the potential insecurity, which needs to be investigated [37]. Research [45,46] shows the major vulnerabilities in cellular networks that lead to IP-based attacks, eavesdropping, spoofing, DDoS attacks, and many other well-known, well studied. Global Navigation Satellite System (GNSS), as an integral part of the inter-vehicular communication system, is also subjected to exhibit system, propagation, and interference-related vulnerabilities, leading to Jamming the service Spoofing the network [47–50]. Similarly, cloud-based beyond vehicular networks is prone to have many vulnerabilities that are a potential issue for the emerging ITS.

Besides, the vehicle is supposed to generate massive data where some are sensitive, such as personal health-related data, vehicle registration, condition or location data, or data about the nearby peer vehicle or cloud. Therefore, these are serious privacy issues that need to pay attention to dealing with identity privacy and location privacy. However, this presentation's scope covers the security supports and related issues with the evolved cognitive engine inside the cloud.

The following section presents some security concerns of the evolved cognitive engine in the cloud of the evolved C-IoV framework. In this short presentation, we have identified the fundamental security issues in relation to the cloud and the ML algorithms with the cognitive engine that may cause security concerns for the proposed paradigm.

8.6.1 Issues Related to the Cloud Computing of the Cognitive Engine

Cloud computing has many unique security concerns that relate heavily to the technologies used within the cognitive engine. The engine relies on the cloud to store the data to allow vehicles to learn patterns and much more; security concerns already present in cloud computing have been considered to IoV. Some high-level security concerns for the cognitive engine on the base of cloud computing/storage are listed as following [51–53]:

1. *Transborder data flow/data proliferation*: One of the significant issues that C-IoV could potentially face with its users is that specific companies can access the stored data with or without permission from the user. This makes the issue of data integrity and privacy a severe and genuine concern for users.
2. *Access*: Since the data is always stored to allow for training, as well as many other uses for cognitive technology within C-IoV, there is the prospect that users' data could be compromised by attackers breaking into the cloud storage that keeps their data.
3. *Multitenancy*: Clouds run on multiple different machines; this leaves the integrity of the data of C-IoV at risk. This leads the cloud to be more susceptible to attacks on the cloud infrastructure.
4. *Trust*: As the C-IoV model stores substantial data relating to the users' information from many different devices, for example, mobile phones and cameras, users have a lack of total trust as there is a significant fear of the systems collapsing and, therefore, the possibility of losing data.

8.6.2 Issues Related to Learning Algorithms in the Cognitive Engine

The proposed cognitive engine in the C-IoV framework impacts the traffic industry in a new and automotive way. However, security breaches into the learning algorithm can negatively impact the users' private data. Security issues related to the machine/deep learning algorithm can make the classification model misinterpret specific data or be taught incorrect data.

There are three classes of concerns with the use of a machine learning algorithm that is needed to be taken into account in realizing effectivity of the cognitive engine:

a. Influence attacks can influence the classifier model by altering or disrupting the classification phase.

b. Security violation is a form of attack aimed at providing false negatives that allow hostile input to a system or possible availability, which focuses on false positives that deny benign input from accessing the system.

c. Specificity, which focuses on allowing a specific intrusion/disruption. This attack also can cause general mayhem in the training model [54].

Three significant security concerns related to machine learning have been identified [29,54–56]. These three security concerns consist of:

1. *Evasion attacks*: This is a form of attack on machine learning that allows the attacker to manipulate malicious samples with the intent to evade detection. This attack is hazardous to any technology using machine learning that connects to the internet because it is designed to bypass classifiers, allowing attackers to sneak into the network without detection.

2. *Data poisoning*: Data poisoning is very different from evasion as instead of avoiding detection, poisoning is about altering the training data for machine learning. This is done by feeding polluted training data into the classifier model, giving rise to what is classified as true and false regarding the attackers' favor. The most common form of poisoning is done by switching the classifiers' understanding of what good inputs are and what are bad inputs. This could potentially be one of the more worrying security concerns for C-IoV as many of the decisions that the C-IoV engine will make can be potentially flipped to have the worst outcomes [57] (e.g., V2V meter distance of safety).

3. *Model stealing techniques*: This security issue is one of the least likely to happen but can still pose a serious concern. This concern is more about recovering models/information that was used for training with the specific use of the training data. This is about how the training models represent intellectual information that has been used to train sensitive data. These forms of data could include anything on users' mobile phones, driving locations as well as medical conditions and more (Figure 8.14).

Issues span further with machine/deep learning for C-IoV when it comes to the data learning algorithm. Because C-IoV is proposed to be one of the recently most advanced and widespread applications of AI, there is a high chance of misinterpretation of the training data without the need of an attacker. The learning patterns in machine/deep learning can be brittle as the model works on data that is like natural data. If unique data that is slightly different from the other training data is used on the learning algorithm, this can cause the model to fail completely. This can bring the theory about how an attacker does not necessarily need to use cyber-attacks to affect C-IoV's AI system [58] negatively. For example, one could cover a "Stop" sign with some tape, and the AI system would not have a clue on how to react; in fact, it might merely resume course and not stop at all Figure 8.15.

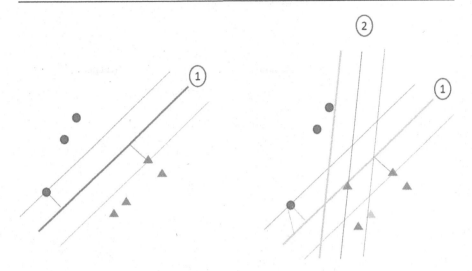

Figure 8.14 Classifier decision boundary from the default (left) being altered from poisoning, causing a massive change in decision choices (right).

Figure 8.15 Machine learning algorithm misses classifying "Stop" sign taken from [59].

Table 8.2 Security Concerns, Threats, and Benefits Comparison within the Cognitive Engine

	Security Cconcerns	Threats	Security Benefits	
			Security Mechanism	Protection Against
Internet Cloud	Trust, Access, Multitenancy, Transborder data flow/data proliferation	Data loss, Insecure interface, Service hijacking, Insider attacks	Secure authentication channel, Secure Over-The-Air updates, Credential Management, Remote monitoring of vehicle activity	Eavesdropping, Spoofing, Malware via updates, Privacy attack
Cognitive learning	Evasion attacks, Data poisoning, Model stealing	Data leakage, automotive car accidents, Unawareness of malware	Authentication, Access control, Secure IoT offloading, Malware detection	Spoofing, Eavesdropping, DoS, Intrusion, Malware, Jamming

A short prospective development with the cognitive engine in the security area compared with existing Internet-based services is presented in Table 8.2.

8.7 CONCLUSION

The advent of artificial intelligence and cloud computing has brought some new prospects for the transportation system's future realization. Simultaneously, new technology faces unique challenges due to the heterogenic structure and critical nature of the transportation system and its application. This chapter presents an overview of the future transportation expectation. Systematically it illustrates the evolution of Intelligent Transportation System, including the recent development of the smart city-centric framework Cognitive Internet of Vehicles. Later it covers the Security, Privacy, and Trust issues related to the emerging intelligent transportation system. More specifically, it discussed the enabling security supports by the evolved framework and the potential attack surface that extends due to the multifarious communication. Overall, the chapter deduced that C-IoV has the potential to meet great expectations by understanding that the technologies involved with the new integrated Cognitive engine will provide significant benefits that can reduce human errors and fatal crashes. This chapter indicates that it has potential for much wide use of cognitive engine technology and therefore further need to explore.

REFERENCES

[1] A. B. o. Statistics. Motor Vehicle Census, Australia [Online]. Available: https://www.abs.gov.au/ausstats/abs@.nsf/mf/9309.0

[2] W. E. Forum, "The Number of Cars Worldwide is Set to Double by 2040." *World Economic Forum, USA2016*, 2016. Available: https://www.weforum.org/agenda/2016/04/the-number-of-cars-worldwide-is-set-to-double-by-2040

[3] N. Dasanayaka, K. F. Hasan, C. Wang, and Y. Feng, "Enhancing vulnerable road user safety: a survey of existing practices and consideration for using mobile devices for V2X connections," *arXiv preprint arXiv:2010.15502*, 2020.

[4] S. Nižetić, P. Šolić, D. L.-D.-I. González De, and L. Patrono, "Internet of Things (IoT): opportunities, issues and challenges towards a smart and sustainable future," *Journal of Cleaner Production*, vol. 274, p. 122877, 2020.

[5] M. Chen, Y. Tian, G. Fortino, J. Zhang, and I. J. C. C. Humar, "Cognitive internet of vehicles," *Computer Communications*. vol. 120, pp. 58–70, 2018.

[6] S. Singh, "Critical reasons for crashes investigated in the national motor vehicle crash causation survey," 2015.

[7] K. F. Hasan, T. Kaur, M. M. Hasan, and Y. Feng, "Cognitive internet of vehicles: Motivation, layered architecture and security issues," in *2019 International Conference on Sustainable Technologies for Industry 4.0 (STI)*, pp. 1–6, IEEE. 2019.

[8] A. Hakkala and O. I. Heimo, "Automobile automation and lifecycle: how digitalisation and security issues affect the car as a product and service?," in *Proceedings of SAI Intelligent Systems Conference*, pp. 121–137. Springer, Cham, September 2019.

[9] K. F. Hasan, "GNSS time synchronisation in co-operative vehicular networks," Doctoral dissertation, Queensland University of Technology, 2018.

[10] T. Lozano-Perez, *Autonomous Robot Vehicles*. Springer Science & Business Media, 2012. Dec 6. Princeton, USA.

[11] W. Xu, H. Zhou, N. Cheng, F. Lyu, W. Shi, J. Chen, et al., "Internet of vehicles in big data era," *IEEE/CAA Journal of Automatica Sinica*, vol. 5, pp. 19–35, 2017.

[12] J. Contreras-Castillo, S. Zeadally, and J. A. Guerrero-Ibañez, "Internet of vehicles: architecture, protocols, and security," *IEEE internet of things Journal*, vol. 5, pp. 3701–3709, 2017.

[13] M. Whaiduzzaman, M. Sookhak, A. Gani, and R. Buyya, "A survey on vehicular cloud computing," *Journal of Network and Computer Applications*, vol. 40, pp. 325–344, 2014.

[14] A. Paul, N. Chilamkurti, A. Daniel, and S. Rho, *Intelligent Vehicular Networks and Communications: Fundamentals, Architectures and Solutions*. Elsevier, 2016. Sep 2. Cambridge, USA.

[15] M. Sookhak, F. R. Yu, Y. He, H. Talebian, N. S. Safa, N. Zhao, et al., "Fog vehicular computing: augmentation of fog computing using vehicular cloud computing," *IEEE Vehicular Technology Magazine*, vol. 12, pp. 55–64, 2017.

[16] H. Lu, Q. Liu, D. Tian, Y. Li, H. Kim, and S. J. I. N. Serikawa, "The cognitive internet of vehicles for autonomous driving," vol. 33, pp. 65–73, 2019.

[17] A. Arooj, M. S. Farooq, T. Umer, and R. U. Shan, "Cognitive internet of vehicles and disaster management: a proposed architecture and future direction," *Transactions on Emerging Telecommunications Technologies*, p. e3625, 2019.

[18] H. Lu, Q. Liu, D. Tian, Y. Li, H. Kim, and S. Serikawa, "The cognitive internet of vehicles for autonomous driving," *IEEE Network*, vol. 33, pp. 65–73, 2019.

[19] E. Britannica, *Encyclopædia Britannica*. Chicago: University of Chicago, 1993.

[20] Y. Qian, Y. Jiang, L. Hu, M. S. Hossain, M. Alrashoud, and M. Al-Hammadi, "Blockchain-based privacy-aware content caching in cognitive internet of vehicles," *IEEE Network*, vol. 34, pp. 46–51, 2020.

[21] K. F. Hasan, Y. Feng, and Y.-C. Tian, "GNSS time synchronization in vehicular ad-hoc networks: Benefits and feasibility," *IEEE Transactions on Intelligent Transportation Systems*, vol. 19, pp. 3915–3924, 2018.

[22] K. F. Hasan, C. Wang, Y. Feng, and Y.-C. Tian, "Time synchronization in vehicular ad-hoc networks: a survey on theory and practice," *Vehicular Communications*, vol. 14, pp. 39–51, 2018.

[23] J. Huang, M. Zhao, Y. Zhou, and C.-C. Xing, "In-vehicle networking: protocols, challenges, and solutions," *IEEE Network*, vol. 33, pp. 92–98, 2018.

[24] M. Priyan and G. U. Devi, "A survey on internet of vehicles: applications, technologies, challenges and opportunities," *International Journal of Advanced Intelligence Paradigms*, vol. 12, pp. 98–119, 2019.

[25] A. Lamssaggad, N. Benamar, A. S. Hafid, and M. Msahli, "A survey on the current security landscape of intelligent transportation systems," *IEEE Access*, vol. 9, pp. 9180–9208.

[26] M. Gerlach, "Trust for vehicular applications," in *Eighth International Symposium on Autonomous Decentralized Systems (ISADS'07)*, pp. 295–304, 2007.

[27] Y. Sun, L. Wu, S. Wu, S. Li, T. Zhang, L. Zhang, et al., "Security and privacy in the internet of vehicles," in *2015 International Conference on Identification, Information, and Knowledge in the Internet of Things (IIKI)* Oct 22, pp. 116–121, 2015. IEEE. https://ieeexplor e.ieee.org/abstract/document/7428337?casa_token=IyxG2Y6xRJEAAAAA:PFE782SSYsFyWhxUMspsowkUAvUGobIB7-0aVL9MRS_8Yco0VzViU2P9tYDheI_xHVY018j.

[28] Y. Li, Q. Luo, J. Liu, H. Guo, and N. Kato, "TSP security in intelligent and connected vehicles: challenges and solutions," *IEEE Wireless Communications*, vol. 26, pp. 125–131, 2019.

[29] G. Xu, H. Li, H. Ren, K. Yang, and R. H. Deng, "Data security issues in deep learning: attacks, countermeasures, and opportunities," *IEEE Communications Magazine*, vol. 57, pp. 116–122, 2019.

[30] Y. Qian, M. Chen, J. Chen, M. S. Hossain, and A. Alamri, "Secure enforcement in cognitive internet of vehicles," *IEEE Internet of Things Journal*, vol. 5, pp. 1242–1250, 2018.

[31] L. Xiao, Y. Li, G. Han, G. Liu, and W. Zhuang, "PHY-layer spoofing detection with reinforcement learning in wireless networks," *IEEE Transactions on Vehicular Technology*, vol. 65, pp. 10037–10047, 2016.

[32] X. He, H. Dai, and P. Ning, "Improving learning and adaptation in security games by exploiting information asymmetry," *2015 IEEE Conference on Computer Communications (INFOCOM)*, pp. 1787–1795, 2015.

[33] V. Mnih, K. Kavukcuoglu, D. Silver, A. A. Rusu, J. Veness, M. G. Bellemare, et al., "Human-level control through deep reinforcement learning," *Nature*, vol. 518, pp. 529–533, 2015.

[34] L. Xiao, X. Wan, X. Lu, Y. Zhang, and D. Wu, "IoT security techniques based on machine learning: How do IoT devices use AI to enhance security?," *IEEE Signal Processing Magazine*, vol. 35, pp. 41–49, 2018.

[35] Y. Xun, J. Liu, N. Kato, Y. Fang, and Y. Zhang, "Automobile driver fingerprinting: a new machine learning based authentication scheme," *IEEE Transactions on Industrial Informatics*, vol. 16, pp. 1417–1426, 2019.

[36] A. L. Buczak and E. Guven, "A survey of data mining and machine learning methods for cyber security intrusion detection," *IEEE Communications Surveys & Tutorials*, vol. 18, pp. 1153–1176, 2015.

[37] N. Benamar, J. Härri, J. Lee, and T. Ernst, "Basic support for IPv6 networks operating outside the context of a basic service set over," *IEEE Std 802.11*, RFC 8691, Dec. 2019, Accessed date: 20 July 2021. Available: https://rfc-editor.org/rfc/rfc8691.txt.

[38] J. Gardiner and S. Nagaraja, "On the security of machine learning in malware c&c detection: a survey," *ACM Computing Surveys (CSUR)*, vol. 49, pp. 1–39, 2016.

[39] K. Iehira, H. Inoue, and K. Ishida, "Spoofing attack using bus-off attacks against a specific ECU of the CAN bus," in *2018 15th IEEE Annual Consumer Communications & Networking Conference (CCNC)* Jan 12, pp. 1–4, 2018. IEEE. https://ieeexplore.ieee.org/abstract/document/8319180?casa_token=nCs6zU4aoUYAAAAA:_AlQA4JpHxPW6NRkc6ZFsKkvwxjxvaF7WK0ynHYm5ad45KzdeUidVU-EdFB7Q0w-4A8cVTK_

[40] S. Woo, H. J. Jo, and D. H. Lee, "A practical wireless attack on the connected car and security protocol for in-vehicle CAN," *IEEE Transactions on intelligent transportation systems*, vol. 16, pp. 993–1006, 2014.

[41] S. Woo, D. Moon, T.-Y. Youn, Y. Lee, and Y. Kim, "Can id shuffling technique (cist): Moving target defense strategy for protecting in-vehicle can," *IEEE Access*, vol. 7, pp. 15521–15536, 2019.

[42] R. Currie, "Hacking the can bus: Basic manipulation of a modern automobile through can bus reverse engineering (white paper)," *SANS Institute*, 2017.

[43] S. Ucar, S. C. Ergen, and O. Ozkasap, "Security vulnerabilities of IEEE 802.11 p and visible light communication based platoon," in *2016 IEEE Vehicular Networking Conference (VNC)*, pp. 1–4, 2016.

[44] N. Lyamin, A. Vinel, M. Jonsson, and J. Loo, "Real-time detection of denial-of-service attacks in IEEE 802.11 p vehicular networks," *IEEE Communications letters*, vol. 18, pp. 110–113, 2013.

[45] R. Hussain, F. Hussain, and S. Zeadally, "Integration of VANET and 5G security: a review of design and implementation issues," *Future Generation Computer Systems*, vol. 101, pp. 843–864, 2019.

[46] J. Cao, M. Ma, H. Li, Y. Zhang, and Z. Luo, "A survey on security aspects for LTE and LTE-A networks," *IEEE communications surveys & tutorials*, vol. 16, pp. 283–302, 2013.

[47] M. G. Amin, P. Closas, A. Broumandan, and J. L. Volakis, "Vulnerabilities, threats, and authentication in satellite-based navigation systems [scanning the issue]," *Proceedings of the IEEE*, vol. 104, pp. 1169–1173, 2016.

[48] E. Falletti, D. Margaria, G. Marucco, B. Motella, M. Nicola, and M. Pini, "Synchronization of critical infrastructures dependent upon GNSS: current vulnerabilities and protection provided by new signals," *IEEE Systems Journal*, vol. 13, pp. 2118–2129, 2018.

[49] M. L. Psiaki and T. E. Humphreys, "GNSS spoofing and detection," *Proceedings of the IEEE*, vol. 104, pp. 1258–1270, 2016.

[50] C. Sanders and Y. Wang, "Localizing spoofing attacks on vehicular GPS using vehicle-to-vehicle communications," *IEEE Transactions on Vehicular Technology*, 2020.

[51] C. Modi, D. Patel, B. Borisaniya, A. Patel, and M. Rajarajan, "A survey on security issues and solutions at different layers of cloud computing," *The Journal of Supercomputing*, vol. 63, pp. 561–592, 2013.

[52] H. Takabi, J. B. Joshi, and G.-J. Ahn, "Security and privacy challenges in cloud computing environments," *IEEE Security & Privacy*, vol. 8, pp. 24–31, 2010.

[53] M. Zhou, R. Zhang, W. Xie, W. Qian, and A. Zhou, "Security and privacy in cloud computing: a survey," in *2010 Sixth International Conference on Semantics, Knowledge and Grids* Nov 1, pp. 105–112, 2010. IEEE. https://ieeexplore.ieee.org/abstract/document/5663489

[54] M. Barreno, B. Nelson, R. Sears, A. D. Joseph, and J. D. Tygar, "Can machine learning be secure?," in *Proceedings of the 2006 ACM Symposium on Information, Computer and Communications Security*, pp. 16–25, 2006. March. https://dl.acm.org/doi/abs/10.1145/1128817.1128824?casa_token=wbSnGd4xyZUAAAAA:pUdvY6RIUR69nX-mP1tCUQItF_mC3gHAjiKh5-Mj-6Br0NxPo8leMa3vD5gBR_gPATfOqIqSlDA

[55] M. Barreno, B. Nelson, A. D. Joseph, and J. D. Tygar, "The security of machine learning," *Machine Learning*, vol. 81, pp. 121–148, 2010.

[56] T. Gu, K. Liu, B. Dolan-Gavitt, and S. Garg, "Badnets: evaluating backdooring attacks on deep neural networks," *IEEE Access*, vol. 7, pp. 47230–47244, 2019.

[57] A. Paul, A. Daniel, A. Ahmad, and S. Rho, "Cooperative cognitive intelligence for internet of vehicles," *IEEE Systems Journal*, vol. 11, pp. 1249–1258, 2015.

[58] O. Simeone, "A very brief introduction to machine learning with applications to communication systems," *IEEE Transactions on Cognitive Communications and Networking*, vol. 4, pp. 648–664, 2018.

[59] T. Gu, B. Dolan-Gavitt, and S. Garg, "Badnets: identifying vulnerabilities in the machine learning model supply chain," *arXiv preprint arXiv:1708.06733*, 2017.

Chapter 9

IT Governance and Enterprise Security Policy in the 6G Era

Mohsen Aghabozorgi Nafchi[1]
and Zahra Alidousti Shahraki[2]

[1]Department of Computer Science and Engineering, Shiraz University, Shiraz, Iran

[2]Department of Computer Engineering, University of Isfahan, Isfahan, Iran

CONTENTS

DOI: 10.1201/9781003121541-9

9.1 INTRODUCTION

The 1G network was an innovation that came out in the 1980s for voice communications. In this generation, analog signals were used to transmit data. Therefore, low sound quality, the lack of wireless standards, hard handovers, and encryption were the concerns of this period [1]. Due to the lack of encryption in data transmission, conversations were recorded and used illegally. So, the security and privacy of individuals were easily threatened [1–3]. Encrypted messages were created by users themselves to avoid any possibility of disclosing the sensitive content of their messages can be considered the first security policies in the first generation of networks. In the early 1990s, with the development of digital systems, the 2G networks began. In this generation, encrypted data services were provided and users could send messages to each other with more confidence [4]. The most important standard in this generation is GSM (Global System for Mobile Communications) [5], which makes use of encryption to increase the security and privacy of individuals to authenticate and protect user data [6]. But one of the weaknesses of GSM is that it only authenticates the user when connecting to the network and does not do this for the devices [7]. Thus, it is possible for illegal devices to connect the network and steal user data [1]. Also, the lack of end-to-end encryption in GSM has increased the risks of attacks [8]. With the rapid development of technology, the year 2000 can be considered the beginning of the 3G networks and services such as web browsing, TV streaming and video services [9]. In the security issues of 3G, problems related to 2G such as attacks have also been transferred to this generation. In addition, it sees all forms of TCP / IP vulnerabilities [10] and weaknesses of the authentication and encryption mechanisms standardized for GSM / UMTS [11,12]. But despite the 3rd Generation Partnership Project (3GPP) AKA Protocol, privacy is still one of the main concerns in this generation [13]. With the launch of 4g networks in 2010, it has given users access to multimedia data like videos and voice calls [14]. But on the other hand, an IP based and heterogeneous network have caused service interruption and hijack the data [15]. Also, mobile phones have faced a lot of malicious (e.g., DoS) attacks, viruses, worms, spam mails and calls and so on [16]. In the fifth generation, with the introduction of new technologies such as IoT, SDN/NFV, virtualization, mobile edge computing, and other technologies will create new challenges in the field of security. On the other hand, the possibility of sharing resources has faced user privacy with new risks [17]. Therefore, in this generation, attention to security policies has been increased (e.g., security policies in edge nodes [18] and Heterogeneous Networks [19]). In the next generation, the sixth generation, technologies such as AI, Molecular communication, Quantum communication, Blockchain, TeraHertz (THz) and the Visible Light Communication (VLC) are used to increase communication capacities. But on the other hand, the complexity of the technologies used in this generation can be considered as important challenges in terms of security and privacy [1]. In 6G, the main security concern is using Artificial intelligence in various fields such as intelligence attacks.

According to this description that provided in the related to different generations of networks, the most important points that can be mentioned are the increase in security and privacy problems and the growing complexity of the technologies in each generation. Therefore, one can understand the role of governments and organizations to overcome these problems that will be one of the main concerns in the near future. In this way, international and national laws, organizational policies, Explainable technologies and users are factors that can play important roles in a security policy framework.

9.1.1 Chapter Roadmap

In this chapter, we discuss about challenges that influence the security policies related to technologies of 6G. The rest of this chapter is organized as follows. Section 2 presents the security and privacy concerns in 6G. Section 3 gives the detailed description of the factors affecting the security policies of the 6G generation. Finally, this paper is concluded in Section 4.

9.2 6G TECHNOLOGIES: SECURITY AND PRIVACY ISSUES

Mika Yliantila and et al describe the challenges that 6G networks will face as follows [20]:

- By increasing the volume of IoT devices (e.g., smart wearable devices, implants, XR systems, haptics, flying vehicles, etc.) in various types [21], providing security and privacy for them as one of the main challenges in the field of 6G development systems.
- With the development of artificial intelligence technologies, distinguishing between real and fake content will not be easy and smart attacks will increase.

9.2.1 AI and 6G

With the remarkable success of the use of artificial intelligence in various fields such as computer vision, natural language processing, and autonomous driving, the use of artificial intelligence capabilities in 6G has received much attention. For example, with the rapid expansion of smart mobile gadgets and the Internet of Things devices (e.g., self-driving cars, drones, and auto-robots), many intelligent applications on the edge of wireless networks will be developed in the near future. But one of the most important issues when people use smart apps is the privacy. Therefore, instead of uploading intelligence apps data in the cloud for model training process, federated learning technology is used [22,23]. Federated learning defines as "a machine learning setting where multiple entities (clients) collaborate in solving a machine learning problem, under the coordination of a central server or service provider. Each client's raw data is stored locally and not exchanged or transferred; instead, Focused updates are updates narrowly scoped to contain the minimum information necessary for the specific learning task at hand; aggregation is performed as early as possible in the service of data minimization" [24].

The major challenges in developing federated learning in 6G networks are personalization, trust mechanisms, and privacy [24]. In the field of learning personalization, designing decentralized algorithms for learning collections based on personalization models [25–27] can play an important role in increasing user trust in AI applications. Privacy is also another challenge of federated learning, which is done by using methods such as adding local noise to user data [26,28] Secure aggregation [29] and secure shuffling [30].

9.2.1.1 Adversarial Attacks

"The term "adversarial attack" to refer to any alteration of the training and inference pipelines of a federated learning system designed to somehow degrade model performance. Any agent that implements adversarial attacks will simply be referred to as an "adversary"" [24]. These types of attacks include data poisoning [31–34], model update poisoning [35,36], and model evasion attacks [31,37]. In another classification, these types of attacks are divided into two groups: training-time attacks (poisoning attacks) and inference-time attacks (evasion attacks) [24]. One of the attacks that can occur in the field of artificial intelligence technologies, especially in federated learning, is the use of model replacement, for example, a word predictor completes sentences with words specified by an attacker [35]. The above shows that security and privacy concerns in 6G are different from other generations of networks and the adoption of artificial intelligence technologies requires a higher level of security. For example, the use of artificial intelligence in medicine such as tumor detection [38] and genomic characterization [39,40]. It can have many positive results and increase humanity's hopes for the treatment of various diseases. But the dangers and attacks associated with artificial intelligence technologies can increase privacy and security concerns about the use of artificial intelligence in the medical field [41] and even reduce trust in such technologies. Therefore, given the widespread use of artificial intelligence in the medical field, it is necessary to consider advanced security rules and policies in order to counter the threats in the field of manipulation of medical data and their dissemination in 6G.

9.2.1.2 Access Control

Lauri Loven and et al. have introduced 6G as a new era of interaction between edge computing and AI methods and mentioned the most important functions of artificial intelligence for edge computing in privacy (fine-grained control, and management of personal data), security (personalization, effectiveness, efficiency) and control (predictive control, decentralized control, predictive maintenance, efficient resource usage) [42]. So, AI methods will play an important role in controlling access and personalization of user data, which should be given special attention in the security policies of organizations.

9.2.1.3 Authentication

AI can be used to authentication of users in the 6G. Continuous authentication model based on monitoring user behavior [43] is one of the topics of interest for organizations to determine the online Authentication of the user during the session. For example, with the development of AI technologies in 6G, it is possible to collect data by motion sensors (mainly, accelerometer and gyroscope) and touch screen mobile phones and analyze user behavior with AI methods for continuous user authentication during session [44]. This could be one of the main facilities in 6G with the proliferation of edge computing and IOT devices. But on the other hand, ethical issues and privacy are main concerns related to apply these methods in organizations. So, The most important question is that whether companies can use AI methods such as federated learning to authenticate their users and regularly monitor them during the sessions or they should use only the old methods that authentication operation are done when users login for first time. For example, Muhammad Sharjeel Zareen and et al. have implemented a machine learning-assisted authentication model for edge devices that could be the beginning of future versions of advanced authentication systems based on AI technologies [45]. Also, Xiaoying Qiu and et al. envision a new Deep learning (DL)-enabled security authentication scheme for improving the security of wireless multimedia networks [46].

9.2.1.4 Encryption of Data

The use of ML [47] and quantum encryption [48] schemes are approaches that can be considered as a solution to increase the communication security of 6G networks [49]. In order to protect the privacy of medical data, William Briguglio et al used a generic machine learning with encryption framework for predicts cancer from a genomic dataset in the field [50].

9.2.1.5 Perturbation

M.A.P. Chamikara and et al. propose a new distributed Privacy-preserving Approach for distributed machine learning (federated learning) in geographically distributed data and systems [51]. This distributed perturbation algorithm can be a solution for increasing privacy and security in 6G.

9.2.1.6 Communication

In order to increase the security of the physical layer in Ambient Backscatter Communications, Tao Hong et al. propose a machine learning based antenna design scheme [52]. So, this research shows that using machine learning capabilities in communication can greatly help improve security at 6G and an issue that can be considered one of the security policies in organizations.

9.2.2 Molecular Communication and 6G

Molecular communication is one of the technologies that can make an important contribution to the development of 6G in the future. But in terms of security, little research has been done on the security of MC links [53]. So, more research should be done on malicious behavior related to this technology so that organizations can implement their security and privacy policies in this area. An issue that can be addressed by enterprises to improve the security of their data transmission is encrypting data during transmission in molecular communications [54–56]. Also, new directions for molecular communication security and privacy are artificial immune systems (AIS), swarm molecular security approaches, and bio-chemical cryptography that more explain with Valeria Loscri and et al. [57]. Also, molecular communication systems provide opportunities for developing new authentication mechanisms [58] that cannot be ignored for increasing level of security and privacy in an enterprise. For example, Sidra Zafar and et al. propose a channel impulse response-based physical layer authentication in a diffusion-based molecular communication system [59].

9.2.3 Quantum Communication

With the sharp increase in traffic volumes in 6G, the need for new technology to transfer this volume of data is felt. Optical infrastructures have this capacity to play an important role in this field [60]. But the issue of security and privacy at this technology cannot be ignored. For this purpose, to increase the security of Quantum communication, Quantum Key Distribution (QKD) can be used as an example of quantum-safe cryptography [61]. So, the development of encryption tools for data transfer with the help of quantum communication can provide the necessary facilities to improve security and privacy in data exchanges. Research into the quantum communication capabilities in the field of security and privacy is just the beginning, but due to the spread of this technology in the 6G, organizations should pay special attention to it in their security policies.

9.2.4 Explainable Artificial Intelligence (XAI) for 6G

With the increasing complexity of human-machine interaction in 6G, one of the issues is the ambiguity of technologies developed with artificial intelligence, which can affect users' trust to this technology. By developing the explainability feature for 6G technologies, trust of users in services such as autonomous driving and remote surgery can be increased. For example, one of the biggest challenges in deep learning is the lack of transparency and trust of users to this technology [62]. Despite the widespread use of deep reinforcement learning for communications and networking in areas such as Network access, adaptive rate control, proactive caching, data off-loading, network security and connectivity preservation, traffic routing, resource scheduling and data collection. But understanding its implications for users is complex, and this can affect users' trust in smart systems [63]. Weisi Guo et al. state that the legal frameworks related to artificial intelligence are at the beginning of the work [62] and there is a need for a comprehensive legal framework for better understanding and explainability of artificial intelligence technologies.

9.3 INTERNATIONAL CYBER SECURITY STRATEGY

With the spread of communication in today's world, the territories and borders of countries are disappearing and the power of local governments to control the Internet and the physical ability to enforce laws in this area is diminishing. But in the world of the Internet, messages are being transmitted without regard to physical restrictions, something that local governments cannot control except by imposing restrictions [64]. Cyberspace is a great place for financial transactions. But on the other hand, these interactions will not be without threats and in order to deal with various scams on the Internet, international organizations must be familiar with the laws of the different countries in which they operate and act in accordance with the laws of different countries. On the other hand, various attacks by hackers at different levels have raised many concerns about the security of organizations, and the most important challenge is to address violations and scams committed in cyberspace. For example, in the international arena, it can be questioned whether different countries can choose the Internet as a place for their hostilities and attack each other's infrastructure using different attacks and if that happens, how can a country affected by these attacks get its legal rights? Or a company affected by the attacks of a hacker based in another country which court should go? Should they go to own country, the country where the hacker acted, or a third country? Therefore, the need for international law to deal with international cyber-crime is one of the most important needs of humanity. The existence of an international law on security issues and cybercrime can also affect the security policies of organizations. And this issue has become more apparent with the expansion of international cooperation between organizations.

In the 6G generation, on the one hand, the emergence of advanced and intelligent technologies, and on the other hand, the expansion of international interactions between different organizations around the world and the development of smart applications in various applications that there is a need for an integrated international law on security issues and cybercrime, regardless of the one-sided views of countries, in order to manage the security problems that will occur in 6G and help develop the security policies of organizations based on it. For example, blockchain technology is expanding rapidly in various aspects of human life and countries have their own policies on this technology. But in the 6G, blockchain technology will be used as a tool in various fields, and for example, traditional contracts will be replaced by smart contracts based on blockchain. By developing an international law to protect the security and privacy, if an organization encounters a security problem in a smart contract, it can act in accordance with the provisions of this law. Also, in general, it can develop its security policies according this international law. Or in the field of AI technologies, the adoption of international laws in order to better understand these technologies can be an important step in increasing user trust in the use of new technologies in 6G. Also, companies that can easily collect and analyze user data in various fields should respect the user's privacy in accordance with international laws and don't make the collected data easily available in business. In the 6G generation, as technologies become smart, attacks and threats will also become smart. Therefore, if user's privacy and security are threatened and harmed by smart attacks, they should be able to compensate under international law. These are just a few examples of the importance of applying an international law to protect the security and privacy of the 6G generation. A generation that records and tracks all human activities with the help of various tools, and human beings are more and more exposed to various dangers.

9.4 NATIONAL CYBER SECURITY STRATEGY

National Cyber Security Strategy is one of the topics that has received special attention in IT governance. Riza Azmi and et al. define National Cyber Security Strategy (NCSS) as "a careful plan or method of protection both informational and non-informational assets through the ICT infrastructure for achieving a particular national goals usually over a long period of time" [65]. Despite the many benefits of a free flow of information, there are countries that restrict this flow for political stability [66]. In 6G when different technologies are used with high complexity will increase concerns about the inability to control the flow of information. Therefore, stricter policies will be applied in the field of 6G communications. On the other hand, advances in 6G technologies may be able to reduce restrictions of countries on the Internet. However, the challenge of countries in relation to the development of communications is not only political, and countries use the Internet as a tool to develop e-government services [67] and the private sector along with governments apply the Internet for e-commerce, e-banking, and their e-advertising [68]. Therefore, a cybersecurity national strategy is needed for cyber activities to combat crimes [69] (e.g., European Union National Cybersecurity Strategies [70]). One of the challenges of a national cyber security strategy is to define borders in cyber space. Because it can be used to deal with jurisdiction issues [64,65]. On the other hand, advances in technology and globalization have changed attitudes toward jurisdiction and border [71]. And concepts such as territorial jurisdiction and universal jurisdiction are becoming more widespread in cybercrime [72]. For example, the importance of artificial intelligence and blockchain laws in various areas of technology such as trade and health can be mentioned [73]. But technology is advancing so fast that law-making and regulatory design must be proactive, dynamic, and responsive [74] to be able to control the challenges related to new technologies well. An issue that is not easily determined in 6G with complex communications. In 6G, the integration of different technologies can be one of the main challenges for countries in defining the boundary and passing laws needed to protect the security and privacy of individuals. Restrictions on various activities may be a temporary solution to this problem but with the advances ahead and strong connections between various groups to achieve different goals such as finance and health, the need for a strong 6G security policy at the national level is well seen.

9.5 ENTERPRISE SECURITY POLICY IN ORGANIZATIONS

In order to have a good security policy in the organization, as much as the system and data must be considered, the employees and the organization's interactions with the outside are also important. Moreover, the rules, ethical standards, and security policies of the organization cannot be ignored [75]. Rainer Diesch and et al. have introduced physical security, vulnerability, infrastructure, awareness, access control, risk, resources, organizational factors, confidentiality, integrity, availability, continuity, security management, compliance, and policy as effective factors on decision-makers in organizational information security [76]. In the following, the effect of these factors is discussed in order to provide more explanations in security policies of an organization in 6G.

9.5.1 Vulnerability

The definition of Vulnerability is: "weakness in an information system, system security procedures, internal controls, or implementation that could be exploited or triggered by a threat source [77]". Due to the high speed of development of various technologies in 6G, organizations must carefully identify and evaluate the vulnerabilities in various technologies and make the necessary decisions. Perhaps the knowledge-based group for recognizing vulnerabilities in the field of security and privacy is one of the groups that every company needs in the near future. This group with their research helps security teams in identifying and controlling vulnerabilities. Also, the development of artificial intelligence technology can play an important role in vulnerability detection. Tools that can diagnose problems and perform configuration optimizations related to the problem [78]. But on the other hand, the vulnerability of the emerging tools for diagnosing problems should not be ignored.

9.5.2 Infrastructure

Understanding 6G infrastructure [79] such as Quantum Communication [60], Ambient Backscatter Communication Systems (ABCS) [80], Blockchain [81], and unmanned aerial vehicles (UAVs) [82] will play an important role in planning, policy-making, and security decisions. Because by recognizing their challenges, more accurate policies can be considered in order to improve the security of the organization against attacks and related damages. For example, to deal with UAV communication threats such as Fabrication, Linking attack, Eavesdropping attack, Distributed DoS attack, and Jamming attack, Blockchain technology can be used to design and implement the necessary security policies to defend against such attacks [81].

9.6 HUMAN CENTRIC CYBER SECURITY VIEW

From the perspective of human centric cyber security, the three components of User, Usage and Usability are considered as effective factors in increasing the security of a system [83]. Factors have to consider seriously and analyze correctly in 6G security policies. In 6G, User data can be easily collected and with analyzing this data, security of users can be threatened. In the following, each of the factors is examined in more detail.

9.6.1 User

9.6.1.1 Demographics and Culture

L Jean Camp et al. believe that it is necessary to consider the role of human in security issues [84]. In their proposed model, the factors of Demographics, risk perception and risk characteristics are mentioned as common factors in increasing vulnerability for online activities. For example, research shows that women are more risk averse, so they face more security risks [85]. On the other hand, risk perception depends on risk characteristics and the availability of risk information. Increasing users' activities and facing various risks on the Internet increase risk perception of users [84]. For example, in the case of phishing, increasing information about the characteristics of this risk can growth the risk perception of user related to this cybercrime in financial transactions and the user is ready to deal with these types of risks.

Demographics, risk perception, and risk characteristics in 6G security policies must be carefully considered. Knowing the characteristics of Demographics can affect security policies because with the advancement of technology, smart attacks can put certain groups of people at risk. Also in 6G, knowing the risk characteristics can help users in risk perception. But the complexity of the technologies offered in this generation can complicate evaluation of risk characteristics for users. And so this makes it difficult for users to risk perception in their activities on the Internet. For example, phishing attacks can be detected using artificial intelligence [86]. But on the other hand, these types of attacks will also be smart [87]. So, detection of these attacks will complicate for the user. Also, because one way to deal with phishing attacks is to train users [88], organizations need to spend more time for training their employees.

Culture can be considered as one of the effective factors in cyberspace security [83]. Culture is "networks of knowledge, consisting of learned routines of thinking, feeling, and interacting with other people, as well as a corpus of substantive assertions and ideas about aspects of the world" [89]. also, cybersecurity culture define as "the intentional and unintentional manner in which cyber space is utilized from an international, national, organizational or individual perspective in the context of the attitudes, assumptions, beliefs, values and knowledge of the cyber user." [90]. Thus, in terms of culture, views of people related to security and privacy in one nation may differ from those in another. For example, research shows that Indians have a high level of trust in government and business organizations that collect their personal information [91], but this is not the case with Americans, who are very concerned about storing and transmitting their data [92].

In the 6G, with the expansion of connections between different societies and the advancement of technology in various fields, knowing the issues related to the cybersecurity culture of different societies, can play an important role in the security policy of international organizations. So, the security policy for Western culture is different from the security policy for Asian culture because they have different perceptions of the risks posed by the Internet. For example, when developing a smart application internationally, security policies in one culture differ from one culture to another, and this imposes limitations on the collection and storage of user data. Also, on the other hand, by knowing the cultural points as it is easy to implement general security policies, hackers can also easily exploit existing security vulnerabilities related to the culture of that community and misuse their information and with developing smart systems in the 6G generation, security vulnerability of users in different cultures can increase.

9.6.2 Usage

Usage emphases on methods used to enhance security in a system which has three components: functional measures, technical measures and legislation, regulations and policies. Functional measures refer to the use of a specific function at a particular time and event such as displaying a warning message to the user when a system encounters a security threat. On the other hand, technical measures try to keep the user away from the details of security issues. However, there are still security problems on the part of the user. For example, despite many advances in password encryption, lack of attention to change the password by the user can increase the security risks of the system against hackers. Also, enacting new laws can also increase the security and privacy of the user in using the system. The adoption of security laws related to IoT can be mentioned as an example [83].

In security policy of 6G, usage factors and the role of the user in increasing security must be effectively considered. One of the most important challenges in this field is to familiarize users with the factors that improve system security and the enactment of laws to protect privacy of users in the face of significant advances in technologies.

9.6.3 Usability

The definition of usability is: "the extent to which a product can be used by specified users to achieve specified goals with effectiveness, efficiency, and satisfaction in a specified context of use." [93]. Also, the important factors that affect the usability of a system are the experience and interaction of users with systems [83].

With the expansion of security concepts and the importance of the role of users in promoting system security, a concept called usable security can be seen in this area [94]. Therefore, with using the provided definition of usability, usable security is the simplification of security steps for users based on previous experiences and interactions of users with the system, in a technique that the users can easily understand the importance of security issues and follow them. An example of usable security research is the usability of authentication methods [95].

In 6G, authentication methods will be significantly improved. Due to the complexity of communication technologies in 6G, the importance of usable security can be realized more than before. Systems that owe their security to advanced artificial intelligence technologies. But on the other hand, understanding them will be very difficult for users and will increase concerns of users about their security and privacy issues.

9.7 CONCLUSION

In the 6th generation, with developing new technologies such as AI, molecular communication, quantum communication, and blockchain, the capabilities of communication networks will increase, but on the other hand, it will raise concerns about security issues.So, in this era of globalization, organizations will face new security challenges. An organization needs security policies to deal with security threats and protect users against threats posed by various attacks. Given the international connections between organizations, international strategies on the Internet can have a direct impact on the security policies of organizations. On the other hand, organizations in their country must be subject to laws that allow them to continue their activities in that country. Also, analyzing behavior of users in their interaction with new technologies can play an effective role in this area. But the complexity of technology cannot be ignored. With the development of artificial intelligence technologies, the complexity of information systems has increased and this can reduce user trust in intelligent systems. So, in the 6G generation, an organization should consider these factors with more priority than other factors in its security policies.

REFERENCES

[1] M. Wang, T. Zhu, T. Zhang, J. Zhang, S. Yu, and W. Zhou, "Security and privacy in 6G networks: new areas and new challenges," *Digitial Communation Networks*, vol. 6, no. 3, pp. 281–291, 2020.

[2] A. I. Gardezi, *Security in Wireless Cellular Networks*. St. Louis: Washingt. Univ. St. Louis, 2006.

[3] A. Gupta and R. K. Jha, "A survey of 5G network: architecture and emerging technologies," *IEEE Access*, vol. 3, pp. 1206–1232, 2015.

[4] S. Dang, O. Amin, B. Shihada, and M.-S. Alouini, "What should 6G be?," *Nature Electronics*, vol. 3, no. 1, pp. 20–29, 2020.

[5] G. Arunabha, J. Zhang, J. G. Andrews, and R. Muhamed, "Fundamentals of LTE," *Prentice Hall Communications Engineering and Emerging Technologies Series*, 2010.

[6] S. Gindraux, "From 2G to 3G: a guide to mobile security," in *Third International Conference on 3G Mobile Communication Technologies*, pp. 308–311, 2002.

[7] G. Cattaneo, G. De Maio, and U. F. Petrillo, "Security issues and attacks on the GSM standard: a review," *Journal of UCS*, vol. 19, no. 16, pp. 2437–2452, 2013.

[8] M. Toorani and A. Beheshti, "Solutions to the GSM security weaknesses," in *2008 The Second International Conference on Next Generation Mobile Applications, Services, and Technologies*, pp. 576–581, 2008.

[9] I. Elsen, F. Hartung, U. Horn, M. Kampmann, and L. Peters, "Streaming technology in 3G mobile communication systems," *Computer (Long. Beach. Calif)*., vol. 34, no. 9, pp. 46–52, 2001.

[10] V. M. Igure and R. D. Williams, "Taxonomies of attacks and vulnerabilities in computer systems," *IEEE Communications Surveys & Tutorials*, vol. 10, no. 1, pp. 6–19, 2008.

[11] C. Xenakis and L. Merakos, "Security in third generation mobile networks," *Computer and Communications*, vol. 27, no. 7, pp. 638–650, 2004.

[12] F. Ricciato, A. Coluccia, and A. D'Alconzo, "A review of DoS attack models for 3G cellular networks from a system-design perspective," *Computer and Communications*, vol. 33, no. 5, pp. 551–558, 2010.

[13] P.-A. Fouque, C. Onete, and B. Richard, "Achieving better privacy for the 3GPP AKA protocol," *Proceedings on Privacy Enhancing Technologies*, vol. 2016, no. 4, pp. 255–275, 2016.

[14] H. Gobjuka, "4G wireless networks: opportunities and challenges," *arXiv Prepr. arXiv0907.2929*, 2009.

[15] H. Alquhayz, A. Al-Bayatti, and A. Platt, "Security management system for 4G heterogeneous networks," in *Proceedings of the World Congress on Engineering*, 2012, vol. 2, pp. 4–6.

[16] Y. Park and T. Park, "A survey of security threats on 4G networks," in *2007 IEEE Globecom Workshops*, pp. 1–6, 2007. doi: 10.1109/GLOCOMW.2 007.4437813.

[17] X. Ji et al., "Overview of 5G security technology," *Science China Information Sciences*, vol. 61, no. 8, pp. 1–25, 2018.

[18] H. Kabir, M. H. Bin Mohsin, and R. Kantola, "Implementing a security policy management for 5g customer edge nodes," in *NOMS 2020-2020 IEEE/IFIP Network Operations and Management Symposium*, pp. 1–8, 2020.

[19] H. Alquhayz, N. Alalwan, A. I. Alzahrani, A. H. Al-Bayatti, and M. S. Sharif, "Policy-based security management system for 5G heterogeneous networks," *Wireless Communications and Mobile Computing*, vol. 2019, p. 4582391, 2019.

[20] M. Ylianttila et al., "6G white paper: research challenges for trust, security and privacy," *arXiv Prepr. arXiv2004.11665*, 2020.

[21] H. H. H. Mahmoud, A. A. Amer, and T. Ismail, "6G: a comprehensive survey on technologies, applications, challenges, and research problems," *Transactions on Emerging Telecommunications Technologies*, p. e4233, 2021.

[22] K. B. Letaief, W. Chen, Y. Shi, J. Zhang, and Y.-J. A. Zhang, "The roadmap to 6G: AI empowered wireless networks," *IEEE Communications Magazine*, vol. 57, no. 8, pp. 84–90, 2019.

[23] B. McMahan, E. Moore, D. Ramage, S. Hampson, and B. A. Y. Arcas, "Communication-efficient learning of deep networks from decentralized data," in *Artificial Intelligence and Statistics*, PMLR, pp. 1273–1282, 2017.

[24] P. Kairouz et al., "Advances and open problems in federated learning," *arXiv Prepr. arXiv1912.04977*, 2019.

[25] P. Vanhaesebrouck, A. Bellet, and M. Tommasi, "Decentralized collaborative learning of personalized models over networks," in *Artificial Intelligence and Statistics*, PMLR, pp. 509–517, 2017.

[26] A. Bellet, R. Guerraoui, M. Taziki, and M. Tommasi, "Personalized and private peer-to-peer machine learning," in *International Conference on Artificial Intelligence and Statistics*, PMLR, pp. 473–481, 2018.

[27] V. Zantedeschi, A. Bellet, and M. Tommasi, "Fully decentralized joint learning of personalized models and collaboration graphs," in *International Conference on Artificial Intelligence and Statistics*, PMLR, pp. 864–874, 2020.

[28] Z. Huang, S. Mitra, and N. Vaidya, "Differentially private distributed optimization," in *Proceedings of the 2015 International Conference on Distributed Computing and Networking*, pp. 1–10, 2015.

[29] K. Bonawitz, et al., "Practical secure aggregation for privacy-preserving machine learning," in *Proceedings of the 2017 ACM SIGSAC Conference on Computer and Communications Security*, pp. 1175–1191, 2017.

[30] A. M. Girgis, D. Data, S. Diggavi, P. Kairouz, and A. T. Suresh, "Shuffled model of federated learning: privacy, communication and accuracy trade-offs," *arXiv Prepr. arXiv2008.07180*, 2020.

[31] B. Biggio, B. Nelson, and P. Laskov, "Poisoning attacks against support vector machines," ICM L'12: Proceedings of the 29th International Conference on International Conference on Machine Learning, June 2012. pp. 1467–1474. 2012.

[32] Y. Liu, et al., "Trojaning attack on neural networks," 2017. URL: https://docs.lib.purdue.edu/cgi/viewcontent.cgi?article=2782&context=cstech

[33] V. Tolpegin, S. Truex, M. E. Gursoy, and L. Liu, "Data poisoning attacks against federated learning systems," in *European Symposium on Research in Computer Security*, pp. 480–501. Springer, Cham, 2020.

[34] G. Sun, Y. Cong, J. Dong, Q. Wang, L. Lyu , and J. Liu, "Data poisoning attacks on federated machine learning," in *IEEE Internet of Things Journal*, doi: 10.1109/JIOT.2021.3128646, 2020.

[35] E. Bagdasaryan, A. Veit, Y. Hua, D. Estrin, and V. Shmatikov, "How to backdoor federated learning," in *International Conference on Artificial Intelligence and Statistics*, 2020, pp. 2938–2948.

[36] A. N. Bhagoji, S. Chakraborty, P. Mittal, and S. Calo, "Analyzing federated learning through an adversarial lens," in *International Conference on Machine Learning*, PMLR, pp. 634–643, 2019.

[37] C. Szegedy, et al., "Intriguing properties of neural networks," *arXiv Prepr. arXiv1312.6199*, 2013.

[38] D. Ardila, et al., "End-to-end lung cancer screening with three-dimensional deep learning on low-dose chest computed tomography," *Nature Medicine*, vol. 25, no. 6, pp. 954–961, 2019.

[39] K. Pinker, J. Chin, A. N. Melsaether, E. A. Morris, and L. Moy, "Precision medicine and radiogenomics in breast cancer: new approaches toward diagnosis and treatment," *Radiology*, vol. 287, no. 3, pp. 732–747, 2018.

[40] H. Lu et al., "A mathematical-descriptor of tumor-mesoscopic-structure from computed-tomography images annotates prognostic-and molecular-phenotypes of epithelial ovarian cancer," *Nature Communications*, vol. 10, no. 1, pp. 1–11, 2019.

[41] G. A. Kaissis, M. R. Makowski, D. Ruckert, and R. F. Braren, "Secure, privacy-preserving and federated machine learning in medical imaging," *Nature Machine Intelligence*, vol. 2, no. 6, pp. 305–311, 2020.

[42] L. Lovén, et al., "EdgeAI: A vision for distributed, edgenative artificial intelligence in future 6G networks," *1st 6G Wireless Summit*, pp. 1–2, 2019.

[43] M. Ehatisham-ul-Haq, et al., "Authentication of smartphone users based on activity recognition and mobile sensing," *Sensors*, vol. 17, no. 9, p. 2043, 2017.

[44] A. Silvelo, D. Garabato, R. Santoveña, and C. Dafonte, "A first approach to authentication based on artificial intelligence for touch-screen devices," in

Multidisciplinary Digital Publishing Institute Proceedings, vol. 54, no. 1, p. 1, Aug. 2020.

[45] M. S. Zareen, S. Tahir, M. Akhlaq, and B. Aslam, "Artificial intelligence/machine learning in IoT for authentication and authorization of edge devices," in *2019 International Conference on Applied and Engineering Mathematics (ICAEM)*, pp. 220–224, 2019.

[46] X. Qiu, Z. Du, and X. Sun, "Artificial intelligence-based security authentication: applications in wireless multimedia networks," *IEEE Access*, vol. 7, pp. 172004–172011, 2019.

[47] Y. Xin et al., "Machine learning and deep learning methods for cybersecurity," *IEEE Access*, vol. 6, pp. 35365–35381, 2018.

[48] Y. Li, P. Zhang, and R. Huang, "Lightweight quantum encryption for secure transmission of power data in smart grid," *IEEE Access*, vol. 7, pp. 36285–36293, 2019.

[49] S. J. Nawaz, S. K. Sharma, S. Wyne, M. N. Patwary, and M. Asaduzzaman, "Quantum machine learning for 6G communication networks: state-of-the-art and vision for the future," *IEEE Access*, vol. 7, pp. 46317–46350, 2019.

[50] W. Briguglio, P. Moghaddam, W. A. Yousef, I. Traore, and M. Mamun, "Machine learning in precision medicine to preserve privacy via encryption," *arXiv Prepr. arXiv2102.03412*, 2021.

[51] M. A. P. Chamikara, P. Bertok, I. Khalil, D. Liu, and S. Camtepe, "Privacy preserving distributed machine learning with federated learning," *Computer and Communications*, vol. 171, pp. 112–125, 2021.

[52] T. Hong, C. Liu, and M. Kadoch, "Machine learning based antenna design for physical layer security in ambient backscatter communications," *Wireless Communications and Mobile Computing*, vol. 2019, p. 4870656, 2019.

[53] T. Nakano, A. W. Eckford, and T. Haraguchi, *Molecular Communication*. Cambridge University Press, 2013.

[54] N. Farsad, H. B. Yilmaz, A. Eckford, C.-B. Chae, and W. Guo, "A comprehensive survey of recent advancements in molecular communication," *IEEE Communications Surveys and Tutorials*, vol. 18, no. 3, pp. 1887–1919, 2016.

[55] Y. Lu, M. D. Higgins, and M. S. Leeson, "Comparison of channel coding schemes for molecular communications systems," *IEEE Transactions on Communications*, vol. 63, no. 11, pp. 3991–4001, 2015.

[56] A. O. Kislal, H. B. Yilmaz, A. E. Pusane, and T. Tugcu, "ISI-aware channel code design for molecular communication via diffusion," *IEEE Transactions on NanoBioscience*, vol. 18, no. 2, pp. 205–213, 2019.

[57] P.-J. Shih, C.-H. Lee, P.-C. Yeh, and K.-C. Chen, "Channel codes for reliability enhancement in molecular communication," *IEEE Journal on Selected Areas in Communications*, vol. 31, no. 12, pp. 857–867, 2013.

[58] V. Loscri, C. Marchal, N. Mitton, G. Fortino, and A. V. Vasilakos, "Security and privacy in molecular communication and networking: opportunities and challenges," *IEEE Transactions on NanoBioscience*, vol. 13, no. 3, pp. 198–207, 2014.

[59] S. Zafar, W. Aman, M. M. U. Rahman, A. Alomainy, and Q. H. Abbasi, "Channel impulse response-based physical layer authentication in a diffusion-based molecular communication system," in *2019 UK/China Emerging Technologies (UCET)*, IEEE, pp. 1–2, 2019.

[60] A. Manzalini, "Quantum communications in future networks and services," *Quantum Reports*, vol. 2, no. 1, pp. 221–232, 2020.

[61] V. Scarani, H. Bechmann-Pasquinucci, N. J. Cerf, M. Dušek, N. Lütkenhaus, and M. Peev, "The security of practical quantum key distribution," *Reviews of Modern Physics*, vol. 81, no. 3, p. 1301, 2009.

[62] W. Guo, "Explainable artificial intelligence for 6G: Improving trust between human and machine," *IEEE Communications Magazine*, vol. 58, no. 6, pp. 39–45, 2020.

[63] N. C. Luong et al., "Applications of deep reinforcement learning in communications and networking: a survey," *IEEE Communications Surveys and Tutorials*, vol. 21, no. 4, pp. 3133–3174, 2019.

[64] D. R. Johnson and D. Post, "Law and borders: the rise of law in cyberspace," *Stanford Law Rev.*, pp. 1367–1402, 1996.

[65] R. Azmi, W. Tibben, and K. T. Win, "Motives behind cyber security strategy development: a literature review of national cyber security strategy," *Australasian Conference on Information Systems*, Wollongong, 2016. URL: https://ro.uow.edu.au/cgi/viewcontent.cgi?article=1044&context=acis2016

[66] S. Arsneault, A. Northrop, and K. L. Kraemer, "Taking advantage of the information age: which countries benefit?," *Public Administration and Public Policy: A Comprehensive Publication Program.* vol. 111, p. 299, 2005.

[67] S. Stier, "Political determinants of e-government performance revisited: Comparing democracies and autocracies," *Government Information Quarterly*, vol. 32, no. 3, pp. 270–278, 2015.

[68] M. E. Porter, "Strategy and the Internet harvard business review," *March*, pp. 62–78. Retrieved July, vol. 20, p. 2007, 2001.

[69] P. de Souza, "National cyber defense strategy," in *Strategic Intelligence Management*, Elsevier, pp. 224–228, 2013.

[70] Europa.eu, "National Cybersecurity Strategies," 2020. URL: https://www.enisa.europa.eu/topics/national-cyber-security-strategies

[71] K. M. Finklea, "The interplay of borders, turf, cyberspace, and jurisdiction: Issues confronting US law enforcement," Congressional Research Service, Library of Congress, 2013.

[72] P. M. Tehrani and N. A. Manap, "A rational jurisdiction for cyber terrorism," *Computer Law and Security Review*, vol. 29, no. 6, pp. 689–701, 2013.

[73] M. Fenwick and E. P. M. Vermeulen, "Technology and corporate governance: Blockchain, crypto, and artificial intelligence," *Texas Journal of Business Law*, vol. 48, p. 1, 2019.

[74] M. Fenwick, W. A. Kaal, and E. P. M. Vermeulen, "Regulation tomorrow: what happens when technology is faster than the law," *American University Business Law Review*, vol. 6, p. 561, 2016.

[75] T. Szuba, "Safeguarding your technology: practical guidelines for electronic education information security," *National Center for Education Statistics*, 1998.

[76] R. Diesch, M. Pfaff, and H. Krcmar, "A comprehensive model of information security factors for decision-makers," *Computers & Security*, vol. 92, p. 101747, 2020.

[77] J. T. Force, "Risk management framework for information systems and organizations," *NIST Special Publication*, vol. 800, p. 37, 2018.

[78] Y. Chen, W. Liu, Z. Niu, Z. Feng, Q. Hu, and T. Jiang, "Pervasive intelligent endogenous 6G wireless systems: prospects, theories and key technologies," *Digital Communications and Networks*, vol. 6, no. 3, pp. 312–320, 2020.

[79] A. L. Imoize, O. Adedeji, N. Tandiya, and S. Shetty, "6G enabled smart infrastructure for sustainable society: opportunities, challenges, and research roadmap," *Sensors*, vol. 21, no. 5, p. 1709, 2021.

[80] N. Van Huynh, D. T. Hoang, X. Lu, D. Niyato, P. Wang, and D. I. Kim, "Ambient backscatter communications: a contemporary survey," *IEEE Communications Surveys and Tutorials*, vol. 20, no. 4, pp. 2889–2922, 2018.

[81] R. Gupta, A. Nair, S. Tanwar, and N. Kumar, "Blockchain assisted secure UAV communication in 6G environment: architecture, opportunities, and challenges," *IET Communications*, vol. 15. doi: 10.1049/cmu2.12113, 2021.

[82] M. M. Azari, G. Geraci, A. Garcia-Rodriguez, and S. Pollin, "UAV-to-UAV communications in cellular networks," *IEEE Transactions on Wireless Communications*, vol. 19, no. 9, pp. 6130–6144, 2020.

[83] M. Grobler, R. Gaire, and S. Nepal, "User, Usage and Usability: Redefining Human Centric Cyber Security," *Frontiers Big Data*, vol. 4, p. 583723, Mar. 2021.

[84] L. J. Camp, M. Grobler, J. Jang-Jaccard, C. Probst, K. Renaud, and P. Watters, "Measuring human resilience in the face of the global epidemiology of cyber attacks," in *Proceedings of the 52nd Hawaii International Conference on System Sciences*, 2019.

[85] C. C. Eckel and P. J. Grossman, "Men, women and risk aversion: experimental evidence," *Handbook of Experimental Economics Results*, vol. 1, pp. 1061–1073, 2008.

[86] A. Basit, M. Zafar, X. Liu, A. R. Javed, Z. Jalil, and K. Kifayat, "A comprehensive survey of AI-enabled phishing attacks detection techniques," *Telecommunication Systems*, pp. 1–16, 2020.

[87] Wired.com, ""Offensive AI: Surfacing Truth in the Age of Digital Fakes," 2020. URL: https://www.wired.com/brandlab/2020/02/offensive-ai-surfacing-truth-age-digital-fakes

[88] H. Shahbaznezhad, F. Kolini, and M. Rashidirad, "Employees' behavior in phishing attacks: what individual, organizational, and technological factors matter?," *Journal of Computer Information Systems*, pp. 1–12, Oct. 2020.

[89] Y. Hong, "A dynamic constructivist approach to culture: moving from describing culture to explaining culture," in *Understanding culture*, Psychology Press, 1st Edition, 2013, pp. 18–38.

[90] A. Da Veiga, "A cybersecurity culture research philosophy and approach to develop a valid and reliable measuring instrument," in *2016 SAI Computing Conference (SAI)*, IEEE, 2016, pp. 1006–1015.

[91] B. Ur and Y. Wang, "A cross-cultural framework for protecting user privacy in online social media," in *Proceedings of the 22nd International Conference on World Wide Web*, 2013, pp. 755–762.

[92] A. I. Antón, J. B. Earp, and J. D. Young, "How internet users' privacy concerns have evolved since 2002," *IEEE Security & Privacy*, vol. 8, no. 1, pp. 21–27, 2010.

[93] International Organization for Standardization, "Ergonomics of Human-system Interaction: Part 210: Human-centred Design for Interactive Systems, 9241-210:2010," 2010. URL: https://www.iso.org/standard/52075.html

[94] M. Theofanos, "Is usable security an oxymoron?," *Computer (Long. Beach. Calif).*, vol. 53, no. 2, pp. 71–74, 2020.

[95] C. S. Weir, G. Douglas, T. Richardson, and M. Jack, "Usable security: user preferences for authentication methods in eBanking and the effects of experience," *Interacting with Computers*, vol. 22, no. 3, pp. 153–164, May 2010.

Index